Praise for *How to Listen When Markets Speak*

"I can't tell you how much I learned from *How to Listen When Markets Speak*. The historical perspectives and insights are something every investor needs to know. Buy this book."

—MARK CUBAN,
founder of Cost Plus Drugs
and longtime *Shark Tank* investor

"Larry McDonald's deep knowledge, experience, and insights have been invaluable in shaping my investment strategies, and *How to Listen When Markets Speak* is no different. It will sit on the edge of my desk, ready for me to refer back to frequently. I highly recommend it to anyone keen to protect their wealth in tumultuous times."

—RAOUL PAL,
CEO and co-founder of Real Vision

"As a journalist who is paid to be skeptical, I have been tracking Larry McDonald's views on markets for many years. His provocative, passionate, and sometimes prophetic insights are always worth pondering, even—or especially—when you disagree, and reading his analyses has often helped me to see situations more clearly. I don't always sit in the same camp, but I appreciate his consistent focus on value investing. His latest book offers a strong riposte to the tech hype, bull-market euphoria, and wishful thinking about a soft landing—it is thought-provoking work, particularly during a time when the global zeitgeist and order are changing in profound ways."

—GILLIAN TETT,
editorial board member and columnist at the *Financial Times*,
Provost at King's College, Cambridge, and author of *Anthro-Vision*

"As soon as I finished *How to Listen When Markets Speak*, I took a long, hard look at my portfolio. Any investor with skin in the game needs to buy this book."

—NIALL FERGUSON,
Stanford historian and author of
The Ascent of Money and *Doom*

"Smart people listen carefully, and they use what they hear to continually question their assumptions. When it comes to markets and their impact on our lives, things change—even the big things. Larry McDonald's *How to Listen When Markets Speak* is a consistently compelling contribution to today's debate on the future of financial markets and a challenge to assumptions that have outlived their value."

—IAN BREMMER,
political scientist and president of Eurasia Group

"*How to Listen When Markets Speak* makes gutsy predictions about seismic shifts in the global economy, advises readers on how to prepare for those shifts, and anticipates trends in almost every asset class while sharing important signals that can give investors an edge in the volatile years to come."

—GREGORY ZUCKERMAN,
author of *The Man Who Solved the Market*
and twenty-year veteran at *The Wall Street Journal*

How to Listen When Markets Speak

ALSO BY LAWRENCE G. MCDONALD

A Colossal Failure of Common Sense

How to Listen When Markets Speak

Risks, Myths, and Investment Opportunities in a Radically Reshaped Economy

Lawrence G. McDonald
with James Patrick Robinson

CROWN CURRENCY
NEW YORK

CROWN CURRENCY
An imprint of the Crown Publishing Group
A division of Penguin Random House LLC
1745 Broadway
New York, NY 10019
currencybooks.com
penguinrandomhouse.com

2025 Crown Currency Trade Paperback Edition

Library of Congress Cataloging-in-Publication Data
Names: McDonald, Lawrence G., author. | Robinson, James Patrick, other.
Title: How to listen when markets speak / Lawrence G. McDonald with James Patrick Robinson.
Description: New York: Currency, [2024] | Includes bibliographical references and index.
Identifiers: LCCN 2023034128 (print) | LCCN 2023034129 (ebook) |
ISBN 9780593727515 (trade paperback) | ISBN 9780593727508 (ebook)
Subjects: LCSH: Investments. | Capital market. | Stocks. | Decision making.
Classification: LCC HG4521 .M3953 2024 (print) | LCC HG4521 (ebook) |
DDC 332.6—dc23/eng/20230807
LC record available at https://lccn.loc.gov/2023034128
LC ebook record available at https://lccn.loc.gov/2023034129

ISBN 978-0-593-72751-5
Ebook ISBN 978-0-593-72750-8

Originally published in hardcover in slightly different form in the United States by Crown Currency, an imprint of the Crown Publishing Group, a division of Penguin Random House LLC, in 2024.

Editors: Leah Trouwborst and Amy Li | Editorial assistant: Cierra Hinckson | Production editors: Robert Siek and Isabella Franco | Text designer: Ralph Fowler | Production: Kevin Garcia and Alison Kaitcer | Managing editors: Allison Fox, Sally Franklin, and Christine Tanigawa | Copy editors: Hilary Roberts and Janet Renard | Proofreader: Muriel Jorgensen | Publicists: Penny Simon and Tara Gilbride | Marketers: Chantelie Walker and Mason Eng
Title page graphic: forwforw/Adobe Stock

Charts: Robbert van Batenburg

Manufactured in the United States of America

1st Printing

First Paperback Edition

The authorized representative in the EU for product safety and compliance is Penguin Random House Ireland, Morrison Chambers, 32 Nassau Street, Dublin D02 YH68, Ireland, https://eu-contact.penguin.ie.

To Anabela, Gabriella, and Marcus,
and to Dad, my mentor for decades.
Without his guidance this book
wouldn't have been possible.

CONTENTS

AUTHOR'S NOTE

This book is the result of fifteen years spent roaming the hallways of global finance. When Lehman Brothers failed, I thought I had lost everything. Like a bird thrown out of the nest, I had to reinvent myself. On that long, sometimes lonely road, publishing the inside story of Lehman's collapse and giving lectures on the economy throughout the world, I somehow amassed a team of brilliant minds who became my brain trust in the coming years. Blessed with good friends and great mentors, I leaned heavily on their wisdom to write this book. For each person who shared their macro lens on markets and allowed me to see with great clarity the ebb and flow of international money, I remain eternally grateful. It is to you that I owe this book.

FOREWORD

NIALL FERGUSON

In *How to Listen When Markets Speak,* Larry McDonald prophesies "a new era of persistent inflation, an escalation in global conflict, a multipolar world teaming up against the United States, the horror of a weakening dollar, a series of sovereign debt crises, and a thundering of capital out of financial assets into hard assets," not to mention "catastrophic shortages of natural resources."

There is always an audience for prophets of doom, as I pointed out in a book of my own—*Doom: The Politics of Catastrophe*—and doommongers have prophesied thousands of the last zero ends of the world. But Larry McDonald is in a different category. The author of the definitive insider's account of the fall of Lehman Brothers, *A Colossal Failure of Common Sense,* he has a remarkable ear for financial markets, the result of decades of Wall Street conversations, going all the way back to the stock market crash of 1987. The message of his new book is not that the world's about to end, but that the global economy is going through a paradigm shift. The markets are already telling us that. You just have to have your ear to the ground, the way McDonald does. Or maybe that should be "your ear to the trading floor."

The trouble with Wall Street chatter is that the ratio of noise to signal is pretty high. To try to strip out the noise, McDonald has developed a model of financial risk based on twenty-one systemic risk indicators, including the corporate default rate, stock market short-interest ratios, and investor sentiment surveys. Since 2010, when he founded *The Bear Traps Report,* he has been one of my favorite channels of communication with that talkative and moody individual known as Mr. Market.

The key thesis of *How to Listen When Markets Speak* is one with which I heartily agree. The end of the Cold War in the late 1980s and early 1990s ushered in a generational financial boom that has lasted close to forty years, albeit a boom punctuated by numerous crises. The principal drivers of the boom were globalization and the integration of Asian labor and savings—not forgetting talent—into an increasingly borderless financial system that successfully harnessed the innovations in information technology emanating from Silicon Valley. These powerful forces drove down inflation from the heights of the 1970s to the low point of 2009.

But that era is now over. What ended it? The prime suspects are central bankers, who grew increasingly reckless in their efforts to stave off crises (notably in 1998, 2001, 2008 to 2009, and 2020) by cutting interest rates and then buying bonds and other financial assets ("quantitative easing"), massively expanding their balance sheets. These measures, McDonald argues, acted as a volatility suppressant, encouraging structural shifts in financial markets in favor of exchange-traded funds, passive investment, and short-volatility strategies. At the same time, China's admission to the World Trade Organization and its securing of permanent normal trade relations with the United States in 2001 ensured a sustained hollowing out of U.S. manufacturing capacity, with all its social and political consequences. Third, fiscal policy—beginning with the Global War on Terror and culminating in the Biden administration's various industrial policy measures—has driven the U.S. federal debt to a height relative to GDP that is unprecedented since World War II. Fourth, the political backlash against globalization has produced a new protectionist (and anti-China) bipartisan consensus in Washington. Finally, the global campaign to discourage investment in "fossil fuels" in favor of "renewables" is leading to an unintended energy crisis.

McDonald's conclusions are bold:

The great migration of capital, moving from growth stocks into value stocks, has only just begun. We are in the first inning. And as every rally in the growth space fails, it will bring more disappointment to those investors who are still searching for the promised land. One day they will grudgingly pack their bags and walk into the value sector. They will see the rally happening in gold, silver, platinum, and palladium.

In other words, the inter–Cold War era of disinflation is over. Inflation is not returning to 2 percent or lower. The dollar is destined for a period of weakness. And investors would be well advised to ditch tech stocks and invest in precious metals, not to mention copper, lithium, cobalt, graphite, and uranium, all of which will be in short supply relative to the ambitious demands of the "energy transition."

Some might say that this makes too little allowance for the likely benefits of further technological innovation (think artificial intelligence) or the potential comeback of secular stagnation as demographics and debt dynamics slow down growth. But McDonald's case for the financial equivalent of a "Fourth Turning" is strengthened by some star witnesses, including such legendary investors as David Tepper, David Einhorn, and Charlie Munger. Interviews with these luminaries, as well as with less-well-known members of McDonald's Wall Street network, are a key part of what distinguishes *How to Listen When Markets Speak* from other books on contemporary finance, most of which ought to be titled *How to Stay Awake While I Pontificate.* McDonald's humility is a rare thing in the financial world. To his credit, he has never forgotten that he started out "as a pork chop salesman along the Cape Cod Canal."

I can't pretend to know the financial future. Back in 2008, my book *The Ascent of Money* did a pretty good job of foreseeing the global financial crisis, but subsequent events caught me out more than once and taught me the valuable lesson that to anticipate markets you really do need to listen before you talk. That's why I became a regular reader of *The Bear Traps Report.* It's why I recommend Larry McDonald's new book. And it's why, as soon as I'd finished it, the first thing I did was take a long, hard look at my own portfolio. I predict most readers will do the same.

INTRODUCTION

A Banquet of Consequences

Sooner or later everyone sits down to a banquet of consequences.

—COMMONLY ATTRIBUTED TO ROBERT LOUIS STEVENSON

After the end of the Cold War, America basked in an unprecedented era of peace and prosperity. International trade flourished in a world protected by U.S. power. The reserve currency generated great wealth, inflation was minimal, and the globe was stuffed with inexpensive commodities. Basically, times were good.

However, these good times led to costly behavior that now impacts our lives. On four major occasions—in 1998, 2001, 2008, and 2020—the Fed and Congress bailed out Wall Street. As a result, the government owes $36 trillion in debt after years of spending wildly beyond its means. The Fed has bought more than $8.5 trillion in bonds, and financial assets have cycled through bubble after bubble.

In 2020, when the COVID-19 pandemic sent financial markets reeling, America reached a tipping point. Russia's war with Ukraine interrupted oil and gas supply lines, and the subsequent inflationary crisis whipsawed the real-world economy into recession. In 2022, we saw a $9 trillion loss of wealth as tech stocks and crypto assets crashed.

This was a seismic shift in the performance of financial assets, and a taste of what was to come. The familiar economic order, the one we had known since the collapse of the USSR, was over.

In the coming decade, inflation will persist, global conflict will escalate, and a multipolar world will team up against the United States. The weakening dollar will materialize as a series of sovereign debt crises, along with a thundering of capital into hard assets. It will be a stark contrast to the previous decades, with the final nail being a catastrophic shortage of natural resources. The demand is on a never-ending upward trajectory.

Why? Europe's Climate Target plan; Biden's original Build Back Better plan; developed countries steaming full speed into carbon neutrality—all without adequate raw materials for solar panels, wind turbines, and electric motors. As nations grow poorer, a natural hunger for oil and fossil fuels will surge, along with fierce competition for global resources.

But since the publication of this book's hardcover edition, another monster has emerged: artificial intelligence. Coupled with crypto currencies, electrical grids are now hopelessly ill-equipped to power the future.

Due to the massive demand for electricity and copper by AI data centers, America faces a daunting challenge: rebuilding its power grid, estimated at a staggering $2 trillion, to fully support AI. The U.S. has dangerously underinvested, particularly in critical areas like nuclear power, leaving it far behind China. This imbalance makes the AI race a genuine national security threat.

Trump recognized this and tasked the Commerce Department to explore tariffs and other measures to cut reliance on imported copper, acknowledging that dependence on foreign sources is a glaring vulnerability. Without a copper surge, America's AI dream collapses.

According to the International Copper Association, data centers in the U.S. alone will require roughly 300,000 to 400,000 metric tons of copper annually. To grasp how severe this is, just look at the current copper supply—it's dangerously insufficient. The copper demand driven by AI infrastructure is completely off the charts.

That's not all, though. The rebuilding of Los Angeles after the 2024 wildfires; of data centers; of Ukraine; of Gaza; and of the U.S. power grid exacerbates an unsolvable issue.

To make matters worse, America's economy is now dangerously out of balance, amplifying the risks of economic disruption. Years of heavy-handed policymaking have destroyed the market's natural ability to price assets accurately. Stocks, bonds, real estate, and commodities have become severely distorted, leaving millions of retirement accounts like 401(k)s and IRAs exposed.

Capital across the economy has flowed blindly into outdated assumptions, built for a world that no longer exists. Tens of trillions have poured into passive investments like ETFs, pushing valuations to irrational levels with little regard for fundamentals. Quantitative trading has multiplied these distortions, creating a ticking time bomb of market risk.

Now imagine a future constantly starved of energy, battered by frequent crises and crashes, where the Fed and Congress have no cards left to play. Investors will be forced to rethink everything they know and reposition dramatically toward entirely new sectors.

But, however grim the economic outlook, this story is not about gloom and doom. Investors are not helpless pawns facing inevitable losses. My goal is not to scare you but to prepare you—to light a path through and around the coming upheaval.

The stakes are sky-high, and the opportunities are even higher. A decade from now, investors who positioned their portfolios ahead of the seismic shifts in global markets—who capitalized on the first-mover advantage—will be the envy of Wall Street.

Meanwhile, investors who still chase the last decade's darlings, pressured by the fear of missing out and trapped in a rearview-mirror mentality, will yearn for a do-over. I've spent practically my entire career on Wall Street, riding the ups and downs of the past thirty years.

In the late 1990s, I co-founded convertbond.com, a website that provided news, valuation, terms, and analysis tools about convertible securities. After that, I moved to Lehman Brothers, where I became one of the most profitable traders in high-yield, distressed debt, and convertible securities.

My first book, *A Colossal Failure of Common Sense,* chronicled the fateful mistakes and hubris that led to Lehman's collapse. Rather than keeping his ear to the ground, our former chairman "secluded himself in palatial offices on the thirty-first floor, far away from the action, nursing ambitions of unfettered growth."

The parallels to our current moment are eerie. Lehman gave me a real-world education in market risk. Watching the cleverest minds on Wall Street succumb to irredeemable logic, heading directly for the biggest subprime iceberg ever seen, left me forever changed.

After the crisis, as the words *if only* slammed repeatedly into my brain, I dedicated myself to spotting early signs of economic danger and opportunity.

Twenty-one systemic risk indicators—many of which mainstream financial models overlook—emerged from my analysis, giving me a razor-sharp gauge for assessing the health of an economy.

Now independent, I founded *The Bear Traps Report*, a macroeconomic financial research platform that helps investors—hedge funds, family offices, and asset managers—navigate an increasingly risky world.

This book will do the same for you.

First, we'll trace the origins of our current economic order, replaying the events, decisions, and economic conditions that created a thirty-year bull market. It's an epic tale of reckless optimism, maddening group-think, and naïve policy.

Although some of this history will be familiar to readers of finance books, we'll approach it as a study of cause and effect. Few investors know how to connect the dots between past, present, and future, and those who can will gain a powerful edge. Then we'll map out the twists and turns of the road ahead.

Though most people alive today grew up alongside a historic rise in financial wealth and are accustomed to relentless asset appreciation, those macro conditions will soon be a distant memory—and much of the "financial wealth" we have accumulated will prove illusory.

In the second half of the book, we'll outline new rules of investing in a radically reshaped economic landscape, including strategies for resisting reactionary narratives and detecting bearish and bullish trends a beat ahead of the crowds.

Along the way, you'll sit down with some of the greatest traders and investors of the past decade, including Charlie Munger, David Tepper, and David Einhorn, getting a front-row seat to the smartest professional money trades in today's markets.

The markets are speaking loudly and clearly; we just need to have the ears to listen.

On the journey ahead, we'll explore the following:

- How the peaceful afterglow of the Cold War's end laid the foundations for an era of disinflation that defined the following thirty years and your investment portfolio.

- Why a sustained era of high interest rates will make the shuddering $33 trillion debt on the U.S. balance sheet impossible to finance, pushing interest payments on the national debt from $580 billion in 2021 to $1.4 trillion in 2024 (more than the government currently spends on defense or Medicare), and how a monumental $200 trillion of unfunded liabilities will increase the risk of a catastrophic default.

- How outsourcing since the 1990s further depressed inflation and facilitated America's now-crushing government indebtedness—and presents you with one of the most compelling investment opportunities in a generation.

- Why countries like Russia, China, and Saudi Arabia are taking steps to transition away from using the U.S. dollar as a reserve currency, further hurting our country's ability to finance its tremendous debts, wreaking havoc on financial markets, and potentially forcing us to slash Social Security, Medicare, and military spending—and how investors can capitalize on the coming era of a weak dollar.

- How inflation is fueling a surge in the power of labor, like that of the 1960s to 1970s, with unions scoring historic wins that ultimately make inflation "stickier," and what this could mean for your portfolio.

- How the West's war on oil and gas, underinvestment in fossil fuels and energy infrastructure, and estranged relationships with Russia and Saudi Arabia will lift the base price of energy—and everything else—to a higher level, and how to get in front of this moneymaking trend.

- How global population growth and mounting demand from the green revolution will contribute to catastrophic shortages of natural resources, and why hard assets, including green transition minerals like lithium and cobalt, will outperform growth stocks, U.S. Treasuries, and passive investment strategies in the coming years.

- How the crypto sales pitch around escaping the centralized, state-controlled financial system relied on a bet that central banks would suppress rates and inject liquidity forever, and how, given its detachment from hard assets, crypto may be even more sensitive to Fed action than stocks or bonds.

- How algorithmic trading fomented a colossal distortion of market risk: a ticking time bomb that periodically leads to extreme spikes in volatility and triggers abrupt market crashes.

- How passive investing and the vehicles intended to democratize finance have fueled bubbles and ideological skew by large market participants, and how America's 401(k) and retirement plans have been hijacked by fourteen stocks.

- Why the classic 60 percent stock / 40 percent bond portfolio—revered as the foundational guidepost for many investors—is dead, and why the forward thinking should embrace a more commodity- and cash-heavy approach to portfolio construction.

We're about to witness a historic, multitrillion-dollar migration of capital—one that ushers in a new class of winners and losers. If you have money invested, this is your story.

Historians William Strauss and Neil Howe suggest history moves through predictable phases: four "turnings" lasting roughly a generation each. Our current cycle began with the post-WWII boom and JFK's assassination, followed by cultural awakenings, economic expansion, and growing polarization.

Now, complacency has bred a crisis. America faces a Fourth Turning, a destructive yet creative reset replacing old institutions with new ones. But first, let's revisit the early 1980s where this story begins: on a road, in the wind, on the backseat of a Presidential motorcade.

How to Listen When Markets Speak

1

The End of an Era

It was the afternoon of March 8, 1983. A tropical breeze swept across endless acres of citrus orchards and into Orlando, fluttering the flags on the limousine pulling up in front of the Sheraton Twin Towers. Immaculate as ever, in a navy suit offset by a white linen pocket square, President Ronald W. Reagan was led to a podium where he delivered a speech that would be remembered for decades. In it, he called the USSR an "evil empire" and took steps to shore up NATO's nuclear deterrent to counteract the Soviet Union's.

The United States and the Soviet Union were already in an arms race that would peak three years after Reagan stepped up to that podium. The Cold War had started in 1947. By 1975, a red line had been carved right down the northern hemisphere, dividing East from West, with the East protected by a Soviet military of 5.5 million men and about twenty thousand nuclear missiles. In the next ten years the number of missiles would double. It was nothing short of a standoff, a display of muscle flexing on the grandest scale, neither camp daring to open a line of communication.

Despite that muscular display, the Soviet Union's economy was in tough shape. The nation spanned fifteen republics, eleven time zones, and a swath of land 6,800 miles wide—from Kaliningrad in the west all the way to a desperately cold spit of land on the Chukchi Sea known as Uelen. But landmass rarely equals wealth, happiness, or opportunity. For the Soviets, it didn't even promise a hot meal. Corruption, the absence of a free market, and a costly proxy war in the Hindu Kush, where the mujahideen were covertly supported by the Pentagon and the Saudis, severely hampered the economy. Images of breadlines and empty supermarket shelves were often seen in Western newspapers.

Reagan's "rhetorical rearmament" achieved its intended effect of rattling his adversary. By 1985, the Soviets had amassed a total of 39,000 nuclear missiles, with close to 6,000 aimed directly at the United States. America met this threat by stockpiling over 21,000 warheads. The world was one technical fault away from total annihilation.

The big man in the White House knew that the USSR could easily buckle under a disillusioned military and an educated populace living in near squalor, with little chance of a better life. Then came the 1986 nuclear accident at Chernobyl and the Politburo's decision to stall the public announcement for two days. Even then, its twenty-second televised statement was vague, assuring listeners that authorities were handling the situation. The surge of radiation poisoning, of course, was not under control. And while the Politburo avoided addressing this new public health crisis, Mikhail Gorbachev, the new general secretary of the Soviet Communist Party and de facto leader of the country, pored over the reports of death, injury, and ruination: across great tracts of land, lives, homes, and even entire towns were torn apart. He wrote afterward that his conscience could no longer be involved with nuclear arms.

Later that same year, a black motorcade snaked through the middle of Reykjavik, Iceland, stopping at a whitewashed building known as Hofdi House. It was a blustery, sodden morning, the skies platinum above the bank of photographers in waiting. Gorbachev, in a knee-length cashmere overcoat, trotted up the steps to be greeted by President Reagan.

Reagan looked at Gorbachev for a beat, at a man born and raised in Soviet Russia under the most hard-line communist rulers: men like Josef Stalin, Nikita Khrushchev, and Leonid Brezhnev (whose eighteen-year reign was defined by economic stagnation). And here was Gorbachev, an educated man standing before the president of the United States, against every possible communist belief. He may have been only five feet nine inches tall, but history would remember him as a giant of democracy. Gorbachev was there to discuss a nuclear arms reduction, for which he would later be given a Nobel Peace Prize. Reagan smiled at him in that classic cowboy way, and the two men shook hands as if they were already friends, the whole world watching. For the USSR, this was a giant step toward dissolution.

. . .

The concept of hope has been one of the most potent forces in the history of mankind.

That simple emotion has been responsible for more victories against the odds than any machine or weapon. It's how the Greeks, desperately outnumbered, defeated ten thousand Persian soldiers in 490 B.C. on the plain of Marathon. It's how Winston Churchill rallied Great Britain and its allies to fight the tyranny of Nazi Germany. And it's how, in the last year of the 1980s, half a million citizens of East Germany staged a mass protest along the perimeter of the Berlin Wall, turning their backs on the bankrupt state. On the night of November 9, 1989, the concrete divider separating East and West Germany was finally torn down.

The Soviet Union was in free fall by late 1991. Despite Gorbachev's hopes for radical liberalization, piecemeal reforms couldn't save an economic system founded on centralized control. On Christmas Day, the bright red flag flying above the Kremlin, with its yellow hammer and sickle representing the solidarity between industrial proletarians and farmworkers, was lowered for the last time. Gorbachev abolished the Communist Party of the Soviet Union and then resigned as president of the USSR.

The collapse of the Soviet Union became the great representation of global peace that settled like a blanket on international trade and free markets throughout the world. The bitter tensions that had plagued geopolitics since the start of the Cold War had finally been extinguished.

But what does the fall of the Soviet Union in the 1990s have to do with your portfolio in the 2020s?

Everything!

Because the collapse of the USSR helped shift the world from a multipolar to a unipolar order, one that revolved around a single dominant player. Backed by an outrageously robust economy and an overwhelming military force, the United States could crush challengers like ants. Under this new world order, a massive, interconnected system of global trade and security blossomed. Countries that took advantage of it prospered. Global trade went from less than $5 trillion in 1990 to $28 trillion in 2022, contributing to an increase in global GDP from $20.7 trillion to $100 trillion.

The unipolar world order entailed many different things across many domains—for instance, reducing the urgency of maintaining large standing armies—but for investors, its most crucial effect was its unprecedented disinflationary power. The surging supply of everything from raw materials (sourced from Russia) to finished goods and cheap labor (sourced from Asia, and especially China) stamped out inflation in Europe and the United States until 2021. Inflation went from 7 percent in the 1970s to 3 percent in the 1990s to 1.7 percent in the 2010s.

This allowed the U.S. Treasury bond yield, also known as the risk-free rate—the fixed rate of return on government Treasuries, which are considered to be zero risk because they are backed by the U.S. taxpayer—to decline from 15 percent in 1981 to less than 1 percent in the 2010s. Declining Treasury yields make fixed-income investments like government bonds less attractive and push investors toward riskier asset classes in search of higher returns. Price-to-earnings (PE) multiples—a measure of how much investors are willing to pay per dollar of company earnings, reflecting general market sentiment—expand when the risk-free rate goes down. Sure enough, the S&P 500's PE ratio went from 7x in the early 1980s to 30x in the late 1990s and in 2021.

This disinflation was one of the most important contributors to the epic bull market in risk assets. Profit margins exploded as financial

S&P Corporate Profit Margin

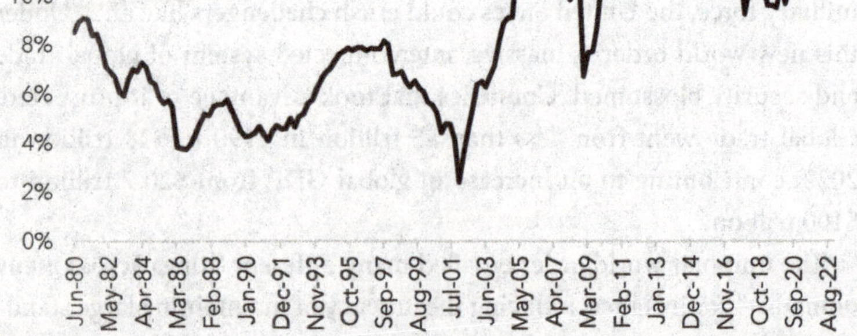

assets—growth stocks and bonds—took off. Investors love a stable, low-inflation environment. It lowers the cost of capital for businesses to invest in and for investors to borrow. The S&P 500 went from 323 in 1990 to 4,800 in 2021, an increase of 1,300 percent. If you'd put $1,000 in the S&P on the day World War II ended, you would have had $23,000 by 1990—but by the end of 2021 that amount would have grown to $343,000. In other words, those three decades of disinflation enabled a radically new approach to portfolio construction.

The World We Once Knew Is Gone

Years ago, I delivered a speech at the conference for the National Bank of Abu Dhabi, where I shared the stage with economic historian Niall Ferguson, former French president Nicolas Sarkozy, and Reagan's close adviser James Baker III. Some of my good buddies thought I was punching above my weight, but all I cared about was that at the end of the week I had a chance to sit down with Baker. The man is not only a Princeton scholar and a former U.S. Marine but also one of the only people to serve as secretary of both the Treasury (under Reagan) and state (under George H. W. Bush). He possesses unparalleled experience in issues of geopolitics and economics, and he opened my eyes to another key driver in both the collapse of the USSR and the suppression of inflation on a global scale: the ferocious control over oil prices the United States established in the mid-1980s.

America forged a real bond with Saudi Arabia in the 1980s, strengthened by mutual interests and mutual trust—a relationship light-years away from the prickly quasi friendship that exists today. Uncle Sam gladly provided the desert kingdom with the firepower and warships it needed to protect its mighty oil reserves, and in return the Saudis agreed to continue trading their oil in dollars. This was known as the *petrodollar agreement.*

The White House used this relationship as a financial nuclear weapon. The Soviet Union was extremely reliant on the export of oil and natural gas to receive hard currencies, such as the U.S. dollar and the deutsche mark. It needed these to buy the many essential goods for which it was not self-sufficient. The United States was keen on limiting Soviet energy exports during the Cold War, but it hadn't been successful in swaying its oil-hungry allies—and European energy dependence on Russia had been of particular concern to Washington. So it struck back. From November 1985 to March 1986, the United States and the Saudis drove oil prices down by nearly 70 percent, decimating the USSR's economic engine. In the early to mid-1980s, oil traded at $24 to $32 a barrel, just enough to keep the Soviet economy afloat. But between 1986 and 1990, when the United States decided to shut down the Cold War and obliterate Russia's economy, it sat on the price of crude like an African bull elephant, capping prices between $11 and $24 a barrel until the USSR had to concede.

I sat down with Baker one memorable afternoon. We were sitting outside the Emirates Palace beside austere, up-lit columns that cast a glow across the veranda. As we sipped our tea in hand-painted china cups, he said something to me I'll never forget. "Larry," he began in a low Texas drawl, "you don't ever want to live in a multipolar world. When I was advising the White House, we had far fewer friends in important places than we do today. Thank God we had the Saudis in our corner. That was an essential ingredient—control of oil prices was paramount."

In his view, the West's control over oil markets not only reduced inflation, lowering the cost of production for many goods and keeping transportation affordable, but also—though it might seem like an extreme imperialist stance—acted as a safety catch on global peace, stabilizing commerce, controlling autocrats, and, of course, shifting the balance of power in America's favor.

Still, geopolitical tensions in the years leading up to the collapse of the USSR had required aggressive military spending, contributing to tremendous deficits and high inflation, including the stagflation crisis of the 1970s.

"In a multipolar world, it's next to impossible to stabilize global markets, especially inflation," Baker explained. "Kind of amazing to think that even my own father spent his entire working life in that environment. Through World War II, Korea, Vietnam. As I said, Larry, war brings chronic inflation, a damn hard thing to stamp out."

He cast his eyes toward the Persian Gulf, as if remembering the 1970s, when OPEC—the Organization of the Petroleum Exporting Countries, a group of nations that now holds more than 80 percent of the world's proven oil reserves and seeks to exert control over the global oil market—imposed embargoes after the United States rearmed Israel for the postwar negotiations. Prices shot skyward and crippled the U.S. economy. Baker shook his head and sipped his tea. We sat there in silence for a beat, the cool desert winds ruffling our hair.

"It's an awful place to be," he continued. "I hope you never experience it."

I was born in 1966, and I'd already seen the images of breadlines and empty supermarket shelves in Russia, as had so many others reading Western newspapers at the height of the Cold War tensions.

But now, decades later, we're watching the tectonic plates of geopolitics shift again—as we'll explore in later chapters of this book.

The Dangerous New Member of the WTO

The college dropout cut a lonely figure as he ran his operation out of a business center in 1990s North Austin, despite the engineering crew scattered around various tables and a busy team collecting orders. Above the door, a blue sign simply read "Dell."

In this small, unobtrusive building, Michael Dell built a historic high-tech empire, inventing customized computers, a concept that wasn't on offer at any retail store. The piles of circuit boards and screwdrivers across the tables in that West Texas workroom represented not just an idea by a young man of irrefutable genius but the future transformation of the entire personal computer industry. Dell quickly realized that if he could undercut the high-street stores and offer "made-to-order" PCs through the mail and later online for less money, there would be no limit to business profits.

Back in 1983 when he drove his BMW to the University of Texas to start his premed degree, there were three dismantled personal computers on the back seat. Those computers were the seeds that would one day grow into the world's largest computer systems provider. The following May, in 1984, Dell dropped out of college. His monthly income was already $80,000. By 1992, at the age of twenty-six, he had become the youngest CEO on the Fortune 500 list, and his company's annual revenue was $679 million.

In 1995, Dell Computer aggressively expanded into every corner of the globe, including Japan, Europe, and the Americas. In 1996, Dell.com launched. Six months later it was banking $1 million a day in online sales. The economic boost of globalization was placed right in the back pocket of Michael Dell.

When China became an official member of the World Trade Organization (WTO) in 2001, multinational businesses—determined to offshore their manufacturing to a place without any potential red tape—romped into China, hired cheap labor, disregarded environmental policies, and started producing their products, chemicals, plastics, you name it, for a tenth of the cost. The 1997 Kyoto Protocol had placed many countries in the developed world—though not the United States—under binding targets to reduce their greenhouse gas emissions below 1990 levels by 2012. Even though the United States never signed on, the Kyoto Protocol raised the specter of imminent climate change regulation that could hurt the U.S. industrial sector.

President Bill Clinton had been lobbying hard for China to become the newest member of the WTO. He was a great ambassador for the institution, believing it could solve many of the world's trade and economic difficulties, and would vouch for any nation that deserved a chance to become a member. Never did he foresee that over the next seventeen years, America would lose 3.7 million manufacturing jobs—and would be left $1 trillion in debt—to China.

Although Dell remained an American business, the computer parts were made in Asia. The low manufacturing costs there were no secret. One man's spending is another man's income, and the wave of offshoring that happened in the ensuing decade is the backbone of how America became saddled with trillions in debt, with a totally hollowed-out manufacturing sector. These events would change the foundation of portfolio construction for decades. In an inflationary regime, hard assets and value stocks outperform. In a deflationary regime, financial assets and growth stocks outperform.

Global markets were soon flooded with cheap "Made in China" clothes, toys, household goods, furniture, and electronics. (On the flip side, the American agriculture sector, the most powerful lobbying force in the world, started to sell huge quantities of corn, wheat, and soy to China.)

INVESTORS TAKE NOTE:
The Relationship Between Offshoring and Deflation

Dell became a textbook example of the massive transition of tech manufacturing from the United States to Asia. The statistics speak for themselves. In 1990, there were 2.1 million workers in the U.S. computer and telecom equipment industry. By 2008, the number of workers had dwindled to 1.3 million, and in 2023, the workforce was down to 1.1 million. Even worse is the semiconductor manufacturing sector. In 1990, there were 660,000 Americans working in the domestic semiconductor industry. By 2008, that number was down to 433,000, and in 2023 it was 392,000. Yet the PC and laptop market sold 326 million units in 2022, more than double the 150 million units sold annually in the early 2000s. Semiconductor revenues almost tripled from $220 billion in 2005 to $600 billion in 2022. Meanwhile, from 1997 to 2015, the consumer price index (CPI) for personal computers and peripheral equipment declined by 96 percent. This level of deflation was not limited to PCs. Television sets registered a similar decline, while audio and photographic equipment declined by more than 60 percent. The immense deflation in so many manufactured-goods sectors was one of the most important factors that helped suppress inflation from the mid-1990s until 2021.

In the coming years, with bipartisan political pressure mounting, onshoring or near-shoring production will inevitably lead to higher prices. Uprooting entire supply chains and building new ones in high(er)-wage countries costs a fortune, and the price is borne by the consumer in the form of inflation.

The pollution in the air above China soared. In one calendar year, China's carbon dioxide emissions embarked on an almost vertical trajectory. In the year 2000, China emitted 3.5 gigatons of CO_2 into the atmosphere—that's 3.5 billion metric tons. By 2010, that number had exploded to 10.3 gigatons, equal to the emissions of the United States,

Europe, and India combined. China's expenditure of coal energy, measured in exajoules (1 exajoule being the equivalent of 174 million barrels of oil or 34 million tons of coal), went from 29.56 exajoules in 2000 to 82.43 by 2013, and that figure has been above 80 every year since then. In simple English, that's burning 2.7 billion metric tons of coal each year. In visual terms, that's about eight thousand Empire State Buildings.

Foreign Treasury Holders and Trade Deficit

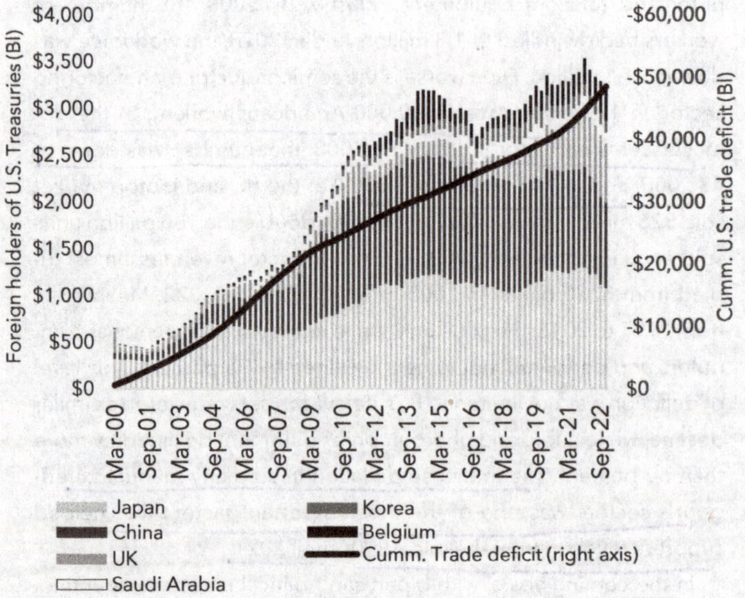

Amazingly, the trade surplus numbers trace the pattern of CO_2 emissions almost to a T. In the year 2001, just before China joined the WTO, the United States exported $20 billion worth of products and goods to China, and in return, the People's Republic sold $100 billion in exports to the United States. A decade later, the figures were alarming. China was selling $375 billion worth of products to the United States, and in return, the United States earned $100 billion exporting to China. That $275 billion difference in 2011 would hit $400 billion in 2021, after China sold $577.13 billion worth of products to the United States.

According to a New York Fed study, China's WTO entry reduced manufacturing price indexes by 7.6 percent between 2000 and 2006. The U.S. Bureau of Labor Statistics (BLS) estimated that a one-percentage-point increase in Chinese import penetration in a given industry led to a three-percentage-point fall in the CPI in that industry, and that this effect on prices started in 2000, when China entered the WTO. Now that the offshoring trend is in reverse, bringing more production back to the United States or neighboring countries will lead to higher costs, resulting in higher inflation at home.

America Beholden to China

David Ricardo and Adam Smith, two of history's most influential classical economists, believed a trade imbalance between two nations would eventually even itself out through the nature of currencies. Economic principles dictated that the currency of the country running a trade surplus would necessarily appreciate against the net importer. This would eventually shrink the trade surplus, thus reestablishing equilibrium between them. But this was not the case when it came to American trade with Japan or the Asian Tigers, and certainly not China. Why? How did this massive trade surplus fester for so long, totally violating classical economic theory? It turns out that the answer is very simple.

Anytime an American firm purchased anything from one of its Chinese suppliers, it paid in U.S. dollars. The normal thing for the Chinese business to do would be to exchange those dollars for yuan, the local currency. This would allow the company to recycle its profits and start the manufacturing and export process all over again, sourcing raw materials, compensating workers, hiring container ships or tankers, and dealing with any other business costs—all using yuan.

But all this currency changing on the Chinese mainland messed around with the price of the yuan. When you buy stacks of your own currency with billions of U.S. dollars, it sends up the value of your currency against the dollar. Big-time. That increases the price of your products abroad, killing the competitiveness of your exports until your currency comes down again. Because China's main competitive advantage was its cheap products, China was decidedly uninterested in this business model.

It didn't take the Chinese government long to move to plan B and put the economic theory of those eighteenth-century classicists in the paper shredder.

What it did has always been a little confusing to non-economists, but it's easy to understand, as long as you can envision two sailboats cutting through the ocean. Imagine one boat represents the U.S. dollar, the other boat the Chinese yuan. The yuan boat has one job. It's not to beat the other boat, and it certainly isn't to let it win. The yuan just has to stay even with the dollar boat and match its speed. If it gets ahead, it lets some air out of the sails. If it lags behind, it tightens the sails. Now pretend those aren't boats and are instead currencies. The Chinese controlled the yuan in exactly the same way against the U.S. dollar.

Whenever the yuan became stronger, the Chinese would sell yuan and buy dollars to weaken the currency. If it ever became too weak, they would dip into their mountain of U.S. dollars, known as their *foreign currency reserves,* and buy some yuan to strengthen it. That's how China essentially pegged its currency to the dollar and ensured that its product prices remained low for the American buyer. Instead of exchanging the dollars, China bought U.S. Treasuries with those dollars—government bonds—and that is one key reason why rates were so artificially low in America for so many years.

And it's also what handed America an almighty mountain of debt and government expenditures. How could a government possibly resist borrowing at rates of 1 percent? How could anyone? Money that cheap, for so long, distorted the natural check on overborrowing that comes in the form of debt-servicing costs. With rates so low, politicians could deficit-spend to high heaven without ever really having to reckon with footing the bill to their creditors. This gave them the financial leeway to borrow more and more, almost in perpetuity.

Low rates are great for consumers and high street borrowers, but there's another side to low rates, one that Main Street rarely thinks about. There is an entire world of corporate credit, which pretty much finances everything on planet Earth. The global economy is run on debt. Nothing really grows from earnings alone. Most companies have a pyramid right next to them, similar to the Great Pyramid of Giza, where Pharaoh Khufu's mummy was installed before final burial in the Valley of Kings. The very top layer, or *tranche,* of that pyramid represents the bank debt; the bottom layer, the one with all the weight on it, represents the equity in a corporation (the dollar value of the company after subtracting all liabilities from its assets, also known as the book value). That's usually the only piece of the capital pyramid Main Street is aware of, but there's an entire world of sophisticated capital above it, all carefully layered in hierarchical fashion, and that is the capital structure that runs the globe.

Each business has this structure, and each business makes a small contribution to the economy by creating transactions and by employing members of the population. That means hundreds of thousands of companies, all creating transactions and creating jobs, until their combined whole is the economy of a country. Across borders, the banking sector transacts with other banks. Lenders lend, borrowers borrow, governments give to other governments, businesses expand overseas, shipping containers representing vast sums of money cross oceans, and in the end this enormous matrix of borrowing and lending, exporting and importing, buying and selling creates the global economy.

In the late 1990s, the hot new sector, the one attracting the venture capital firms, was technology. The dot-com world is ingrained in our lives now, but back then, it was as if a new world were upon us, and it created a digital gold rush on Wall Street. Venture capitalists thought they were financing a renaissance, much like the one in Florence in the 1500s, and the investment banks jumped headlong into the speculative equity investments of the latest tech companies. They cast aside any semblance of economic guidelines like earnings and valuations. They wanted to finance the next Microsoft or AOL, Yahoo! or Amazon. Low rates pushed the boundaries of risk, a pattern we will see over and over as this story unfolds. But the promise of fortunes on the information superhighway totally clouded Wall Street's judgment.

That clouded judgment made a lot of people very rich, including our friend Michael Dell. His company's stock soared sixtyfold in five years. But in the halcyon days of the 1990s bull market, a lot of companies that had no viable business model and no path to profitability launched initial public offerings nonetheless. There are plenty of examples, but one that remains stuck in my memory is drkoop.com, the health information website founded by former surgeon general C. Everett Koop. In the dot-com frenzy of 1999, this online doctor IPOed at $9 and ran all the way up to $36, giving it a $1.9 billion market cap on revenues of a measly $43,000.

A year later it would trade at 20 cents. But there were also major companies that lost all sense of reason. WorldCom, Enron, Tyco, Adelphia, and others used the wide-open capital markets and blindly optimistic investors to fund a debt-fueled expansion. And they did not hesitate to falsify the books to make it all work.

MASTERS OF INVESTING WEIGH IN

An Interview with André Esteves

I could hold my own at New York cocktail parties on the subject of post–Cold War economics, but it wasn't until April 2022 that my hazy grasp on the relationship between geopolitics, inflation, and disinflation was brought into focus.

The summer had cooled off in São Paulo, South America's largest city, where 21 million inhabitants lived in the most immense urban sprawl I had ever seen. After delivering a speech on macrofinance to a group of hedge fund managers, I was driven through the Itaim Bibi district, São Paulo's upscale business zone, where most of corporate Brazil has offices in the glitzy high-rises that shape the skyline. The car turned onto Avenida Horácio Lafer, named after the outstanding Jewish political leader, paper industry scion, and former minister of finance under President Getúlio Vargas. He died in Paris in 1965, the same year the United States rapidly increased its war presence in South Vietnam. And here I was, three blocks from my final stop, to meet with another giant of Brazilian finance, a man who had spent his career sparring, grappling, and ground-fighting with high inflation.

We pulled into the giant portico of a mirrored-glass high-rise. Moments later, an elevator whisked me to its fourteenth floor, where BTG Pactual is headquartered. Across the wide, brightly lit foyer, a man in a white shirt and pressed khakis walked toward me. He had dark hair covering his brow, metal-framed glasses, and the quintessential look of someone who had built a financial empire that spanned the globe. It was André Esteves, the founder of the largest investment bank in Latin America.

I followed André down the hallway, onto a sky bridge that overlooked a trading floor. "That's where my office is, right in the action. It's the only way, as you say in America, to keep your finger on the pulse," he said.

A CEO, right down on the trading floor with his team. I had so much respect for this, and he knew it. In all my years at Lehman, I never saw our CEO in that environment. Not even once.

"A lot of people come to Brazil, and they think only of football, the rum parties, the beautiful women," he added. "But in finance, we've always been in a different world than the United States. We live with inflation and have done so for many years. But I think, now America will have a similar problem. And you have no idea how to handle it."

That was a sharp observation for early 2022, because the markets hadn't woken up to the reality of real inflation. Not yet. In fact, nearly everyone in D.C. was characterizing the recent uptick in prices as transitory, a lingering aftereffect of the COVID-19 pandemic.

"Will it be as bad as Brazil?" I asked, with an edge of concern.

"Maybe. You can never tell. But it won't be fleeting, like Washington believes. History tells a different story."

I glanced at André, but I didn't want to interrupt. This was a special moment for me. I have a lot of respect for the man, and it was an honor to be there on the sky bridge with him.

"There's always been a strong connection between geopolitical tensions and inflation," he continued. "The last thirty years have been a walk in the park, nicely controlled by the United States. The markets were on an almost uninterrupted bull run."

"Caused by the fall of the USSR, right?" I blurted, but I had a feeling this was only a part of the answer.

"I guess so. . . . That was the last bastion of conflict. And when it fell, we knew it would open up the world to 2 billion more consumers and eventually make China the factory of the world. We're unlikely to see that again in our lifetimes."

As his words sank in, I looked down at the market tickers, remembering the days when I also reported to the trading floor at six o'clock sharp every morning.

"Amazing how the Chinese came to dominate manufacturing, isn't it?" I said. "They practically monopolized it."

"It was . . . and for Brazil, it was an epic development. My country benefited from their insatiable demand for all sorts of essential commodities. Iron ore, soybeans . . . China bought it all. We grew from a $390 billion economy to $2 trillion, a marker we hit last year."

"Just goes to show, doesn't it?" I remarked. "Cheap labor can change the world."

"Cheap labor?" André looked at me quizzically with a half smile. "This is what everyone thinks, but it's a little misguided. Because it's not cheap labor as a single entity. The key word is 'access.'"

"What do you mean by that?"

"It's to do with the international security of trading routes. It's what makes trading possible. It lowers the costs of shipping goods all over the world. As geopolitical tensions drop, the ease of overseas manufacturing increases, along with offshoring labor costs. Exporting commodities is a breeze. So for the consumer it means anything from cheap underwear at Walmart to iPhones from Apple, manufactured with cheap coal and labor.

"One needs to understand that the highly deflationary, east-west, just-in-time supply chain model that thrived from 1990 to 2020 doesn't look the same in a multipolar world. I see a north-south supply chain developing in this hemisphere, between North and Latin America. So many jaded U.S. companies want peace of mind in a post-COVID world. Near-shoring, friend-shoring, backup supply chains, whatever you want to call it, it's on the way. To some extent, it's here now and it is far more inflationary."

I stood there for a moment, digesting what André had said. Then we walked away from the sky bridge, toward a window at the end of the corridor. "The USSR's dissolution ushered in a thirty-year period of disinflation," he continued. "But I'm sure you know all this. Putin's war will do no favors for Europe, which is completely reliant on cheap Russian energy and metals. And what about the Chinese production miracle? Their factories inundate the world with clothes, iPhones, laptops, and electric vehicle batteries! You think this war will do anything for trade? Think about it. Does America even have the leverage anymore to stop this? I suspect countries will start fleeing from the dollar over time, don't you?"

We arrived at the window, which was just large enough for us to peer between the high-rises and far into the distance, where the crisp air of the city became a dust-filled sepia.

"In the end," André continued, "it's not just easy money that causes inflation. It's risky geopolitics. Look again at the last time the West suffered from it. You'll have to open the Korean War chapter in your history book, when the North invaded the South. A proxy war against the threat of communism. Then there was Vietnam and the Yom Kippur War. Nearly twenty years of attrition warfare. Do you think for one second Asian goods could be as cheap as they are today with all of that going on?"

"Of course not."

"Fuel costs, shipping costs, security risks. It would hardly be worth it . . . not with Southeast Asia on fire. That's why there was inflation in the United States from 1965 to 1982."

"What do you think the next decade looks like, given the war in Ukraine?"

André checked his watch before he answered. "We're on the other side of the mountain now," he said. "The West is where Brazil has been far too often, with high inflation and subpar growth. Brazil has gone through multiple periods of hyperinflation, the most recent being in the early to mid-nineties, when inflation rates reached 5,000 percent. But even in 2021 the rate of inflation was as high as 30 percent. A large public sector, combined with mounting budget deficits and limited foreign trade, leads to sharp price increases from time to time that take years to bring under control. That's a much harder world to invest in. Just look at the S&P 500. It still trades at eighteen times earnings. But our Bovespa index is less than seven times. Here, we're used to consistent inflation. Five, sometimes 10 percent. But for the U.S. this is going to be a hard lesson to learn."

"You think it will stick around for a while?"

André processed the question very carefully, and when he did answer, he nodded sorrowfully. "Inflation is a very tricky phenomenon, my friend. When it arrives, it gets under the rug. It hides under the seat cushions. It's one of those things that has a way of sticking around for years."

Standing across from him, I was struck by his statement. I thought of hedge fund icon Seth Klarman, who once said that investing is the intersection of economics and psychology. I realized at that moment that André had mastered that craft.

On the long flight home, as the plane crossed Brazil's northwest border with Colombia, the consequences of the end of the great era of deflation began playing out in my mind. Life would be different: more expensive and more uncertain.

And André was correct. We are entering a multipolar world, and it will dramatically alter the economic landscape in the years to come, ushering in a new set of winners and losers. As for its implications, this book lays out, chapter by chapter, exactly how investors must be positioned for the coming storm.

The market has spoken. And right now, it's time to listen.

2

America Crosses the Rubicon

A bad economist will pursue a small current benefit that is followed by a large disadvantage in the future, while a true economist will pursue a large benefit in the future at a risk of suffering a small disadvantage immediately.

—FRÉDÉRIC BASTIAT

Economics is a study in cause and effect. In geopolitics, in global finance, and on the trading floors, we always dial back the years to find the root cause of any market boom, bust, or reset, replaying the pivotal moves on the financial chessboard to understand how America and the West arrived at where we are today.

In this chapter, we'll revisit the first colossal asset bubbles of the modern era and the role that governments played in inflating them, and in responding when these bubbles finally burst, leaving the economy in shambles. We'll examine how one faraway bubble sent ripple effects around the world, leading to a near-death experience for the U.S. stock markets—one that forced the Federal Reserve to change its policy forever, with enormous consequences for the economy.

Our journey starts in the land of the Rising Sun and eventually takes us to the pastoral suburb of Greenwich, Connecticut. That's when the hedge fund Long-Term Capital Management (LTCM) threatened to annihilate the global markets. It might have happened twenty-five years ago, but it still has everything to do with your portfolio in the modern age. Because when the Fed rescued that hedge fund, it started an era of unprecedented Federal Reserve activism, propping up markets every time real trouble knocked on the door. After LTCM, we saw bailout after bailout—each one bigger than the last, each one occurring in a time of low inflation and in a geopolitically safe, unipolar world. This gave the Fed a big arsenal of firepower with plenty of cheap money to bail out financial markets. But today, times have changed. We're in an inflationary regime, and the world is not nearly as safe. We're facing a new cold war and an era of high rates.

The Fed's choices will be very different during the next market crash. It can either do nothing, letting it all go to hell, or rescue the markets with another multitrillion-dollar bailout. If it opted to bail out the market once more, the terrifying price would be something nobody in the West has seen since the 1920s. Back then it was called hyperinflation, which is devastating for economies and investors. But we're getting a little ahead of ourselves. First we need to discuss the butterfly effect that landed America in this tragic mess.

Somewhat surprisingly, we can trace that effect to a Kawasaki GPZ900R motorcycle, the famous Ninja, first spotted in the classic 1986 movie *Top Gun* with Maverick on board, speeding through Miramar on his way to Kelly McGillis, with Berlin's "Take My Breath Away" on the soundtrack. On the streets of America, among the high-speed junkies, the eighties were about Japanese motorcycles, and as a country, Japan was booming.

The brilliance of the Japanese was their ingenuity. Japan is a country with no natural resources, pretty terrible farmland, and not a ton of real estate, and its nearest neighbors are communist China and the eastern seaboard of Russia. Yet the Japanese made themselves into the second-largest economy in the world. The key was superior manufacturing, and they flooded the world market with cheap, fast, smart, and reliable technology. They were on fire. Products included not just the high-performance engines of Yamaha, Suzuki, Mitsubishi, and Honda but also consumer electronics. Japan was the dominant global force with brands like Pioneer, Sony, Kenwood, and the gaming empires of Sega and Nintendo, not to mention Toyota, the master of just-in-time production management.

But for every winner, there is also someone who suffers. America was receiving bitter complaints from the likes of General Motors and Caterpillar to rally Congress and suppress the Japanese export market, because the Japanese competition was decimating their sales. In the early 1980s, the United States placed restrictions and tariffs on Japanese imports, but those did little to slow things down. Finally, in September 1985, five world economic leaders wielding Mont Blanc pens met in New York's finest hotel to sign what is known as the Plaza Accord and try to cool off the angrily strong dollar. They were Gerhard Stoltenberg of West Germany, Pierre Bérégovoy of France, James Baker III of the United States, Nigel Lawson of Britain, and Noboru Takeshita of Japan. The agreement led to a 25.8 percent decline in the dollar over the next two years and a big appreciation in the German mark and Japanese yen. The latter rose 100 percent over the same time frame. A surge like that placed Japan's economy at risk of a deep recession because of how reliant it was on export-based industries.

Think of currencies and export markets as sitting on old-fashioned scales. Finding that perfect balance is a very difficult task. If currencies get too strong, it kills the export market, as the goods and services exported will be less affordable abroad. Weaken the currency, and demand for exports will go up.

Now, before everyone signed the Plaza Accord, Japan had a relatively weak currency, and the U.S. dollar was very strong—good for Japan, but bad for the U.S. exports. (We'll get to the advantages of a strong dollar in a later chapter.) That's why GM and Caterpillar were kicking up a fuss. A Japanese stereo was cheap when bought with American dollars. But after the accord, the dollar became drastically weaker against the yen. So while an American consumer still paid the same number of dollars for the stereo, each dollar was worth less. In effect, Japan received less money for the stereo. The tables had turned, and Japan's rampant export industries were in trouble.

In response to this, Tokyo started the first experiment with central bank activism. The Bank of Japan slashed interest rates in half to bolster the Japanese economy, fueling an unprecedented asset bubble. When that bubble finally popped a few years later, the bank started buying hundreds of billions of bonds in the market and eventually dropped interest rates below zero. This became the blueprint for the Federal Reserve and the European central banks. We would witness it fifteen years later, when these central banks bought trillions of bonds to combat a recession. The Fed dropped rates to zero, and the European Central Bank even went below zero.

The initial rate cuts by the Japanese central bank in the mid-eighties made borrowing money much cheaper for the Japanese people, creating an epic credit bubble, a real estate bubble, and a stock market bubble. Meanwhile, the Land of the Rising Sun had become the envy of Asia, and it wasn't long before neighboring economies tried to duplicate its success. These economies became known as the "Asian Tigers"—South Korea, Taiwan, Hong Kong, and Singapore—and the "Tiger Cubs"—Indonesia, Malaysia, the Philippines, Thailand, and Vietnam. Not China. It wasn't yet free of the quagmire of communism, but its capitalist neighbors learned from the excellent example set by Japan, ramping up a massive export economy based on brainpower and hard work.

Nikkei During the 1980s Bubble Economy

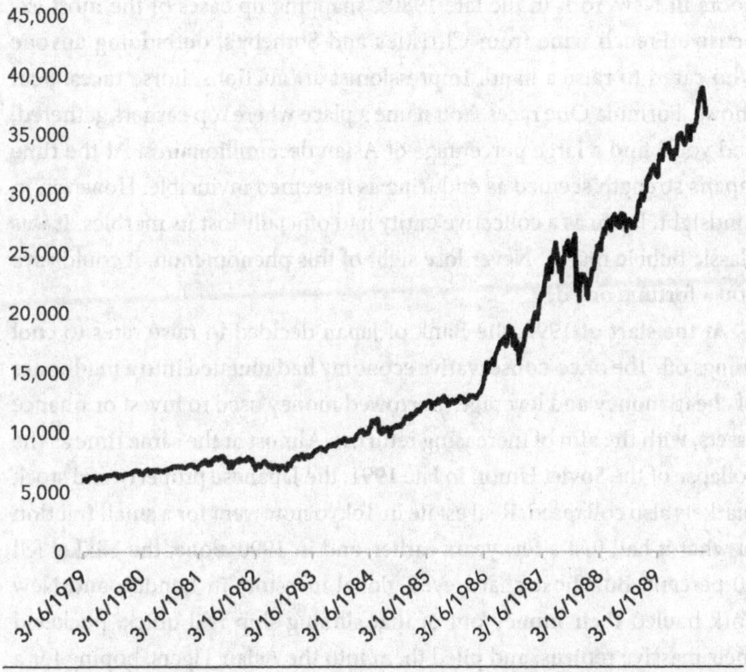

In the 1980s, institutional investors in the West had quickly latched on to the booming markets in Asia. There's a great line from Gordon Gekko, the villain of Oliver Stone's iconic film *Wall Street,* uttered into his cellphone one morning on the beach: "Money never sleeps, pal." It really didn't. Not anymore. Traders in the United States and Europe scoured every time zone for the best returns on capital. They poured money into the Asian Tigers, hoping each could be the next Japan, which itself was in the process of completing the most epic asset bubble the world had ever seen.

With their wealth, the Japanese bought land, stocks, and collectibles, often financed with cheap money, courtesy of the Bank of Japan. At its peak, Tokyo's real estate could sell for as much as $139,000 a square foot! Even now, penthouses overlooking Central Park in Manhattan go for $6,500 per square foot, which is widely considered among the most expensive real estate in the world. If not, it's right up there. At one point, the grounds of the Imperial Palace of Tokyo were worth as much as the entire state of California. Between 1986 and 1989, Japan's Nikkei stock index rose a staggering 200 percent. Japanese businessmen lined auction house floors in New York in the late 1980s, snapping up cases of the most expensive French wine from Christie's and Sotheby's, outbidding anyone who cared to raise a hand. Impressionist art auctions, horse races, boat shows, Formula One races. You name a place where top earners gathered, and you'd find a large percentage of Asian decamillionaires. At the time Japan's strength seemed as enduring as it seemed invincible. However, in hindsight, Japan as a collective entity had officially lost its marbles. It was classic bubble mania. Never lose sight of this phenomenon. It could save you a fortune one day.

At the start of 1990, the Bank of Japan decided to raise rates to cool things off. The once-conservative economy had mutated into a madhouse of cheap money and leverage (borrowed money used to invest or finance assets, with the aim of increasing returns). Almost at the same time as the collapse of the Soviet Union in late 1991, the Japanese property and stock markets also collapsed. Real estate in Tokyo now went for a small fraction of what it had just a few years earlier, and in 1990 alone, the Nikkei fell 50 percent. But those sharp-eyed global investors in London and New York hauled their money out of that sinking ship real quick, pocketed their massive returns, and piled them into the Asian Tigers, hoping for a carbon-copy performance.

INVESTORS TAKE NOTE:

The Importance of the Japanese Asset Boom-Bust for U.S. Markets

After the implosion of asset prices, the Japanese economy entered a decade-long period of deflation. Ben Bernanke, who became chairman of the Fed in 2006, gave a speech in 2002 titled "Deflation: Making Sure 'It' Doesn't Happen Here." He laid out a playbook to avoid the deflationary trap of the Japanese economy. This became the blueprint for the Fed's monetary policy after the 2008 financial crisis. In line with his speech, Bernanke dropped rates to zero and started large-scale asset purchases by the Fed (Bernanke called it the modern equivalent of printing money). Twelve years later, Bernanke's successor did the same thing in response to the COVID-19 crisis and the plunge in the stock markets. We now know that this policy, commonly known as quantitative easing (QE), primarily inflates financial assets such as stocks and bonds, while also exacerbating income inequality by keeping asset prices like houses and commodities artificially high.

By 1992, Japan had cratered and was left with a long runway of deflation—this was the start of its "lost decade." At the same time, the Asian Tiger economies began to rise. Same playbook as Japan, but they study their history in that part of the world and try never to repeat the mistakes. This time, they intended to avoid rapid currency appreciation, which had effectively set in motion the historic boom-bust that ravaged Japan. Each country pegged its currency to the U.S. dollar, the global reserve currency (aligning its exchange rate with the value of the dollar). This kept any currency fluctuations to an absolute minimum and made it easier to attract global institutional investors, who took sizable positions in Korea and Hong Kong stocks. The pegs also removed any need to hedge currency exposures. Once the lavish table was prepared, Southeast Asia sat down to enjoy the inevitable banquet of their success. Not in their wildest dreams did they imagine that dessert would never be served.

The Asian economic boom followed a very similar pattern to Japan's, starting out with a huge trade surplus—that's when a country sells more than it buys—and this glut of cash created easier borrowing and attracted hordes of foreign investors. The bust side of the equation was a different story. Wary of getting wiped out like their Japanese counterparts, the local business elite were watching the influx of money from a local perch. This gave them a very sharp lens on the economy and allowed them to spot any shift in sentiment—putting them first in line for the life raft if the ship hit an iceberg. From 1994 to 1996, the Asian Tigers and the Tiger Cubs went through a period of economic growth that could only be described as unprecedented. South Korea, Singapore, Thailand, Malaysia, and Indonesia experienced GDP growth rates of 8 to 12 percent. Between 1990 and 1997, the Philippines' stock market soared 250 percent, Indonesia's 160 percent, Malaysia's 140 percent, and Taiwan's 80 percent. It was like a giant flood tide that raised sea levels in every harbor, and halfway around the world in a sleepy corner of Greenwich, Connecticut, that tide had started to breach the seawalls.

A revered hedge fund had been riding the wave of an almost uninterrupted, low-volatility bull market like few others. Just since its inception in 1994, it had achieved a spectacular 300 percent return. But global markets were about to have a rendezvous with destiny, and the hedge fund's days were numbered.

The Birth of Bailout Nation

In 1997, a man named John Meriwether from Chicago's South Side, the pioneer of fixed-income arbitrage, was in his fiftieth year. He had a face still plump with youth, a boyish shock of brown hair, and an expression of pride that often comes with giant financial success. Throughout his life, he'd stamped his tickets, too. First with a hotshot degree from Northwestern, then with a master's from Chicago's Booth School of Business, and finally with a reputation for brilliance on Wall Street, which is no easy task. And now John Meriwether presided over a hedge fund that was the talk of the town. Two of his partners had just been awarded a Nobel Prize in economics.

Meriwether's hedge fund was the legendary LTCM. (Anyone knowledgeable in financial history knows its story, but few make the connection between it and the asset price inflation that came to define the early twenty-first century.) In 1994, its first year in business, the fund's return was 21 percent, in the following year 43 percent, and in its third year 41 percent. Its staggering success was built on one small word that has caused more financial pain than anything else in history: leverage. It's a highly addictive drug, because the returns can be so outlandishly big if you get it right. Get it wrong, and you might end up without a place to live.

LTCM was an arbitrage fund, which at its core meant that it exploited market inefficiencies. Its bread and butter was fixed income—securities that pay fixed interest or dividend payments until their maturity date, generally considered low-risk—with a particular focus on government bonds. Sometimes two different issues of the same Treasury bond with maturities six months apart can have a slight difference in price. When I say "slight," I mean something like 12 cents. The classic *arb trade* (sometimes referred to as the basis trade) would be going long on the lower-valued bond (a bond that doesn't trade very often, described as being "off the run"), betting on a higher return, and shorting the higher-valued bond (a more liquid bond that trades more regularly, or is "on the run").

When the two bonds eventually fell into line, the hedge fund made the spread (collected the difference). Inside the fund, a sophisticated computer model flagged arbitrage opportunities. And Meriwether's fund bet big. It placed enormous trades on one position. If it went the wrong way, the traders didn't panic. They doubled the bet, over and over again, until the trade finally turned in their favor.

But LTCM's success was starting to work against it. An army of copycat traders all over the place was squeezing it out of its best trades. Meriwether had hired the best mathematicians from Harvard and MIT, even nurtured and trained them over many years. But LTCM's footprint on the market was too big now. The smart money was on to its tricks. The fund needed a new edge, even if it meant venturing outside its area of expertise.

INVESTORS TAKE NOTE:

How Important Trends in Foreign Exchange Can Help You Make Money

While most emerging-market currencies were pegged to the dollar in the 1990s, after the crisis the currencies became freely floated and important leading indicators for investors. When it comes to listening to markets and looking for telling signals, we are grateful to Jens Nordvig, founder of Exante Data and MarketReader, in the foreign exchange arena. Jens has been a longtime mentor and adviser to our team. After more than a decade at Goldman Sachs and Nomura, Jens commands the highest respect on the Street and, in our opinion, is a true Hall of Famer. When we think of the late 1990s and early 2020s in foreign exchange there are some striking similarities.

At our client conference in Panama in November 2022, Jens made several key observations over dinner. "From June of 1995 to September of 2001, the dollar appreciated over 51 percent, one of the most significant bull runs of all time," he said. "The current up cycle in the dollar started in October of 2008, and by September of 2022 the greenback had appreciated by 62 percent." That's the second-biggest run since the 1960s, and according to Jens, this bull is long in the tooth. "Most telling," he continued, "is the rising bullish corre-

In 1997, LTCM stepped away from American shores and started investing vast sums of money in emerging-market debt and foreign currencies. The hedge fund took positions in the Norwegian krone, Brazilian and Russian bonds, and Danish mortgages; it made investments in the Greek economy; it shorted massive tech companies like Microsoft and Dell; it was even short Berkshire Hathaway—believing the company was overvalued relative to its holdings. But LTCM itself didn't know the value of the holdings, which were mostly private. Its entire portfolio was a poisonous matrix of longs and shorts, bets that something would move one way while another asset would move in the opposite direction.

lation across the tertiary foreign exchange space, giving off a sharp bear signal for the U.S. dollar coming out of the flows using our 'MarketReader' technology."

The point Jens was making is this: When you see the second- and third-tier currencies all start to outperform the U.S. dollar together, at an accelerating rate of change, this is a signal that some hot capital flows are starting to come back into emerging-market currencies. Jens carefully measures this rate of change. He's constantly on the lookout for acceleration points. "Elephants always leave footprints, Larry," he told our clients. By late 2022, similar to the post-LTCM era in the late 1990s, there was a grueling bear market for emerging-market currencies. As a cold winter creeps into spring, there's a frost-covered beauty across the meadow, but not a soul can be found. The once hubris-filled crowd has run for the hills, and all the wounded dollar bears that were dancing victory laps have gone into hiding. After the bear's mauling, the genesis of a new bull market is a lonely yet peaceful place. In the months well before "the turn," we must meticulously measure the capitulation climax (the speed at which the patrons are running from the smoke-filled theater). At the heart of our work is avoiding the bear traps but being there for "the turn." In this case, Jens has identified key signals pointing to a turn in the great U.S. dollar bull run; the greenback plunged over the next several months. Bravo, Jens.

The hedge fund had counterparty risk stuffed into the coffers of financial companies all over the world. (That type of risk is related to the possibility, or even probability, that the other party involved in a transaction will default on their contractual obligation.) It had credit default swaps (CDSs), stock options, and short positions on stock options hedged against five-year CDS contracts. The fund's leverage, or debt-to-asset ratio, was an astronomical 30:1, with off-balance-sheet derivatives (derivative positions that do not appear on the balance sheet) of well over a trillion dollars.

There is a valuable lesson here. Success often breeds complacency around risk management. We saw this at Lehman, and it applies to small investors as well. Excessive confidence leads to hubris. It lures investors with a small, manageable stack into what you could call the centipede trade, where they have too many legs. As hedge fund legend Mike Gelband once told me, holding too many positions often translates into being "too big to succeed." Whenever you're investing and there is a moment when you feel over your skis, get smaller and regroup.

Big names on Wall Street were raising doubts about the fund's ability to weather a storm. Its entire risk model was powered by previous market behavior. The fund's success relied heavily on the market continuing to do the expected—on the past being a reliable predictor of the future. But what if something nobody expected happened? Could LTCM bring down the entire financial system?

In mid-1997, fault lines began to surface in the Asian economy. Trade surpluses had turned into deficits, and the capital flow from the West started to slow down, dropping to $26 billion from $54.9 billion the previous year, practically a 50 percent decline. It wasn't dire, not yet, but it wasn't great. These countries had received massive inflows of capital, but their currencies were pegged to the U.S. dollar. This led to an expansion in money supply and inflated property prices while the central banks sat with their hands tied behind their backs. When international investors realized how overvalued and bubbly these markets had become, they rushed to withdraw their capital. They exchanged local currency for dollars and yen, and pulled their money back home so quickly that it caused a balance-of-payments crisis. In other words, Asian central banks no longer had the reserves of foreign currency that they needed to maintain their peg with the U.S. dollar. The seeds of the crisis first sprouted in Thailand and Malaysia, and it wasn't long before the entire region had caught a cold.

On July 2, 1997, Thailand broke the peg and devalued its currency in a desperate move by the central bank to throw the economy a lifeline. Within weeks, the Thai baht dropped 20 percent to a record low. Then Malaysia's central bank imposed severe restrictions on capital outflows and offshore trading to keep the ringgit afloat, but that autumn the currency would drop by 48 percent. Global macro hedge funds caught on quickly and started to short the currencies of these countries. Three days later, the Philippine peso was devalued. Then Indonesia widened the trading band around the rupiah—giving the pegged currency more leeway to fluctuate, which is usually an ominous sign. In mid-August 1997, Indonesia gave up on the trading band and allowed the currency to float freely, which triggered an 85 percent plunge over the next twelve months. The repeated currency interventions in the summer of 1997 signaled to the entire investment world that there was blood in the water, and investors wanted out. The International Monetary Fund had to step in with multibillion-dollar bailout programs for the Asian countries and imposed all kinds of reforms—including the abandonment of their pegs to the U.S. dollar.

Renowned hedge fund manager Kyle Bass once told me that "the adjustment mechanism for troubled countries is a much weaker currency. It's very difficult to go through a hard restructuring [default] and become competitive once again as a nation unless you have a currency adjustment mechanism that's associated with your restructuring."

The seismic collapse of Asia really caught the academics off guard, especially since they were a group relying on computer algorithms. They had never been on a trading floor before. That's where the rubber meets the road, where hotshot analysts determine value and a sixth sense for real danger keeps you from hitting an iceberg. It's also where a pit boss might yell at you from across the floor, "The past is never a reliable predictor of the future!"

Nasdaq Composite (Rose 278% After LTCM Bailout)

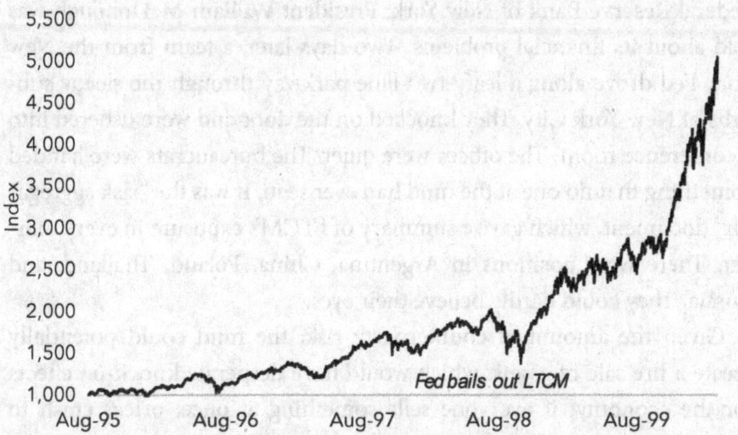

In May 1998, Meriwether's portfolio lost 6 percent of its value. In June, 10 percent. July was worse, racking up an 18 percent decline. In August, while most fund managers were out in the Hamptons or cruising the Med on a chartered boat, the stock market plunged and LTCM lost $553 million. Virtually all of its positions went against it. In a completely unexpected move, Russia, reeling from the Asian crisis and the gigantic plunge in oil demand, defaulted on its debt. This was the knockout punch for Meriwether.

When global markets go into a tailspin, investors stampede to safety. And safety means U.S. Treasuries. Yields are lower, of course, but preservation of capital is all people want in a bear market. LTCM had mountains of bonds hedged against U.S. Treasury bonds, which it sold short in vast numbers. And it was an awful time to be short.

By the end of that month, shortly before Labor Day, 44 percent of LTCM's entire portfolio had gone up in smoke. Four weeks later, its performance had fallen off a cliff, and by the time the sugar maples in Vermont had turned an autumnal red, LTCM was down 83 percent. Now it was teetering on the edge of bankruptcy, and institutions all over the country were about to go down with it. Somebody had to step in.

On September 15, 1998, famed investor George Soros told Congress that the global capitalist system was "coming apart at the seams," adding that "instead of acting like a pendulum, financial markets have recently acted more like a wrecking ball, knocking over one country after another." Three days later, officials from the Greenwich hedge fund contacted the Federal Reserve Bank of New York. President William McDonough was told about its financial problems. Two days later, a team from the New York Fed drove along a leafy two-lane parkway through the sleepy suburbs of New York City. They knocked on the door and were ushered into a conference room. The offices were quiet. The bureaucrats were handed something that no one at the fund had ever seen. It was the "risk aggregator" document, which gave a summary of LTCM's exposure in every market. There were positions in Argentina, China, Poland, Thailand, and Russia. They could hardly believe their eyes.

Given the amount of counterparty risk, the fund could potentially create a fire sale of assets, which would have desperate knock-on effects for the economy; if everyone sells something at once, prices crash to nearly zero as liquidity dries up. As McDonough famously said, "Markets would . . . possibly cease to function." That's when the decision was made. The Federal Reserve orchestrated a bailout of LTCM, pressuring a consortium of U.S. and European banks to buy the assets. The Fed had concluded that LTCM was too big and could not be allowed to fail.

Credit, Equity, and Bank Lending

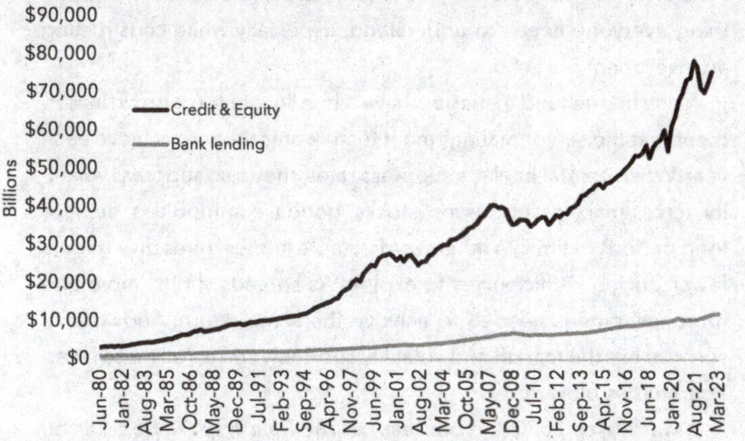

This was a wakeup call for Fed chairman Alan Greenspan. He realized that corporations were obtaining much more of their financing through the financial markets than from banks, leaving the U.S. economy dangerously dependent on those markets. Consider that in 1998 total bank lending was around $3 trillion, while the U.S. stock and credit market had a combined market cap of more than $20 trillion; today, total bank lending in the economy is about $12 trillion, while the total size of the equity and corporate bond market is almost $75 trillion. This made the Fed's conventional tools that directly impact bank lending—such as interest-rate policy—much less effective. From that day forward, Fed policy became almost exclusively focused on the stock and credit market, or, in the Fed's jargon, "financial conditions."

The bailout of LTCM by the Fed sent a clear message to every financial institution in the country: *If you get too big, if you become an out-of-*

INVESTORS BEWARE:

What Blew Up LTCM Also Led to an Implosion of Several Hedge Funds in March 2020

The connection between the blowup of LTCM in 1998 and the colossal COVID-era bailouts is more than just a coincidence. It's something everyone needs to understand, especially while constructing an investment portfolio.

Many hedge fund managers have a hurdle rate, a return on investment that the senior management team wants them to achieve each year. When central bankers suppress rates, they also suppress volatility across many asset classes (stocks, bonds, commodities, etc.) for long periods of time. In other words, stable interest rates give traders fewer pricing inefficiencies to exploit. As spreads shrink, more and more leverage is needed to achieve the same return. And when a surprise hits the market and volatility suddenly spikes, all these leveraged trades blow up.

It was March 2020 and our team at *The Bear Traps Report* was on the phone with one of our favorite macro investors in the hedge fund space, Joe Mauro. He'd spent thirteen years at Goldman Sachs, mainly as a partner. His understanding of rates, government bonds, and foreign exchange—along with a broad macro understanding of commodities—was at the highest level on Wall Street. There are those moments in a career on the street when you have a conversation with someone that opens your eyes to the bigger picture. This was one of them.

Across stocks, bonds, and nearly all asset classes, markets were becoming an out-of-control inferno. Spreads were blowing out, and the buyers were gone, providing exactly zero bids for anything. Everything was for sale, and even though COVID was a threat, there was something else impacting asset prices.

"What's going on, Joe?" I asked. "This is nuts. I haven't seen anything like it since Lehman."

"They really have 'em by the short hairs!" he fired back.

Joe was referring to the large leverage inside the relative-value hedge funds. The systemic risk of the situation would force the Fed to respond in a big way. He went on to explain how the Fed had suppressed rates for so long that the "leverage buildup" across at least a dozen funds was unimaginable. Once again, institutions were too big to fail, but this time it wasn't limited to just one or two banks. It was spread out across multiple hedge funds. At least a dozen funds were up to their eyeballs in the *basis trade,* popularized by LTCM, and in the *relative-value trade,* another strategy that takes advantage of minute price distortions. These firms were preposterously overleveraged: some levered 20:1, others as much as 30:1.

"Everyone thinks this is a COVID-19-driven sell-off," Joe continued. "The fact is, the cards on the table make LTCM look like a Sunday picnic. This could get real big, real fast. Maybe twenty times larger. This pandemic is triggering a colossal leverage blowup across multiple hedge funds simultaneously. Washington will have to back up the truck for this one. . . . [It's] maybe three to five times bigger than Lehman. The consequences will be a game changer. It's going to impact all asset prices, and will radically change portfolio construction for the next decade."

The lesson here? This was LTCM on steroids and the deadliest pandemic in a hundred years forcing a public policy response more than three times larger than that of the great financial crisis. The bottom line: Central bankers are trying to smooth out the ups and downs of the business cycle, but they are just sowing the seeds of a much bigger blowup down the road.

control pile of debt that puts the entire financial system in jeopardy, we won't let you go down. Uncle Sam will bail you out and support the financial markets no matter what. This act changed the course of financial history forever. America had crossed the Rubicon—the point of no return.

After the LTCM bailout, we entered an era of government accommodation, which, like the Chinese currency pegging, changed the landscape of business forever. Financial accommodation comes with various weapons at the government's disposal. Not Gatling guns, not tanks, and not Scud missiles, but these weapons were far more dangerous. You wouldn't ever go into battle with them, but if you were trying to destroy a global economy, they would do nicely. I'm talking about interest rates, printing presses, or bailouts.

In the spring of 2001, the dot-com bubble well and truly imploded. Private capital and speculative fervor finally dried up, and valuations plummeted from their stratospheric heights. Technology companies across America were stacking the furniture, preparing to close up shop. Armies of nerds were out of work. The great craze that had taken over the markets was ending. The tech boom had gone on for about four years, which is about right for a bubble, and then everything collapsed like a flan in a cupboard. Those who exited made out like bandits. But as for those left holding the bag in the summer of 2001, it was sad to watch the expressions on their faces as they peered into the bag at their shattered dreams, at the millions in profits that had disappeared like a puff of gunpowder smoke.

Old-fashioned value investor Warren Buffett, who had stood in Sun Valley in 1999 and delivered a speech to the titans of technology—Bill Gates, Michael Dell, Larry Ellison—explaining why he would never invest in one of these overpriced tech firms, now sat in his office in Omaha sipping a Cherry Coke with a wry smile on his face. The 10 percent owner of the world's number one drinks company had avoided a crash that had wiped out several hedge funds and exposed frauds like Enron and WorldCom. The Nasdaq index looked like it had been hijacked by a bungee jumper, dropping 80 percent since its peak. The new nirvana was over. It was time for America to dig out the suits and ties once more, and get back to work like sensible adults, trudging back into an economy that was figuratively hungover. It was lackluster and kind of depressing once all the dot-com fun had been washed out. The Fed stepped in with a rate cut, just to put a little pep in the economy's stride, but that

September, on the eleventh, at 8:46 A.M., American Airlines flight 11 crashed into the World Trade Center's North Tower. At 9:03 A.M. United Airlines flight 175 crashed into the South Tower.

The markets did not open that day. They remained closed for the entire week, which marked the longest shutdown since the Great Depression. When the New York Stock Exchange's opening bell rang again on September 17, markets went into a tailspin. The Dow ended the day off 7.1 percent, a new record for daily losses on the index. The S&P 500 index plummeted 11.6 percent, and the tech-heavy Nasdaq dropped 16 percent. In total, $1.4 trillion in value was lost.

In the Eccles Building on Constitution Avenue in Washington, D.C., Alan Greenspan sat with his Federal Open Market Committee (FOMC), wearing a grim expression. Somehow, this act of war on the American economy rested on his shoulders. The U.S. transportation system had been shut down until further notice, and the capital markets had frozen over. Nobody in the country knew when the next plane would take off. The airline business and the hotel business are tied at the hip, and both industries were suddenly in big trouble, creating a massive credit risk that poured right into the insurance industry with a $40 billion bill. And it had happened in the blink of an eye. One morning there was peace. The next day, America was at war. Economically as well. And it had been all year, in a sense. The 9/11 attacks were another major kick in the pants. And so, two days after the attacks, the Maestro, as Greenspan was called, started the first of another six rate cuts.

Going into the new millennium with interest rates relatively high, the Fed had plenty of weapons to fight a war with the market. Its guns, so to speak, were fully loaded, and it had stockpiles of ammunition, with more on the way. The sovereign balance sheet, which is government debt in layperson's terms, was healthy. When 2001 began, the federal funds rate stood at 6 percent. Before the year was through, however, the Fed had cut interest rates a staggering eleven times, all the way down to 1.75 percent in December. After 9/11, the Fed went on a rate-cutting program of fifty basis points a month—that's half a percent—for four months in a row. Remember, low rates mean cheap capital, which means easy money. Every consumer wins. This provided sufficient liquidity, and by some act of mercy from the heavens, markets normalized quickly after the World Trade Center attacks.

But a new phrase was creeping into market lingo, and that phrase was only two words long. In fact, it was only two syllables, but it's part of the reason why we are now, as of this book's writing in 2023, facing a sovereign debt crisis with ~$33 trillion on the government's balance sheet and more than $200 trillion of unfunded liabilities that can never be paid. That phrase was "Fed put."

The phrase was born from the Fed's response to downward moves in the market and Greenspan's propensity to throw out a life raft when things went awry—the failure of LTCM, the dot-com bust, the 9/11 terrorist attacks. Every time there was a disaster, the Fed was there, making sure the markets, left to their own tendencies, didn't cause another Black Monday. Our old friend Adam Smith, the classical economist, with his invisible-hand-of-capitalism theory, probably would have been in disbelief at an FOMC meeting in the early 2000s. Think of the New York restaurant scene. If you ever visit the city and you come across a restaurant that's too expensive and the food is no good, you can almost predict it will go bust within six months. It's the most brutal market I know of, and capitalism is actually functioning extremely well in that market. But that's what's lacking in global markets these days. When the policymakers don't allow the business cycle to function, allow things to go bust, you get a buildup of rot, and that enables foul play, because the bad apples aren't flushed out of the system. If New York restaurants received bailouts all the time, it would be the worst dining scene on earth! But instead, it's one of the best.

Market stress builds over time, much like mildew or moss on a brick wall. It requires a regular cleaning crew to smarten the place up and get everything looking sharp again. That's what a capitalist market does, very naturally, when left to its own devices. But when Greenspan kept backstopping these disasters, the bad apples in the market never went away. They were just hidden by all the lifeboats, and they would one day wind up on the sovereign balance sheet.

We need to listen when markets speak, especially at turning points of colossal secular change. That is where billions will be made and lost. Think of the early 1980s, at the end of the high-inflation regime, on the doorstep of the deflation era. Value stocks and commodities dominated for more than a decade. By 1981, most of the capital in the S&P 500 was in stocks adjacent to the "real" economy. This was at the end of a decade of sustained inflation and a major tailwind for hard assets. More than 27 percent of market value was tied up in the energy sector, 12 percent in industrials, and 10 percent in materials. Think of a jaw-dropping 50 percent of the market's valuation in these three hard-asset-centric sectors. In contrast, financials claimed a measly 6 percent.

Fast-forward to 2007—after almost two decades of deflationary pressure, easy leverage, and the Fed put—and it was a totally different story. Before the momentous Lehman Brothers collapse, financials became the biggest sector and sucked up almost a quarter—24 percent—of total value. Meanwhile, energy had dropped down to just 12 percent, industrials to 8 percent, materials to 4 percent, and utilities to 2 percent. It's also worth noting that in 1980 information technology composed 10 percent of market value, which shot up to an eye-watering 35 percent in 2000 at the peak of the dot-com bubble, after which it sank back down to 12 percent in 2007. During the 1990s and the 2000s, the center of gravity in American business shifted completely, especially at the top. The economy of the multipolar world order (1968–1981) was centered on commodity extraction and industrial production. The economy of the new, unipolar world order of sustained peace and free trade was all about finance and tech. Markets reacted to this shift in nearly euphoric fashion.

By 2021, $20 trillion of wealth was found in just one hundred stocks inside the NDX (Nasdaq 100). This was the most crowded trade in the history of asset bubbles (an overwhelming majority of investors piled into these Nasdaq stocks). Over and over the lesson is clear: Whether it was big oil in 1981, tech stocks in 2000, or financials in 2007, when a sector is dominant over an extended period of time, this is where the most significant downside is lurking. When the buy-in to the prevailing investment narrative is that loud, run, don't walk, the other way.

As the genesis of a large secular change is upon us, it's very difficult to read the tea leaves in real time, but if you look carefully, all the signs are there. And our team spends every day searching for these signs.

Leverage Is a Hell of a Drug

The word "systemic" was not part of everyday life on the trading floor at Lehman Brothers. It didn't really surface until we started to analyze the sheer risk of certain balance sheets and imagine the consequences if one of those gigantic dominoes tumbled. We looked at Fannie Mae and Freddie Mac, which owned hundreds of billions of dollars in mortgage bonds. They were backstopping the entire system that was stuffed with subprime—people who couldn't pay after their rates reset. My dear late friend, the irreplaceable Larry McCarthy, described those two companies as "nothing more than government-funded, positive-carry hedge funds." In 2007, we saw one shadow bank after the next implode. Our group at Lehman was out in front of this, and we shorted the subprime mortgage broker New Century, big-time, to hedge our long positions in the housing sector. But what ultimately led to our failure was the same malady that killed LTCM: leverage.

But the Lehman story and the crash of 2008 are yesterday's news now. For this story, the mechanics of how it happened and why it happened would clutter up the narrative. What we need to know is that it did happen, and the government bailed out the entire financial system instead of letting it implode. The low interest rates the Federal Reserve set from 2001 to 2003 created the housing bubble with cheap money and easy lending standards and kept crooks like Bernie Madoff from being exposed, and the Fed put rescued the entire house of cards when it came tumbling down.

The public policy response to the financial crisis in 2008 was the equivalent of Hiroshima, in terms of financial weapon usage. But what were the ramifications over the next decade? The Fed did fix the credit markets, companies kept their doors open, and the financial system stayed alive. But in life, everything comes with a trade-off. And you have to expect one after throwing $5.7 trillion at a crisis (see estimate on page 44). That disrupts the balance of nature too ferociously, and it must create terrible unintended consequences. In order to understand where we are today, with a mountain of debt the size of the Himalayas, we must explore the experimental drugs the Federal Reserve used after Lehman Brothers, and the devastating side effects that could one day obliterate the markets.

3

The Dazzling Obamas—and the Dying of the Light

January 20, 2009, was icy cold and blustery, but more than 2 million people had crowded into the nation's capital to witness the historic event with the theme "A New Birth of Freedom." Barack Obama had won the 2008 general election comfortably, ending eight years of Republican government. He promised hope to a nation reeling from crisis: an end to the Iraq War, a solution to high healthcare costs, a plan to address climate change, and, most of all, a plan to fix the economy. During the last months of George W. Bush's administration, the U.S. government had spent trillions to bail out the country's collapsing economy. The Fed alone had bought $1.3 trillion worth of troubled assets, on top of the alphabet soup of lending facilities it had created (TALF, AMLF, TSLF) to unfreeze the credit markets. In December, it had begun buying $600 billion worth of agency mortgage-backed securities from newly nationalized Fannie Mae and Freddie Mac.

On March 6, the S&P 500 briefly touched the ominous 666 level. J. P. Morgan dipped below $11, which was, incidentally, "the greatest buying opportunity I've ever seen," said our longtime friend Doug Kass on CNBC. Everyone was on edge, awaiting the next move from the inexperienced Fed chief, Ben Bernanke.

But this brilliant economic scholar, a Harvard undergrad and an MIT PhD in economics, was out of firepower. The federal funds rate was at rock bottom. For all the trillions they'd thrown at the crisis, it was a black hole that inhaled money at an unstoppable rate.

Bernanke had studied the Great Depression extensively while in academia, and he was terrified that the U.S. economy would slip into a catastrophic deflationary spiral, as it had during the 1930s. He was crossing into uncharted territory with his latest idea—a brand-new form of monetary policy known as quantitative easing. As we discussed in chapter 2, Japan had experimented with this in the late 1990s and early 2000s, but Bernanke believed the Fed needed to go in much bigger than the Japanese had ever dared to go. The bombshell of Lehman Brothers had pushed the country all the way to the brink of financial ruin. Desperate times called for desperate measures.

And it worked! In March 2009, the Fed promised to buy $1.25 trillion in agency debt and Treasuries, which immediately set off a frenzy of stock buying and a new bull market. Wall Street never looked back, and by the

How Much Did the Government Spend Because of the 2008 Financial Crisis?

Let's start with the Fed's response to Lehman's collapse, because that is easiest to measure. By the end of the first quarter of 2010, the Fed had bought $1.5 trillion in assets under its newfangled quantitative easing program. This wasn't enough, and QE part 2 and QE part 3 followed, and the Fed injected a total of $3.5 trillion of liquidity from 2008 until 2014. The $700 billion Troubled Assets Relief Program (TARP) bank bailout fund was later reduced to $475 billion. Fannie and Freddie were bailed out for a little less than $200 billion, while Citi alone received $400 billion in assets, debt guarantees, and other government assistance, and Bank of America $100 billion. Morgan Stanley received $100 billion from the Fed in October 2008 so that it could report third-quarter results with "ample liquidity." In addition to that, the administration passed the $900 billion American Recovery and Reinvestment Act in early 2009 to help revamp the moribund U.S. economy after the Lehman collapse. The government ran budget deficits of well over $1 trillion from 2009 until 2012. Excluding these deficits, the bailout tab was $5.7 trillion, which is more than former bailout czar Neil Barofsky's $4.6 trillion total bailout estimate.

end of 2009 the S&P 500 had rallied 68 percent. There were a lot of smiles, a lot of backslapping, and a lot of self-congratulation. But—and I remember it well—the smartest risk advisers I knew were uneasy, alarmed by what the Fed was doing and the sheer magnitude of debt Congress had approved.

Despite the stock market rally, the recession continued. Workers, especially low-skilled workers, faced a dire lack of opportunity. Many lost their savings, jobs, and homes. As assets ballooned in price, the richest 1 percent of Americans suddenly had more wealth than the entire bottom 95 percent!

Detroit had once been the most successful city in the country, if not the world. In 2009, it was on its knees. Auto manufacturing plants were abandoned. Almost a third of the city's houses had been vacated. Same in other heartland manufacturing capitals: Youngstown, Buffalo, Flint, Gary, and St. Louis.

What had caused the demise of the American manufacturing economy? You couldn't blame Lehman Brothers for everything. One of the root causes was thousands of miles away, in China, the people's benighted republic. When it joined the WTO in 2001, there were 17.5 million American manufacturing jobs. By 2007, 3.5 million of those jobs had been axed, and by 2009, only 12.8 million people were still employed in manufacturing. That's 5 million workers displaced. Although the share of American workers employed in the manufacturing sector had been declining since the end of World War II, the pace had accelerated wildly. Employment for workers who graduated from high school but not college (construction workers, mechanics, and manufacturers) had declined from 37 million in 2000 to 33 million in 2010. This was the plight of the blue-collar worker. And it was marching America onto a collision course with dangerous civil unrest.

President Obama was desperate to sort out the plight of the Rust Belt, and he had the perfect platform. His party had won control of the House, the Senate, and the presidency—something coveted by every administration in history. And Larry Summers, director of the White House economic team, helped him hatch a plan. Summers was a brilliant economist. He had entered MIT at sixteen, and Marty Feldstein had been his PhD adviser at Harvard. Feldstein practically invented Reaganomics.

In 1999, Summers had helped Bill Clinton dismantle the Glass-Steagall

Act, the removal of which ended up being one of the major gateways to the collapse of Lehman. Now he had to deal with its unintended consequences. First on the agenda was saving the automakers. GM and Chrysler, hard hit by Japanese competition and decades of grotesque mismanagement, were teetering on the edge of the abyss.

By May 2009, the U.S. government had bought 72.5 percent of General Motors in a debt-for-equity exchange. That kept 5,700 Canadians out of the soup kitchens that winter. The total rescue cost was about $51 billion, plus another $17.2 billion to the company's mortgage bank, GMAC Finance, which had been hammered by the housing crash.

Obama's economic team then made an unprecedented move. GM was forced into bankruptcy, and its private bondholders were thrown under the bus, forced to take equity shares that were worth much less than the bonds. Meanwhile, the unions hit gold, pocketing twice as much of the equity for their pension claims. This trashed all legal precedent by putting senior bondholders at the back of the line. Until then, priority of payment had been decided by a bankruptcy judge, but the administration flipped two hundred years of bankruptcy law on its head. Once politics overtakes the rule of law, it's a very slippery slope. (Just ask investors in Venezuela and Argentina.)

Chrysler met a similar fate. It, too, was forced into Chapter 11 and given a debtor-in-possession loan of $8 billion, and 50 percent of the company was sold to Italy's Fiat for a song.

NAFTA—the North American Free Trade Agreement—had a lot to do with all this. A friendly partnership between the United States, Canada, and Mexico signed in 1995, it had been a wrecking ball for U.S. auto workers. Even after the bailouts and promises to keep jobs at home in 2009, manufacturing continued to be moved to Mexico, where labor was cheaper.

The Demise of the U.S. Auto Industry

American automotive employment went from 2.2 million jobs in 1992 to 1.8 million in 2023, despite the massive influx of foreign car companies' manufacturing plants into the United States. GM had 800,000 U.S. employees in 1990 and just 167,000 in 2023. Ford had 400,000 U.S. employees in 1990 and only 170,000 in 2023. In 1994, America made more than 500,000 cars per month. That had dwindled to 300,000 per month by 2008 and 200,000 by 2018. The COVID-19 crisis hampered production even further, and the figure is now down to a little more than 150,000 units per month. More and more U.S. production has moved abroad.

To illustrate: In 2004, 74 percent of all cars built in North America were manufactured in the United States. Just a fraction were made within Mexico's borders—a mere 9 percent. Canada manufactured the remaining 17 percent. But ten years later, things had changed dramatically. Mexico's share of auto production had doubled to 20 percent, at the expense of the U.S. business. Mexico had the added attraction of being relatively close to home, unlike China on the other side of the Pacific Ocean. When cars are being shipped over long distances, that matters.

Online vs. Department Store

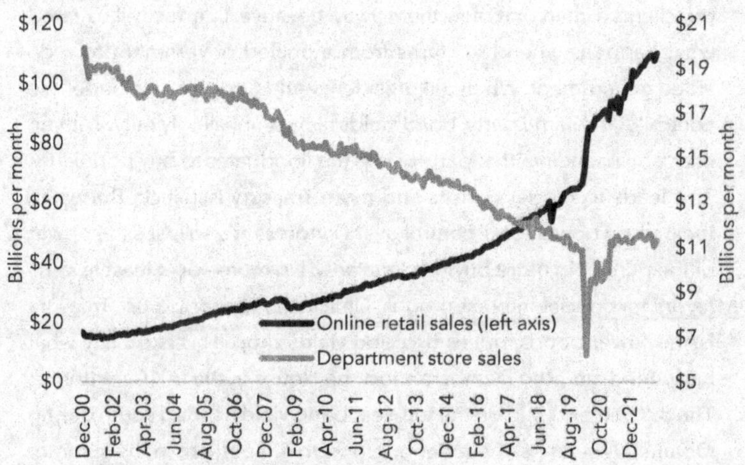

The rise of robots in manufacturing also laid waste to thousands more jobs across the country. Where would all those displaced workers go? When the Model T came along, it created entire industries, places like tire shops, oil change outfits, car washes, and more; out-of-work buggy whip salesmen and blacksmiths had lots of new opportunities. The same can't be said now for those whose automotive jobs have been eliminated.

For a while, it seemed like the retail sector might offer hope. But with the rise of online retail, many of those jobs began to disappear as mall after mall went out of business.

The Obama administration was aware of all the problems but had no lasting solutions. And so, in the sacred tradition of politicians, they threw money at it. Unemployment benefits skyrocketed, and Obamacare was rolled out across the nation, as were green energy subsidies, mortgage relief programs, and solar subsidies. Total bill: $1.3 trillion for the taxpayer.

INVESTORS TAKE NOTE:

Bonds Love D.C. Gridlock

It was our top strategist, Robbert van Batenburg, who told us about the market implications of Obama's midterm elections. He showed our clients a chart that blew them away, because it perfectly illustrated what happens when D.C. turns from a unified government to a divided government. When the presidency and Congress are under the control of the same party, bond yields almost unfailingly rally. With no check on spending, that party opens the floodgates to buy popularity. This leads to bigger deficits and more Treasury issuance. But when the party in power loses control over Congress, it also loses the power of the purse. No more buying popularity. No more—or at least fewer—favors for special interest groups. Deficits no longer go up, Treasury issues fewer bonds, prices rise, and yields drop. This is exactly what happened after the Democrats lost the House in the 2010 midterms. The 3.6 percent yield on the ten-year bond yield headed south during Obama's two terms, meandering down to 1.4 percent in the summer of 2016.

Sometimes the best trades are the simplest to understand. So, we went long bonds in October 2018 ahead of the midterms. The House flipped to the Democrats, and bonds enjoyed an unprecedented two-year rally. That autumn, ten-year yields were trading above 3 percent. Two years later they hit 0.5 percent in the eye of COVID-19 crisis. That was an unbelievable 50 percent return on the long bond in two years.

The spending plans and the explosion in income inequality exacerbated the polarization of the American public. Tea Party protests sprang up all over the place, in defiance of the mounting debt on the U.S. balance sheet. The deficit spending continued—another $1.3 trillion in 2010. But then the U.S. political machine slammed on the brakes.

In the midterm elections in 2010, the Republicans crushed the Democrats in the House. The Democrats surrendered sixty-three seats that day, their greatest loss since 1926, and Congress swung decidedly out of their control. From that day on, Obama's plans would be met with gridlock. Almost as soon as they took their seats in the House chamber, Republicans pulled out every stop to slash the country's deficit spending. In 2011, they pushed budget sequestration, threatening a national default to force Obama and the Democrats to agree to $2.4 trillion in budget reductions over ten years. Republicans kept their power over America's purse throughout the rest of Obama's presidency, and they did indeed cut the deficit—from $1.4 trillion in 2009 to $680 billion in 2013.

With the country whipsawing back toward austerity, the markets—addicted to stimulus—were floundering again. They simply wouldn't rally without the Fed's help. And that's exactly what they received.

Treasury Yields Under Unified and Divided Government

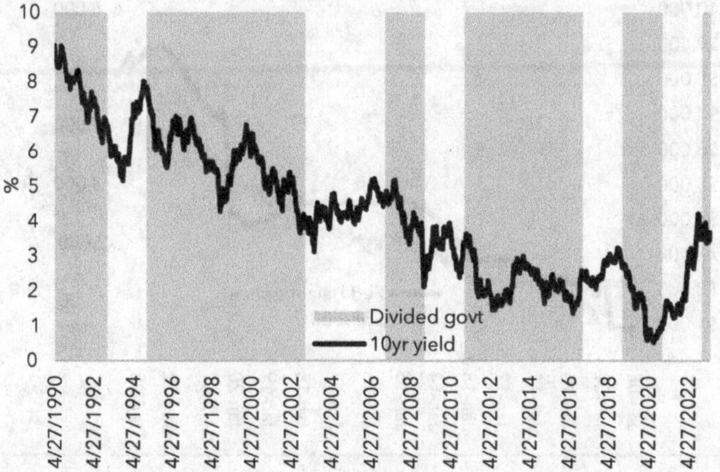

In 2011, America proved once again that its engineering was the best there has ever been. I'm not talking about cars. I'm talking about finance. The media dubbed the plan Operation Twist. The Fed was now buying long-dated bonds and selling the equivalent in shorter maturity dates—going long the thirty-year and short the two-year. Because the rate of inflation—and future expectations—remained so doggedly low, the Fed wanted to suppress interest rates further by any means necessary and push yields through the floor to jump-start economic growth. The next year, 2012, the Fed, unsatisfied with the result, embarked on a $1.7 trillion bond-buying program.

Did that make stocks go up, you might be asking? It was like attaching one of Elon Musk's Falcon 9s to the S&P 500—that's nine Merlin engines powered by liquid oxygen and rocket-grade kerosene propellant, more than 1.7 million pounds of thrust at sea level. The answer is yes. Hell, yes! Stocks surged higher. From the summer of 2012, when Bernanke announced QE3, until the middle of 2014, when the program ended, the S&P rose more than 50 percent.

As in March 2009, however, the stock market rally didn't touch the overall economy. In the following years, real GDP growth never exceeded

Impact of Fed Stimulus on S&P

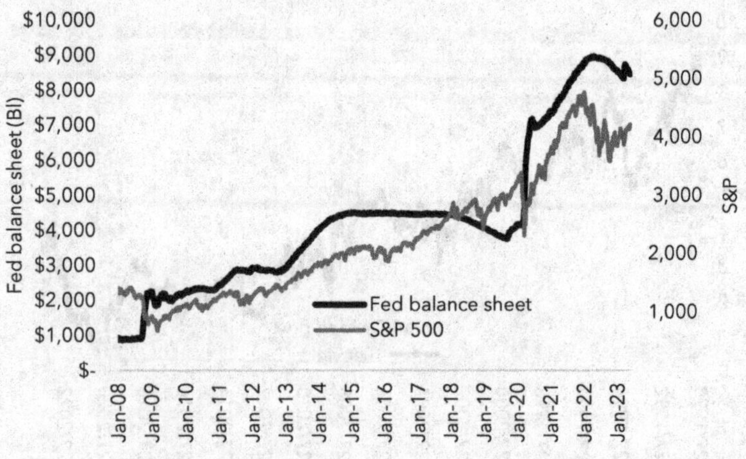

2.5 percent. The dejected masses were still struggling to put food on the table and keep the lights on. The Fed's plan was to bolster bank lending and allow companies to invest in the economy. But instead of lending, banks were parking money in very low-risk assets—U.S. Treasuries—and, for reasons that we will go into later, corporate America was hoarding cash and buying back their own stock.

Do you remember the correlation between rates and prices? It's a classic cause and effect. Low rates mean cheaper loans, which artificially inflate prices, especially when it comes to big assets like houses, which require big loans. This kept real estate prices high, which kept rents high. Vast numbers of low- and middle-income families found themselves unable to purchase homes or faced increased financial burdens related to homeownership. High expenses made life tougher than ever and exacerbated inequality even further, until America ended up with the greatest explosion of inequality since the Gilded Age.

I now welcome, ladies and gentlemen, one of the dullest subjects in finance: secular stagnation. This is an economic state of affairs in which the private sector has made a definite decision to hoard cash and not invest. In normal environments, low rates are supposed to encourage investment and growth, but that wasn't happening in 2012 to 2014, despite the Fed's best efforts. That's because banks, businesses, and households were focused on rebuilding their balance sheets after the carnage of the financial crisis. Consumers postponed purchases, and businesses postponed investment.

The plan was to end QE once the holes in banks' balance sheets—estimated to be nearly $5 trillion—were plugged. Lower interest rates meant the assets the banks held increased in value. But it lasted far longer than that.

Meanwhile, artificially suppressed interest rates gave seniors and pensioners less income on which to live. Seniors tend to hold most of their savings in municipal bonds and other fixed-income investment products. Many were already struggling with the aftermath of the Lehman crisis. In a way, QE delivered a wealth transfer from the retirees to the banks. Long after the banks were healed, this wealth transfer from old people to banks continued. With many Americans repairing their own balance sheets, the low rate of return on fixed income further eroded households' ability to spend. This was one factor in the slow-growth years following the Great Recession.

But the Fed didn't want to see it that way. When growth didn't occur, the bond-buyback programs became bigger. The Fed hopped from QE1 to QE2, and then swiftly onto QE3, right up until its balance sheet had

INVESTORS TAKE NOTE:

How QE Drives Up Stocks and Bonds

Market liquidity is one of the single biggest factors driving stock prices up and down. Increasing liquidity will put more money into the financial markets, which find their way into stocks and bonds. On the other hand, removing liquidity drains cash from the markets and tends to put pressure on stock and bond prices.

But how does the Fed add and subtract liquidity from the market? When the Fed buys a bond, it takes a bond out of the hands of investors in exchange for cash. It puts that bond into its account and will hold it until maturity. This exchange injects liquidity into the market because the investor now needs to redeploy that cash. Imagine when the Fed buys trillions of U.S. Treasuries, which they do under a QE program. It leaves investors with trillions of cash and the Fed with a mountain of risk-free bonds that are no longer accessible to investors. These investors need to buy new bonds with that liquidity to replace the ones the Fed purchased from them. But because of all these bonds that the Fed has been buying in the market, the bond yield is now so low that they no longer meet the required minimum yield for investors.

Lots of institutional investors such as insurance or pension funds need to buy low-risk fixed-income assets that have a minimum rate of return. So, these investors search elsewhere for bonds with an adequate return, and they end up buying investment-grade corporate bonds. But this puts pressure on those yields and eventually creates a shortage of Investment Grade bonds. All this creates a sliding scale whereby investors are forced into asset classes they would otherwise not need to consider. It's a dynamic that drives down yields across reached $4.5 trillion. Remember, that's the balance sheet of the Federal Reserve. It's not the same thing as the national debt, which was up in lights near Manhattan's Bryant Park on a big digital clock, the brainchild of the real estate tycoon Seymour Durst. The speed at which it counted was breathtaking. The United States was printing roughly a

---

the fixed-income markets, and lower yields generally are bullish for stock prices as it makes stocks more attractive relative to bonds. It also allows well-capitalized companies to issue debt at artificially low interest rates and use the proceeds to buy back their own stock. Take, for example, Apple. Since 2012, the company has issued $130 billion of debt to help pay for $500 billion of its own stock repurchases.

There is more to it, though. The Fed itself has very little cash on the balance sheet, so it buys these assets with credit that it creates at commercial banks. So, if the Fed buys $100 billion of Treasuries, the reserves at the commercial banks go up by the same amount. That reserve at the commercial bank balance sheets is used to buy more assets. Since 2008, regulations have become much stricter and limit the assets that banks can hold on their balance sheet to the safest assets, primarily Treasury bonds. So that's what these banks do: They buy more government bonds. In other words, every time the Fed buys a big chunk of bonds, it creates an asset at the commercial banks with which they also buy Treasury bonds, so it's a double whammy of bond buying.

From 2024 through 2026, $2.9 trillion of U.S. corporate debt will mature (including high-yield bonds, investment-grade bonds, and leveraged loans). If the Fed really stays "higher for longer" with interest rates, this colossal debt load will need to be refinanced at much higher yields. Zombie companies and an epic default cycle will litter the field. Remember, much of this debt was issued between 2020 and 2021, when bond yields were meaningfully lower. An eye-opening example is the Apple AAPL 2.55 percent bond due in 2060. The paper was sold to investors in 2020 at par (100 percent of face value) and traded at 60 cents on the dollar by 2023. Investors will need to stay on high alert.

---

million dollars a minute. When the Obama administration walked into the White House in 2009, the national debt sat comfortably at $10 trillion, exactly 68 percent of GDP. By the end of fiscal year 2014, it had climbed to $17.8 trillion—101 percent of GDP. For the first time since World War II, America owed more money than the economy produced.

By 2016, as Obama began his final year in office, the fresh-faced optimist of eight years earlier looked world-weary, and his once jet-black hair had turned silver. America was in trouble. It wasn't just the lost jobs and all the debt, nor was it the political divide. There was a terrible drug problem killing Americans, especially in the Rust Belt. So many unemployed and underemployed working-class people were dying from overdoses, suicide, and alcohol-related afflictions that the U.S. life expectancy—which had risen steadily for decades—had begun to decline. Princeton professors Anne Case and Angus Deaton famously used the phrase "deaths of despair" to describe this trend. Professor Nathan Seltzer's 2020 study "The Economic Underpinnings of the Drug Epidemic" points out that manufacturing job losses predict a substantial share of drug and opioid overdose deaths for both women and men. If we look at the map of U.S. manufacturing employment, it overlaps quite accurately with the rate of drug overdoses.

Goldman Sachs dug deeper into the data to analyze the disparity in the American labor force. It observed that the U.S. prime-age participation rate, meaning the percentage of those between the ages of twenty-five and fifty-four who are in the labor force, was lower than that of most other advanced economies. Alan Krueger, who was chair of Obama's Council of Economic Advisers, has documented that nearly half of prime-age men who were not in the labor force took pain medication daily, and almost 20 percent reported poor health. Equally striking was the fact that the female prime-age participation rate in the United States had stalled since 2008, while in other advanced economies the number had kept climbing.

Over the last ten years, more than a billion iPhones have been made in Chinese manufacturing plants powered by coal. Exporting our green guilt to China while simultaneously harming job prospects in the Rust Belt, creating an uneven playing field for American companies, makes little sense. It's an unsustainable path with significant political ramifications. Although carbon reduction goals are commendable, meeting them will be impossible without China playing a more active and constructive role. In 2022, China built six times as many new coal plants as the rest of the world combined. And it has continued the "permitting spree" for coal power plants that began in 2022, with 52 gigawatts (GW) of new coal power permitted in the first half of 2023, according to a report by the Global Energy Monitor (GEM) and the Centre for Research on Energy and Clean Air (CREA). This means that coal power capacity could increase by 23 percent to 33 percent from 2022.

More than those of any other developed country, American firms and consumers embraced cheap imports, especially from China. While many other developed countries have policies to protect their industries and workers against this ferocious competition, politicians and Wall Street were focused on the deflationary effects of cheap imports. Low inflation meant low rates, which buoyed stocks and bonds, while Washington was able to finance ballooning deficits at rock-bottom rates. It seems increasingly clear that the price of all that was millions of lost jobs and opportunities, a decade of secular stagnation, and hundreds of thousands of unnecessary deaths.

Between 2008 and 2016, the national debt didn't just increase; it almost doubled, rocketing from $10 trillion to $19.5 trillion. As the middle class was hollowed out by globalization and a loss of purchasing power, money fled overseas in the form of trade deficits and returned to Wall Street as bond purchases. The inequality turned America into a winner-take-all society. Big corporations could borrow a few ticks above the fed fund rates, roughly 1.5 percent. But small business owners, the lifeblood of the real economy, were fleeced by their local banks with 6 percent and 7 percent loans, or corporate credit cards with 18 percent interest rates. They couldn't compete. Between 2007 and 2019, American corporate investment-grade debt—that of the biggest and safest companies—grew 3.7 times over, or by $4.5 trillion. In comparison, high-yield debt, the stuff that funded small or medium-sized firms, grew by just 1.6 times. The cheap credit allowed behemoths like Amazon, Home Depot, and Starbucks to borrow money cheaply and then use it to wipe out smaller businesses.

The minuscule cost of capital gave the biggest firms yet another mechanism to press their advantage: stock buybacks funded by the cheap debt. When a company buys back its stock, it reduces the number of shares trading on the open market, which drives up the price. Investors obviously love this, because it increases the value of their portfolios and, unlike for dividend income, they don't have to pay taxes on those gains until they sell. In 2009, before the era of secular stagnation and zero interest rates, companies in the S&P 500 collectively spent $137 billion on stock buybacks. The following year, that number more than doubled to $285 billion. By 2012, it hit more than $500 billion and would remain above that mark through the rest of the 2010s.

Small businesses were losing out to the big guys not only because of the massive disconnect in interest rates but also because the investment capital wanted to be where the stock buybacks were happening. Most of the buybacks during the 2010s happened in the tech and financial sectors, further widening the gap between the system built on secular stagnation and the real economy. All told, the overflow of cheap debt and leverage enabled by the Federal Reserve fueled $5 trillion in buybacks during the 2010s. No one is asking the most important questions. How much is cheap debt and financing distorting the value of the S&P 500 through an unsustainable pace of stock buybacks?

Per our friends at *The Wall Street Journal*, the percentage of profits enjoyed by the top one hundred companies shot up from 52 percent in 1997 to a staggering 84 percent in 2017 and nearly 90 percent in 2020.

The secular stagnation economy, and maybe even the whole arrangement since the end of the Cold War, just wasn't working for Rust Belt manufacturing workers, small business owners and employees, and the middle class.

There was another issue, too. The European Central Bank had started buying billions of euros' worth of bonds every month while the Fed was beginning to sound hawkish (threatening interest-rate hikes). This led to a rapid strengthening of the dollar against other currencies. A strong dollar sounds good, right? Wrong. As we discussed in chapter 2, it wrecked the competitiveness of American industry because it made our products more expensive for other countries to buy. In 2015 and 2016, the United States shed fifty thousand more manufacturing jobs, mostly because of this dynamic.

According to the Bank for International Settlements, the amount of dollar-denominated debt outside the United States, both government and corporate, doubled by nearly $13 trillion between 2010 and 2020 and grew

INVESTORS TAKE NOTE:

Corporate Buybacks Are the Single Largest Source of Demand for U.S. Stocks

The companies in the S&P 500 buy on average between $600 and $800 billion of their own stock per year. This is a development that gained popularity by the turn of the twenty-first century, based on the idea that corporations, if they cannot find a better return on their investment, should use their capital to repurchase their own stock.

When the Fed suppresses the cost of capital for longer and longer periods of time, capitalism stops working properly; it becomes a two-tiered system instead. Cheap debt gives the biggest firms insurmountable advantages.

S&P 500 Stock Buybacks (per Half Year)

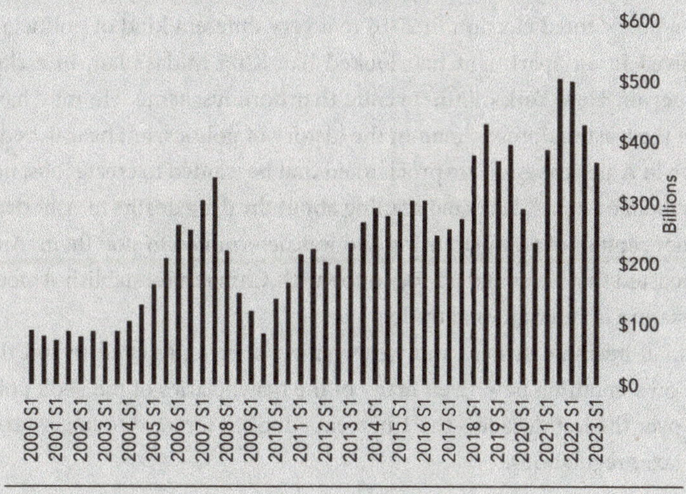

to a level more than six times as large as it had been in 2000. The world was loaded up to the gills with credit, and every time the dollar went up in value, that credit became more expensive to service and weighed heavier on balance sheets. If the U.S. Dollar Index (DXY) moves 10 percent higher, a $1 billion debt in the emerging markets becomes $1.1 billion. A U.S. dollar moving higher became far more destructive, and even more deflationary. In effect, the Fed had begun setting monetary policy for the entire world, and a strong U.S. dollar was now a global wrecking ball. Roughly 40 percent of S&P 500 revenues are generated outside the United States, and a stronger dollar makes U.S. products more expensive.

On the back of the Fed's hawkish rhetoric (threatening interest-rate hikes), manufacturing output around the world plunged, instigating a global earnings recession and chopping stock values by nearly 20 percent. This also prompted the People's Bank of China to devalue the Chinese currency in the summer of 2015. Remember, China pegs its currency to the dollar, so if the dollar goes up, so goes the yuan. By devaluing the currency, China stayed competitive while U.S. manufacturing languished.

Hope for change had faded, and the Democratic Party was about to lose a presidential election in 2016 to a very different kind of politician. He lived in an apartment that looked like King Midas's lair, in a skyscraper on New York's Fifth Avenue that bore his name. He may have been the least diplomatic man in the history of politics, but he touched a nerve in America's soul. He proclaimed that he wanted to create jobs, not ship them overseas. He hated reading about the drug deaths in America's former capitals of manufacturing and was determined to stop them. And he boasted that he would go toe to toe with China to reestablish America's stature in international trade.

Small business owners and weary citizens were prepared to roll the dice on something new. Even many of the beneficiaries of the Fed's policies over the last decade—the 1 percent—looked forward to lower taxes and laxer regulations.

4

The New Washington Consensus

In 1975, Steven Spielberg directed *Jaws,* a blockbuster movie about a killer shark that terrorized beachgoers on a fictionalized version of Martha's Vineyard. I grew up on Cape Cod, right across the Vineyard Sound from the real island, so this was my home turf—but the film hardly scared me. There weren't any killer sharks on the Vineyard or Cape Cod, or anywhere nearby, for that matter. In fact, nobody I knew had ever seen one—at least, not in Massachusetts. I jumped in and out of those waters all summer without a second thought. Later on, I found out that in 1936 there *had* been a fatal shark attack on the Cape, but that was so long ago, nobody ever thought about it.

But then everything changed in 2018. That's when a great white shark attacked a sixty-one-year-old neurologist named William Lytton from Scarsdale, New York, ten feet off the coast of Cape Cod. He was airlifted to Boston, where doctors had to pump twelve pints of blood into him to save his life. Three weeks later, a great white shark killed Arthur Medici, a twenty-six-year-old college student from Brazil, while he surfed just off the shore of Wellfleet, an idyllic beach town on Cape Cod's National Seashore famous for its oyster shacks. Though his death sent shock waves rolling through the region, panic over shark attacks had been building since 2014. That year, a different great white knocked two women out of their kayaks in Plymouth.

But what caused the shark problem on Cape Cod to explode? What tipped the balance of nature and led the number of different sharks detected in the region per year to jump from just 11 in 2013 to 132 by 2021?

What turned Spielberg's *Jaws* from improbable fiction into regular headline news?

It turned out to be governance. Perhaps well-intentioned, but ill-considered. In 1972, Congress passed the Marine Mammal Protection Act, which protected all mammals in U.S. oceans, including seals, which just so happened to be the great white shark's favorite meal. In 1997, lawmakers went on to designate sharks themselves as a protected species in most federal waters, and eight years later they became protected in Massachusetts state waters as well. These legislative changes rendered both sharks and their food sources immune from molestation and capture—terrific news for them, but detrimental and sometimes deadly for Massachusetts beachgoers. Policymakers had no idea that legislation to protect sea life would unleash the world's most feared animal upon the public. With just a few strokes of a pen, Congress and state lawmakers inadvertently turned the Cape Cod coast into the North American equivalent of Gansbaai in South Africa, which has the most shark-infested waters in the world.

This chapter isn't about sharks, the ocean, or Cape Cod. Rather, it's the story of how the unintended consequences of naïve and one-dimensional public policy thinking has spawned terrifying dangers for America's financial markets. All the trillions in accommodation Bernanke had thrown at the markets in five years in the form of QE had become the playbook of central banks across Western Europe and the United States. But what happens when volatility is suppressed for years and central banks come to the rescue at any sign of danger? It injects a misguided sense of safety into markets and lures investors into dangerous waters.

The Phantom Menace Inside the Market

In early 2016, markets were again flashing red, with the high-yield bond market in flames. Central bank chief Janet Yellen joined forces with her colleagues in Europe, Japan, and China to respond. Under what became known as the Shanghai Agreement, they performed another round of monetary stimulus and publicly vowed not to raise rates anymore.

Volatility faded away, sending markets back on a bull run—until later that spring, when the United Kingdom voted to pull out of the European Union and shook markets once more. But the Bank of England marched right into the inferno on day one, armed with a fire hose, and announced a massive bond-buying program. This immediately put out the flames and calmed the nerves of rattled investors, and the markets quickly recovered. But if central banks continually suppress volatility, preventing market corrections by deploying lifelines at the first signs of trouble, the market professionals will figure out one thing real fast. And that's how to get rich. But scheming the markets has always had a nasty habit of ending in tears.

One summer weekend in 2017, the *Bear Traps Report* contributor Robbert van Batenburg explained to me the nuances of volatility trading—and the dangers incurred by its rising popularity. Robbert had become a close buddy of mine when we worked together on the global macro desk at Société Générale. He has a razor-sharp mind, always wears fitted tailored suits, and has the angular looks of Willem Dafoe. It was one of those rare days in July, when a cool westerly was blowing through the city, stamping out the sultry summer heat. We arranged to meet on the docks downtown and head to Grand Banks, an oyster restaurant on the deck of an old schooner named *Sherman Zwicker.* In midsummer, the Hudson River is the place to be, even if you're still tethered to the dock.

Robbert had emigrated to the United States from the Netherlands in his early twenties and had fought his way up to be an influential market consultant at the biggest French banks in New York. He developed a gift for building key relationships with institutional clients, gaining trust with his European charm, asking the right questions, and making jaw-dropping discoveries.

When I showed up, he was by the gangway. Robbert was always a few minutes early. We found two stools at the bar. It was packed, but the noise was civilized, subdued by the breeze off the Tarrytown Narrows.

"Larry, our job is to take a piece of information and surround it with evidentiary corroboration. This is mosaic research, something we live for," Robbert said. He spoke with a Dutch accent, though his English was honed at Columbia, where he had earned a master's in international finance. "There's a ticking time bomb in the markets. The popularity of volatility ETFs has ballooned in the last several years, and the problem is,

INVESTORS TAKE NOTE:

The Risky Business of Volatility Strategies

Volatility is a concept that most individual investors hear about only on CNBC in the midst of a violent correction. The volatility index, known as the VIX, is the primary measure of how rocky the stock market seas are. In comparison to a severe storm, a VIX reading above 30 is a category 3 hurricane, and one above 40 is a violent category 5. If you own a volatility ETF during a significant equity market drawdown, returns can be 30 to 60 percent. It's all about your entry point and timing. When someone says they are "long volatility," all that means is they are betting on a move lower in the equity market, the S&P 500.

Let's say it's been a good year, and heading into September your portfolio is up 15 percent. One way to protect those gains is to sell some of your holdings. The problem is, this creates a taxable event. There are capital gains, and Uncle Sam needs revenue, as we well know.

One way to protect some of your gains without a large taxable event is to buy a volatility ETF. If you're up 15 percent, why not use 2 percent of the profits to safeguard your stack?

Outside periods of large market declines, volatility tends to be well-behaved and trades mostly in a very narrow range. During those times, most investors give it little attention and investment advisers and brokers use volatility to generate extra income for their clients. They do this by selling options to pick up a little extra income. If you are selling volatility, you are the "house," or the casino. Investors want to pay for insurance, and when you sell volatility you can reap attractive rewards if the market stays calm. In this case you are shorting the VIX.

Options can be bought or sold on an index such as the S&P or the Nasdaq or an individual stock. Option prices have a volatility premium embedded in them. When a stock or an index is very volatile, that premium is very high. In an orderly market, the volatility premium is rather low, but it's still worth selling to collect income if the broker thinks volatility will remain stable in the near term. Also, when there is an event pending on a stock or an index, such as an earnings report or a Federal Reserve interest-rate decision, volatility tends to be elevated. But once the earnings are out or the policy meeting is over, the volatility premium collapses and the seller of the option pockets the premium. These are short-volatility strategies, and investors can also play those through inverse volatility ETFs such as the ProShares Short VIX Short-Term Futures ETF (SVXY) and the -1x Short VIX Futures ETF (SVIX). So, when volatility goes down, these ETFs go up. But as we saw in early 2018, if the market goes into a violent sell-off, these ETFs can quickly lose a lot of their value.

An example of a long volatility strategy would be to buy options, which will go up in price if volatility spikes. Alternatively, investors can buy long volatility ETFs such as the iPath Series B S&P 500 VIX Short-Term Futures ETN (VXX) or the ProShares Ultra VIX Short-Term Futures ETF (UVXY). The problem with these ETFs is that they hold a futures contract on the VIX because the VIX itself is an index and doesn't trade. Since the ETF primarily holds the futures closest to expiration, the ETF must roll the assets every month into the next month's VIX future. The result is that the ETF loses a bit of its assets every month on the "roll," which leads these ETFs to grind lower over time if the market remains stable. Most investors therefore use these ETFs to hedge against a surprise sell-off. Otherwise, for investors to profit from these long volatility ETFs, they really need to be confident that a market correction is around the corner; if it isn't, they remain stuck in them as the price gradually drifts lower day after day. Never, ever forget that leveraged ETFs should be rented for short periods of time—not owned. The cost of rolling futures contracts is very expensive over time.

volatility strategies are a corner of the investment world that is often overlooked by the financial media."

As we sipped cold white Burgundy and watched the shuckers rip the shells off bluepoints and Wellfleets, Robbert explained a market scenario that made my hair stand on end: "It is dominated by geeks, especially French quants. The French Cartesian education system pushes out an endless cadre of math graduates year after year, and the best find their way to the derivatives departments of banks and hedge funds in London and Manhattan. That's where they focus tirelessly on esoteric topics such as volatility trading strategies."

A platter of fresh oysters on crushed ice was placed in front of us. It included lemons and mignonette, but I never use either of them. I like the brine, the ocean scent, the cream of the shellfish. For me, oysters have always been a liqueur from the sea. No acid required.

"How long were you working with these French banks?"

"Must be about ten years . . . make it thirteen if you count BNP Paribas."

Since then, Robbert had joined one of the biggest of the new breed of market makers that specialize in arbitraging ETFs. As a top strategist, he had a bird's-eye view of every trading desk in that firm, and he was shocked to see what had happened in volatility, or the VIX. These days it's known as the fear index.

"We both know that volatility measures how much uncertainty there is about the future price of the underlying asset," he told me. "If uncertainty goes up, it means volatility goes up and stocks go down. If there is a lot of uncertainty, such as during the Lehman crisis, volatility is extremely high. Wall Street has made it easier to gauge that volatility by creating the VIX. This index is normally between 10 and 15, but during such a catastrophe, it went as high as 90, which is an extreme level never seen before."

He continued. "Think about the spike in the VIX that happened during Lehman. I mean, you were right there. The day it hit 90, I honestly thought the world was going to cave in."

"My world did cave in that day."

"Both of our worlds. The point is, it took almost six years for that volatility to calm down. A literal nightmare for individual investors, but for option traders it was a nirvana because that volatility makes options more expensive."

"Amazing how the scars of Lehman lasted until 2014," I added.

"They did, my friend. It took six years for the VIX to return to its baseline of fifteen. And this was with the help of central banks everywhere propping up markets. But now astute investors are selling volatility at every turn. Now more than ever."

"Why is this a time bomb? How will this eat them alive if the markets are so tranquil?"

Robbert picked up an oyster and, with the skill of someone who had grown up on the coast of northern Europe, tipped it out of the shell and started chewing. "This will require a bit of an explanation, but essentially, shorting volatility is now one of the most crowded trades on earth. They're piling into inverse volatility ETFs, such as the VelocityShares Daily Inverse VIX short-term ETN (XIV) and the ProShares Short VIX Futures ETF (SVXY)."

"Will central banks stop all this accommodation one day?"

He turned the empty shells face down on the ice. A strong gust billowed through the restaurant. A couple of women reached for their pashminas and hugged them around their shoulders.

Robbert cleared his throat, took a sip of water. "It's not really about that. It's about how much money is piled into these short-vol ETFs. They're literally as popular as Cabbage Patch dolls in the 1980s. Everyone, from financial advisers to fund managers, is generating extra income under the guise of yield-enhancing strategies."

As I listened to him, I found myself feeling a little anger at all the market accommodation. Maybe I was a dyed-in-the-wool laissez-faire free-market capitalist, but the amount of money that had been pumped into the market was sickening. "This is what artificially low rates do to a market, right? They entice people into products they have no business being near."

"Exactly," said Robbert, his eyes gleaming with the sheer horror of a market spiraling blindly into a brick wall. "I think 90 percent of the buyers out there are totally oblivious to the risks. Other forces are at play. Passive funds and quant funds are a monster now . . . close to 70 percent of daily stock market trades, buying the market every day with volume-weighted average prices. This suppresses volatility even more. And it feeds on itself, like a negative feedback loop.

"All this indiscriminate buying by these passive investors puts downward pressure on volatility, and as it goes down, these passive investors mechanically increase their exposure to equities even more.

"Larry . . . I'm not just talking about a couple of extra funds piling into these strategies. Volatility selling has exploded higher. In just a couple of years, assets in these ETFs have increased sixfold. Literally every investor is selling volatility and collecting premiums. And that's why the SVXY, that innocuous little ETF never mentioned on the news, has gone up 600 percent in the last fifteen months. Together with hedge funds and options structures, I calculate that there is as much as $2 trillion of capital linked to short-volatility strategies now."

I sat there for a minute, looking out across the restaurant, wondering how many volatility shorts were surrounding us. I could see over Robbert's shoulder the light blue mirrored skyscraper representing American financial strength—the Freedom Tower—looming over the Battery neighborhood, the one just south of Wall Street.

By that summer of 2017, the looming tax cuts had put the markets in ecstasy, and the S&P was grinding higher every day. Ultimately, there were only three trading days in that entire year when the S&P 500 went down more than 1 percent. This had never happened in the history of the stock market.

"It has been the easiest trade in the world!" Robbert exclaimed. "But the beast inside the market is lurking, just in the shadows. Kinda gives me the creeps."

"You think the markets will sell off? I don't understand how that can happen."

"Now it gets complicated," he replied. "It's to do with 'vega,' this crazy Greek word that only about five people on Wall Street understand. Vega measures how much the price of an option changes in response to a 1 percent change in volatility. So . . . vega tells you how much the price of an option will change if there is a change in how uncertain people are about the future price of the underlying asset. For example, if uncertainty increases and volatility goes up by 1 percent, the price of an option with a high vega will increase by more than the price of an option with a low vega.

"You have to follow this vega carefully. Because this is when the beast will move out of the shadows and pounce on investors like a phantom."

I sipped my wine and placed it back on the bar carefully.

"The VIX is now trading around ten and has been for many weeks," Robbert went on. "But if some unknown unknown hits the market, the index could pop from ten to eighteen. Easily. That's only three points above the base level of fifteen. Still a modest level, but in percentage terms, how much is that an increase?"

"Ten to eighteen? That's 80 percent."

"Right, an 80 percent increase. Let's take a more extreme scenario. Imagine a 3.5 percent drop in the S&P 500. Today that's about a twelve-point jump in the VIX, equal to 120 percent. And still, we're only talking about a VIX at twenty-two. It's not like Lehman or anything. It is the percentage move that determines the vega risk, not the amount of volatility.

"So here's the math that's going to kill everyone who's short volatility. Because when you're short volatility, you're also short vega. And right now the amount of vega in inverse VIX ETFs is about equal to $200 million. The managers of these ETFs, just like bookmakers at the Belmont Stakes, have to balance their risk on the day. If the VIX spikes one percentage point, they have to buy $200 million of VIX futures to mitigate that exposure. But if we get a real spike, like the twelve-point move I just mentioned, they would need to buy seventy thousand VIX futures to offset that risk. And those seventy thousand futures add up to $37 billion. Can you imagine being short that? There are not even close to that many VIX futures available for that amount of hedging. You will end up in the graveyard."

"That's insane," I said, remembering how the markets had crashed in 2008. It will always haunt me, how the liquidity ran dry and nobody could get out. "This will overwhelm the market, won't it?"

"It can't miss."

"Jesus Christ," I muttered, almost unable to believe such intense risk was once again buried in the markets.

"And guess what? VIX ETFs are not the only ones short vega in size. Hedge funds are short another $250 million in vega. They're all short volatility, starving for yield. Even Main Street investors are short $700 billion of options now. But everyone is basically in the same trade, and they're all oblivious to the total lack of liquidity if the market took a nasty turn."

I sat there, gobsmacked, thinking of all the investors who had casually marched straight into the Valley of Death.

"What would happen if a crisis like that happened?" I eventually asked.

"It would wipe out those ETFs, and everyone who owns them."

One week later, we published a letter explaining all these dangers of being short volatility. But the S&P 500 kept grinding higher, every day, all the way until the end of the year. By New Year's Eve it was up 20 percent. That stern warning we had sent to clients globally was making us look like the boy who cried wolf. I had always had my doubts about passive investing, especially with all the trillions of dollars that had been flowing into passive ETFs over the past decade. Still, I was shocked by what Robbert was telling me. I wondered if what he was saying would ever really come to pass.

Then it all started to happen, a few weeks into 2018 on one uneventful morning in late January.

The Day of Volmageddon

On Wednesday, January 22, 2018, a team of press reporters filtered into the Oval Office to watch the president sign new tariffs on Asian washing machines and solar panels. They were relatively small tariffs, but instead of aiming just at China, they encompassed the whole of Asia. This sparked protests and mass grumblings from South Korea and China but was lauded as a great move by American steel and appliance workers.

But the markets sided with Asia this time. For the first time since Trump walked into the White House, they were angry. On Monday, January 29, they started to crash. Volatility, tracked by the VIX, the famous fear index, rocketed 270 percent in a single day. (As a basic rule of thumb, every time the stock market goes down, the VIX goes up.)

It was a stunning event. Nobody could believe their eyes. Had 9/11 happened all over again? Had another Lehman collapsed? Not exactly. This was a short-covering rally (a frenzy of short-sellers closing out their positions). Perhaps the worst one I'd ever seen. The markets had been so tranquil for so long, investors thought the safest bet on the Street was to short volatility. Clearly the president was going to send the markets up indefinitely. But the beast inside the market hated the change from tax cuts to tariffs.

VIX Volatility Index

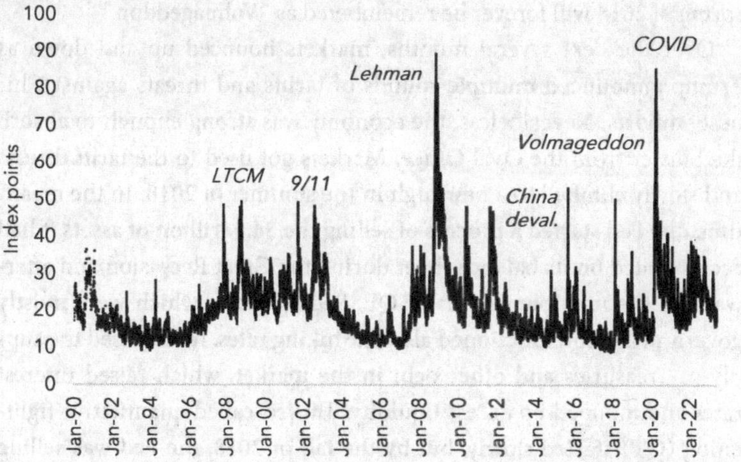

And it caught everybody off guard, especially that armada of investors who were short volatility. And the more investors unwound their positions, the higher volatility spiked. Remember, you have to buy to cut a short position, not sell. That nasty volatility spike was like a released spring that had been coiled for fourteen months. VIX ETF managers were panic-stricken, clamoring to buy VIX futures contracts as the vega levels annihilated their funds. They were forced to buy every VIX future in existence to rebalance their portfolios, but by 4:00 P.M., the close of the market, they knew it was over. There weren't enough futures in the world to satisfy their desperate needs.

Next, it hit every single short-vol trader right between the eyes. And there were thousands of them, all running for the exits. But the margin clerks, the back-office managers who lend traders the capital to trade with leverage, were on them like a pride of lions, and by the afternoon of Friday, February 9, they had all been skinned alive. The margin clerks had taken the traders ruthlessly out of their positions, something they are allowed to do if the traders' collateral is at risk of being wiped out. The ultimate yield-enhancing trade had been dragged underground by the Grim Reaper. Five years of gains were given back in a week. That's what happens when your investment strategy is the equivalent of stepping in front of a freight train to pick up a dollar bill. Those two weeks in the spring of 2018 will forever be remembered as "Volmageddon."

Over the next several months, markets bounced up and down as Trump announced multiple rounds of tariffs and threats against Chinese imports. Nevertheless, the economy was strong enough to absorb the bluster from the Oval Office. Markets got used to the tariff threats and slowly climbed to a new high in the summer of 2018. In the meantime, the Fed started a process of selling the $4.5 trillion of assets it had accumulated on its balance sheet during the Great Recession and afterward in the multiple rounds of QE. Selling these, which were mostly government debt, functioned also like hiking rates. It increased the supply of Treasuries and other debt in the market, which raised interest rates and mopped up excess liquidity. This so-called quantitative tightening (QT) started slowly, but by the fall of 2018, the Fed was selling $50 billion in Treasuries and securitized mortgages every month. At the same time, it was raising the federal funds rate at each meeting. In total, it raised rates by 1.5 percentage points and lowered its balance sheet by $340 billion. The Fed embarked on this substantial hiking cycle because financial markets and the broader economy at the time appeared so fundamentally strong. By the waning days of 2018, however, markets had started to falter.

In the last three months of the year, the S&P fell by 20 percent. Trump tirelessly lambasted the Fed for its unwillingness to ease up on the monetary tightening, but to no avail. QT put the brakes on the economy, which was buoyant in 2017 and most of 2018 but was now slowing down fast. Fed chair Jerome Powell wouldn't back down for months. Eventually, however, he saw the damage his policies were inflicting on the markets and the economy. In early 2019, he threw in the towel. That was the end of rate hikes. And the markets came roaring back. From the lows of December 2018, the market soared 39 percent by the end of 2019. The rally was sometimes rudely interrupted by Trump lobbing more trade-war threats at China, but by September 2019, the mercurial Trump was

Nasdaq -3% Drawdowns Come in Bunches

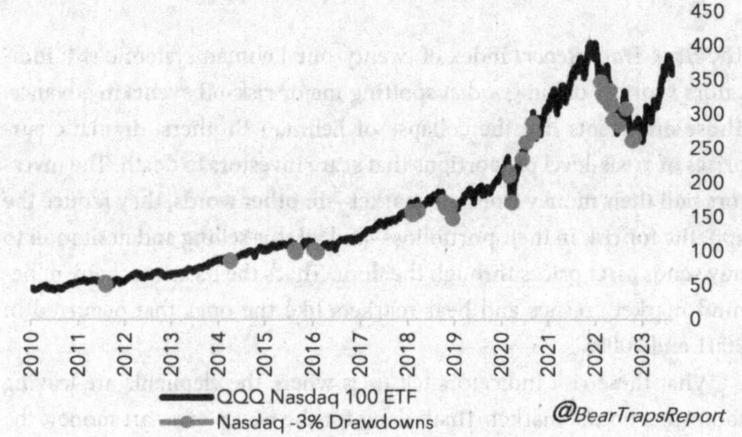

gunning for the 2020 general election. A trade deal with China would appease the markets, create a détente between the two economic superpowers, and place him in a powerful position to ramp up his campaign machine.

On January 15, 2020, Trump walked into the East Room of the White House with Liu He, China's vice-premier, to a brass rendition of "Hail to the Chief." He approached the podium, followed by Vice President Mike Pence, Treasury Secretary Steven Mnuchin, and Ambassador Robert Lighthizer, the U.S. trade representative. The president sat down at a wooden desk to the left of Liu, and both men signed the agreements, bound in the classic black leather holders familiar from executive orders. Trump wore his signature self-congratulatory smile as he leaned over and shook hands with the Chinese delegates. The markets rallied hard before the ink was even dry on the page, with the Dow hitting 29,000 for the first time in months. Trump was brimming with reelection confidence.

But inside the Chinese government, word had come down that a mysterious virus was spreading in Wuhan, one of the country's largest cities.

The Risk Indicators Flashing Bright Red

The *Bear Traps Report* index of twenty-one Lehman systemic risk indicators is pretty damn good at spotting major risk-off events in advance. Those are events like the collapse of Lehman Brothers, dramatic surprises of crisis-level proportions that scare investors to death. The investors pull their money from the market—in other words, they reduce the appetite for risk in their portfolios—and all this selling and hesitation to buy sends asset prices through the floor. That's the basic mechanism behind market crashes and bear markets like the ones that occurred in 2001 and 2008.

What these risk indicators tell us is where the elephants are leaving footprints on the market. That's slang for the waves of smart money, the first movers, the big stacks of capital being skippered by some of the smartest money managers in the world. It's what all investors should follow to stay one step ahead. Most days, those indicators are pretty tranquil, with maybe one or two flickering minor concerns.

In late January 2020, however, many of our systemic risk indicators were flashing red, picking up on the fact that we were on the precipice of an international nightmare. On the surface, markets hadn't yet reacted, but underneath, we could see the rumblings of something big starting to develop.

This was especially true in the economically sensitive parts of the market. They were selling off hard. Copper was in free fall, bonds were rallying—the classic risk-averse capital taking over from volatile equities—and transportation sector stocks (airlines, rental cars, hotels, UPS, and FedEx) were selling off each day, scrabbling for a bid but in vain. It was like sitting in Kenya's Masai Mara, where the red oat grasses flourish, and suddenly a dust cloud at the base of Kilimanjaro moves swiftly across the African savanna as a tight parade of bush elephants charges out of a forest. The question is, what's frightening them?

Back at our office we were on high alert, imploring investors to chop down risk. We had seen it all before, in the weeks leading up to September 15, 2008. And we could clearly see the shift in sentiment as dark storm clouds gathered once again. Money poured out of high yield; capital was hiding out in the Nasdaq. In fact, in February 2020, the Nasdaq

100 went up nearly every day—8 percent in less than three weeks. Day by day the evidence of the pandemic's threat grew. The amount of attention focused on COVID-19 cases coming out of Asia was exploding each evening as news stations pounded the story across the globe.

As the risk of a deflationary shock rises, the first thing you see in equity markets is a move into long-duration growth stocks. Likewise, capital allocators start to look for perceived safe places, and that's why megacap technology stocks like Apple, Microsoft, and Google catch the bid—all in preparation for the coming storm.

Around February 20, our team noticed a massive acceleration in the flow of capital into the consumer staples ETF, the XLP, and out of the consumer discretionary ETF, the XLY. The XLP ETF is stuffed with names like Procter & Gamble, General Mills, Coca-Cola, and Hershey—American companies that outperform in recessions. Normally, capital flows into consumer staples at a snail's pace that could bore anyone sideways, but that week our model picked up a stampede. At first it was moving at ten miles per hour, then twenty, and suddenly it ripped to ninety miles per hour. That's known as "rate of change." Investors were jumping over their seats to get into these stocks.

As we stood there stunned by the amount of capital romping into America's most unexciting stocks, I shouted across the trading floor, "Hey, Chris, come over and take a look at this, will ya?" We shared office space with the brilliant Chris Brighton, a partner at the highly respected boutique rates shop Astor Ridge. Chris understands the inner workings of interest-rate derivatives better than just about anyone else. It was like sharing an office with Paul Tudor Jones.

Chris, who'd been riding high that month, positioning his clients in long-duration U.S. Treasuries, walked into our office and saw the charts of the two ETFs flickering in front of us. His face took on an uncharacteristically grim expression.

"Wow," he said. "We're seeing the same dynamic in [interest] rates. Everyone's piling into the thirty-year U.S. Treasury." It had started on January 8. For the next month they moved from 2.36 percent to 2 percent (equivalent to the bond appreciating by 7 percent). "There has been a deep, endless bid, day in and day out," Chris noted. Not everyone has a proper grasp of the importance of the Treasury markets and bonds, but they are almost always a leading market indicator. Fixed income has the best sniffer on earth. As the risk of recession rises, bonds pick up the scent well before stocks.

"Let's model out [interest] rates," he barked. "Copper, oil, consumer staples against discretionary, and don't forget the transports. We need to measure the synchronicity and rate of change."

In other words, how many sectors were changing tack, and how quickly was it happening? How many elephants were moving, and how fast?

When we ran the data, the results were bloodcurdling. No one, not even Chris, a New York veteran of the fixed-income markets, had seen anything like it. At least, not since the Lehman crisis.

Markets were sending a clear message.

"Jesus Christ," said Chris. "If this gets as bad as I think it could, we might have to shut the office."

That was the first moment it really hit me.

"Holy shit," I said to nobody in particular.

I picked up the phone and, without hesitating, dialed ten digits, connecting straight to the desk of Gillian Tett, the U.S. managing editor of the *Financial Times.* She is one of the greatest financial journalists in the world and has a Rolodex with connectivity to all the key players in U.S. finance. Her pen was powered by a mind nurtured at Clare College, one of the oldest colleges at Cambridge University. Gillian is English, gifted with a calm, upper-class accent, and when she answered the phone, I recognized her voice immediately.

It's always an honor to be quoted in one of the world's most respected business newspaper, but I carefully laid out the findings of the day before, about the rates of change and how synchronously these assets were moving (meaning how much they were trading in line with each other) and the impending death spiral facing the markets. She didn't interrupt me while I spoke, and when I paused, all I could hear was the very faint echo of my voice. I waited for a reaction, but there was only a long silence and the distant sound of scribbling. Gillian then asked me one question, in a tone of voice that betrayed nothing: "How bad will this be?"

"Bad," I said. "Our indicators tell us we're very close to a Lehman-like drawdown."

On February 21, the Nasdaq plummeted 4 percent, the biggest drop in fourteen months. After a long period of time in a tranquil, low volatility market, the first 3 percent drawdown for stocks often signals near-term trouble to come. On February 23, Gillian Tett published those exact words in the *Financial Times*. That week the S&P dropped by 12 percent. On March 16, the market tanked by 12 percent. That was the largest single-day percentage drop in history after Black Monday in 1987. By late March, the S&P 500 had collapsed by 35 percent. That, by the way, is technically known as a bloodbath. Markets were acting like a bucking bronco. Not even Tuff Hedeman, the three-time Bull Riding World Champion, could've stayed on this one. It was flinging its riders all over the place, left, right, and straight over its head.

Ten days later, the Fed dropped rates to zero and began to roll out an unparalleled quantitative-easing and emergency-lending program. It was 2008 all over again but faster, bigger, and stronger. Ben Bernanke probably would have fainted, but the new chairman was a cold-blooded killer in comparison. Jerome Powell, with a political science degree from Princeton and a JD from Georgetown Law, hatched a QE program that dwarfed all previous QEs combined. He announced a smorgasbord of new programs to backstop every major corner of the credit markets, from money markets to junk bonds. By June, the Fed's balance sheet had expanded by $3 trillion. Within a year it would be $5 trillion, bringing the balance sheet of assets owned by the Federal Reserve to an astounding $9 trillion in March 2021. If that number wasn't on a computer screen but was instead exchanged into dollar bills, the stack of them would reach 612,000 miles high—2.5 times the distance to the moon.

The U.S. government opened the floodgates with spending at the same time. The world was ending, and the only thing that could save it was a fire hose of money flowing directly from Washington. The Trump administration threw away any semblance of caution, strapped a breeze block to the accelerator, and ratcheted up the debt to levels nobody had ever imagined. In March, Republicans and Democrats in Congress came together to pass the largest financial rescue package in American history, the $2.2 trillion CARES Act.

This massive bill was passed with lightning speed and allocated spending across the country's economy. It propped up floundering state and local governments, funded loan programs to support small businesses, and even sent no-strings-attached money to every American household. Commentators might quibble about the CARES Act's impact on the American economy for a long time, but the country did manage to avoid a real recession during the chaotic, crazy year of 2020. Of course, it added trillions to the national debt and a new menace on the horizon: inflation.

Assets across the board roared back, starting the last week of March, when it was clear that the Fed was going to roll out a $6 trillion asset purchase program and the CARES Act was going to pass. Around mid-April, though, they started to flatten out. It wasn't really clear whether we were headed for a bull market or something much choppier.

Remember how our index of twenty-one Lehman systemic risk indicators spots risk-off events? It does a solid job at picking up risk-on events. Those are the opposite; they're when investors envision bright days ahead and increase their level of risk by buying stocks, bonds, and other assets. This, of course, sends prices skyward.

While stocks were still searching for a more consistent direction, our twenty-one Lehman systemic risk indicators were flashing risk on. And that signal came from the credit markets. Over the years, it's been one of the best risk indicators we know. While investing in equities, many professional or institutional investors look for confirmation or vetoes from high yield. That's the credit markets. And the most important question boils down to something very simple: When equities want to party all night long, do the credit markets feel the same way? The answer to this question is often the only one you'll need.

Bond traders tend to be exceptionally good at measuring risk. They're just about the sharpest guys in finance. In some cases they can see the future earlier than anyone else. So, when they load up on high-yield, they're confident.

At the beginning of the work-from-home era, our team had a conversation over Zoom with Brian Maggio. He's a hedge fund manager and an outstanding trader. More than a decade before, he ran the financial credit desk at Lehman Brothers. Back then, he helped put our team into Countrywide credit default swaps. These were bets on the default of the mortgage giant. But in Q2 2020, there were still a lot of equity bears around, betting against a recovery during the near peak of COVID economic stress.

Brian gave our team a stern warning that day. "Don't, for chrissakes, be short here, Larry. Equities are going to rip." He said it like his life depended on it. Brian was telling us repeatedly, "When you see CCC-rated bonds outperforming equities to this degree, it's incredibly bullish for the stock market. You have to buy, buy, buy!"

CCC-rated credits are high risk, the worst and sketchiest of the junk bonds. But this was inside baseball for Brian. Trading was in his blood. And just like a man batting close to .400, he was dead right.

CCCs bottomed out on March 23, 2020, and peaked at a yield of 19 percent! The yield is normally around 11 percent. By April 17, 2020, they'd dropped to 14.4 percent, and by June 5 they hit 10 percent. Meanwhile, equities were range-bound between April 17 and May 17, whereas high-yield junk credit became 2 percent tighter, which is a significant amount for bonds. But after mid-May, equities caught the scent like a pack of bloodhounds and went on an unstoppable bull run through the start of September. Over the years, if you listen to markets, you will find that significant moves in credit markets (bonds) tend to lead equities.

The trick to finding the best information, and uncovering the mysteries that lie beneath the surface of markets, is developing relationships. (Even better if they're spread across different asset classes.) You can piece together the puzzle if you know how to ask. Like the legendary Jim Rohn always said, "Success in life is not about being a hard worker. Most of us can manage that. It's about being a great asker."

That's how we met Boaz Weinstein, Hall of Famer in the cross-asset space—which means he studies different asset classes to find value and opportunities. Boaz is a chess master who started working on Wall Street at fifteen. Today he runs the hedge fund Saba Capital, and he and his team are always on the lookout for dislocations, always asking questions. Across the corporate bond market, are collateralized loan obligations trading rich or cheap compared to high-yield bonds? How are junk bonds priced relative to equity volatility? Is the VIX trading expensive to the high-yield market?

"Larry, markets speak to us through important divergences," said Boaz, the master of picking up on those signals.

When it comes to equities, some stocks are loaded with leverage on the balance sheet. Veteran credit investors like Boaz remind us to always look at the entire capital structure. Think of a company as an apple pie with ten pieces. If eight of the slices are debt and only two represent equity, investors in the stock are at a huge disadvantage. The total enterprise value of the company includes all the equity market capitalization value, plus the face value of the debt, minus the cash the company has on the balance sheet. Too many equity investors will look at a stock and not understand that it may be only a small slice of the total picture.

In the case of a heavily leveraged company, when the bonds are trending upward while the stock remains within a specific range, it signals a bullish outlook for equity investors. On the dark side, if the bonds are being sold and are underperforming, this can serve as a notably bearish leading indicator. In a highly leveraged company, where the capital structure is predominantly composed of debt, creditors wield *much* greater influence compared to equity holders.

The moral of the story? Listen to the credit markets. That'll often get you out of harm's way or, better yet, put you in a sweet spot for a great trade.

Best Performing Stocks of 2020		
Name	Sector	% Change
Tesla	EV	750%
Enphase	Solar	591%
Moderna	Vaccines	448%
Etsy	Retail	300%
Solaredge Tech	Solar	239%
Carrier Global	Airco	217%
Nvidia	Semis	125%
Generac	Generators	125%
Paypal	Payments	117%
Albermarle	Lithium	108%

Best Performing Stocks of 2021		
Name	Sector	% Change
Devon	Oil & gas	189%
Marathon	Oil & gas	145%
Fortinet	Software	143%
Ford	Autos	136%
Bath & Body Works	Retail	129%
Moderna	Vaccines	128%
Nvidia	Semis	124%
Diamondback	Oil & gas	123%
Nucor	Steel	120%
Gartner	Software	110%

Best Performing Stocks of 2022		
Name	Sector	% Change
Occidental	Oil & gas	119%
Constellation Energy	Oil & gas	107%
Hess	Oil & gas	94%
Exxon	Oil & gas	89%
Marathon	Oil & gas	88%
Schlumberger	Oil services	82%
Valero	Refiners	77%
Apa	Oil & gas	75%
Halliburton	Oil services	75%
ConocoPhillips	Oil services	72%

The Beast of Inflation Comes Out of Hibernation

By the end of 2020, the S&P 500 had rallied 70 percent from its March lows. The tech-heavy Nasdaq surged 90 percent, especially the biggest lockdown beneficiaries, like Amazon, Netflix, Facebook, and Apple. As the investors believed deflation was here to stay, megacap growth stocks finished the year up 120 percent, whereas megacap value stocks were down just under 1 percent, the largest one-year divergence ever recorded outside the dot-com era.

In November, Trump was voted out of office. The Nasdaq had soared 172 percent and the S&P rallied 83 percent during his four years in office. The Fed's balance sheet had doubled to $8.5 trillion, and the U.S. government debt went up by $7.8 trillion. And despite all the dialogue, the big new friendships, and the flights back and forth between China and the United States, the annual trade deficit was still well over $300 billion.

U.S. Monthly Budgets Deficits (1980–2023)

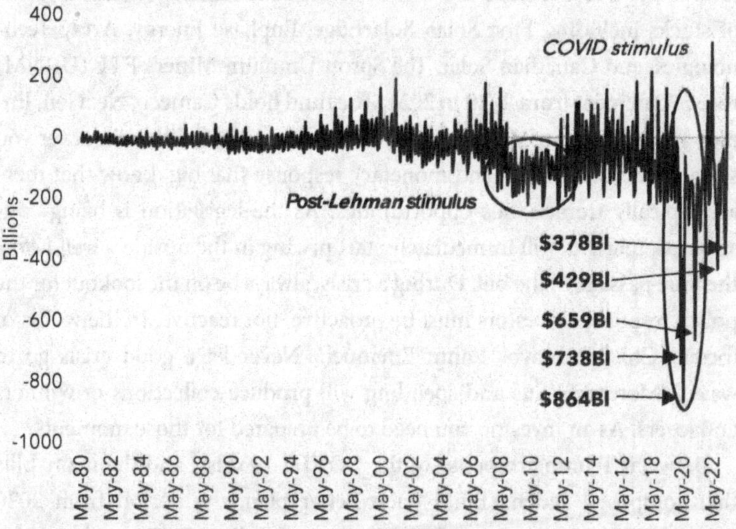

New president Joe Biden wasted no time. In a statement released on March 31, 2021, he promised "to reimagine and rebuild a new economy." This meant more spending. Lots of it. Supposedly, all of this would be paid for by raising the corporate tax rate to 28 percent and, of course, incurring *even more* debt. In the March 31 statement, Biden also pitched a proposal to use federal authority to overhaul states' "right to work" laws, which would massively bolster labor union power nationwide. The American Jobs Plan was just one part of a broader focus on what Biden called "Build Back Better," a theme of his campaign that envisioned massive, ongoing infrastructure spending to transition America's economy to carbon neutrality.

No matter the party, this kind of stimulus can be a real boon for investors. Our team held conference calls, alongside David Metzner and his second-to-none political advisory firm, ACG Analytics in Washington, D.C., with our biggest clients about this very subject later in 2020 and into 2021. We saw it as key for investors to position themselves in and through the fiscal and monetary response via solar and uranium names. With fiscal policy of this size, the investment windfalls can be mind-blowing. For example, the Invesco Solar ETF (TAN) rose 490 percent from the March 2020 lows to the October 2021 highs. This investment vehicle contains a basket of stocks including First Solar, SolarEdge, Enphase Energy, Array Technologies, and Canadian Solar. The Sprott Uranium Miners ETF (URNM) rose 570 percent from 2020 to 2021. The fund holds Cameco, NexGen, Energy Fuels, Denison Mines, and others. As long as you live, whenever you see a government fiscal and monetary response that big, know that there are typically tremendous opportunities. As the legislation is being constructed, markets will immediately start pricing in the upside—well *before* the final passage of the bill. During a crisis, always be on the lookout for the policy response. Investors must be proactive, not reactive. In the words of former Chicago mayor Rahm Emanuel, "Never let a good crisis go to waste." More stimulus and spending will produce collections of winners and losers. As an investor, you need to be prepared for those moments.

Between Trump's response to the COVID-19 crisis and the many bills that composed Biden's Build Back Better plan, the period from 2020 through 2022 was an orgy of government spending. In December 2020, right before he left office, Trump signed another $900 billion aid package that included checks to every household. After he took the reins, Biden passed a further $1.9 trillion of stimulus through the American Rescue Plan Act in March 2021, including even more checks. In November 2021, he signed the $1.2 trillion Infrastructure Investment and Jobs Act. The next year, Congress passed yet another spending deluge called the Inflation Reduction Act, with almost $500 billion in subsidies to promote the adoption of electric vehicles and solar energy. All told, 44 percent of all U.S. dollars ever created were turned out in 2020 and 2021. On top of Trump's $7.5 trillion, Biden tacked on another $5 trillion to the national debt during his tenure. Together, these two increased the debt by 50 percent in seven years.

Total U.S. Federal Debt

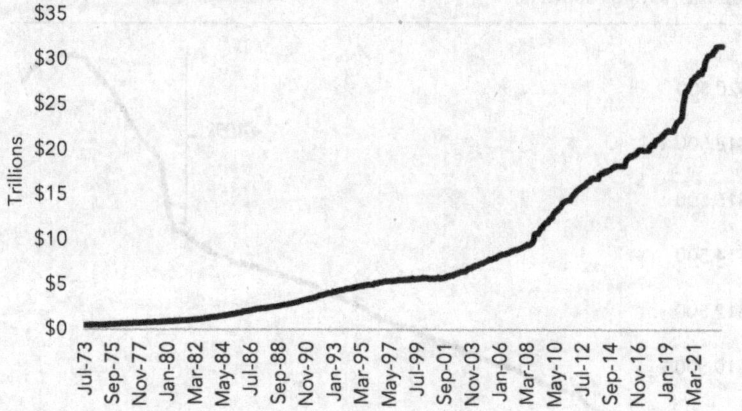

Inflation stems from an increase in both the supply and the velocity of money. In other words, if the government prints $1 trillion and locks it in a sealed vault for a decade, that won't move inflation at all. Much of the stimulus was aimed at restoring bank balance sheets during the Great Recession in 2008 and 2009. But if it were to take that trillion, or even more, and deposit it directly into millions of Americans' bank accounts, inflation would soar. That's exactly what happened between 2020 and 2022.

The COVID-19 pandemic also shifted the balance of power in American business from ownership to labor. To support workers during the lockdowns, the federal government passed emergency unemployment insurance that lasted through September 2021 and issued three rounds of direct stimulus payments. This gave workers a leg up and strengthened their position in collective bargaining and pay negotiations. A lot of workers permanently left the workforce, primarily through early retirement. More stayed home, too, creating a labor shortage. Over the past few years, calls for union membership at Amazon, Walmart, and Starbucks have exploded, as have wages at those companies and others like them. These three companies are three of the largest employers in the world. Amazon fulfillment center minimum wages increased from $15 per hour in 2018 to more than $19 in 2022. Similar trends manifested at Starbucks, where unions also forced the company to change its divi-

M2 Money Supply
(includes cash, checking accounts, money market funds, time deposits, savings deposits)

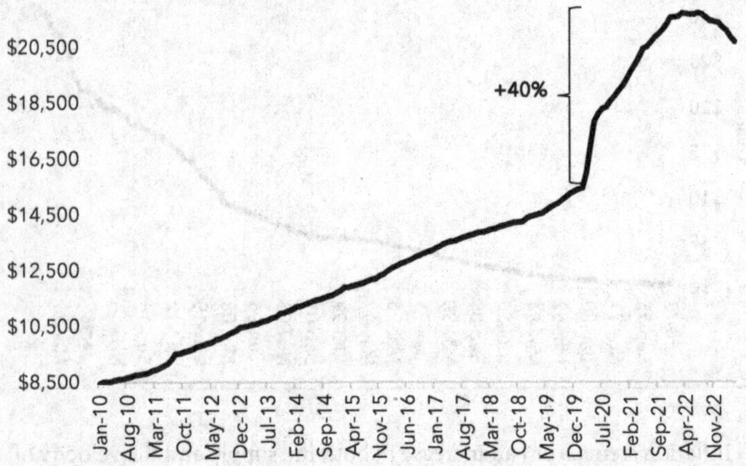

dend policy. In 2022, unions nearly crippled American freight transportation by threatening a strike at Union Pacific Railroad, which was averted through wage increases. The company cited this as a major drag on its earnings. These are the types of things we haven't seen in America for a long time, not since the 1968–1981 period.

Over the past three decades, outsourcing and right-to-work legislation crippled the power of unions and deflationary pressure hurt workers' ability to negotiate higher pay. Inflation empowers labor unions because more workers join them when they're getting screwed by declining purchasing power. The higher wages enabled by labor unions increase inflation even more, creating a self-strengthening cycle. This will make inflation stick around for a long time and create a hard-to-stamp-out environment. The Atlanta Fed's wage tracker shows that even as CPI inflation came down in 2022 and 2023, wage growth remained high. The increased power of unions is starting to show itself in our politics. The approval rating of labor unions rose from a historic low of 48 percent in 2010 to a near-all-time high of 71 percent in 2022, most of that increase coming during the pandemic.

The old Washington economic consensus was thoroughly deflationary: Open international markets, outsource to the developing world, and don't meddle with the private sector unless necessary. These policy motifs lowered prices across the board by helping to reduce the cost of labor, commodities, and transportation of goods around the world. The new Washington consensus is by and large inflationary: trade wars, reshoring of industrial capacity all paid for by stupendous deficit spending (see the $280 billion CHIPS Act). At the same time, we've rolled out aggressive foreign sanctions. It's a multipolar world, with expensive possible global conflicts on many fronts. Add in the resurging power of labor, and you've got a recipe for one thing above all: rising prices for the long haul. Buckle up!

Core CPI (yoy)

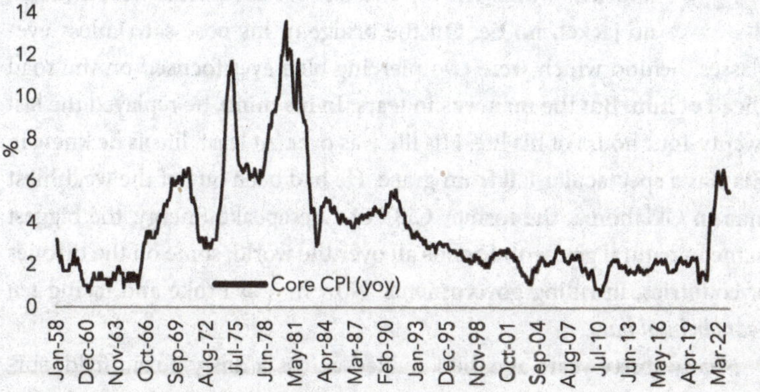

5

Fossil Fuels Paving the Way to the Green Meadow

Aubrey McClendon's gray hair was swept off his brow, his knuckles white. The top two buttons of his shirt were undone, no jacket, no tie. On the bridge of his nose sat rimless eyeglasses, behind which were two piercing blue eyes focused on the road ahead of him. But the man was in tears. In his mind, he replayed the last twenty-four hours of his life. His life was over. At least, life as he knew it. His was a spectacular fall from grace. He had been one of the wealthiest men in Oklahoma, the former CEO of Chesapeake Energy, the biggest name in natural gas, with friends all over the world, some on the thrones of countries, in ruling governments. Now he was broke and facing *ten years behind bars.*

Nearly thirty years ago, he'd walked across a dusty Texan field, surrounded by vertical rigs pumping oil and gas, and saw the future, clear as day. His lifelong friend Tom Ward, the man with whom he'd co-found Chesapeake Energy, was likely at his side, both of them bedecked in Stetsons and cowboy boots as they looked out across the land. They would scrap vertical well drilling altogether and pile every nickel they could find into lateral drilling, freeing natural gas from craggy, unsuspecting shale formations. *Fracking.*

The men went on to create a colossus in the energy markets, ramping up Chesapeake's market cap to $37 billion—an outrageous amount of money.

But then the Lehman crisis hit them on the chin, exactly when their balance sheet was stretched like a bungee cord right across Texas and Oklahoma, on the brink of snapping. Energy prices crashed to a level almost as low as their subterranean fracking drills. Natural gas fell from $15 to $4, and suddenly all the leverage, the enormous piles of money borrowed for exploration and land leases, came at them like a pack of starved wolves. Chesapeake's debt hit $21 billion at the end of 2008, and the company was burning through $5 billion in cash every year. Its stock fell from $62 to $12 in a matter of weeks, and its market cap cratered to $115 million. But the crash of 2008 wasn't the end of the road.

As we all know, the government bailed everyone out and propped up the financial system, exacerbating the festering wound of government intervention left by Long-Term Capital Management's failure. Tampering with markets is a dangerous game. They are delicate systems with endless subtleties, great living organisms with millions of finely balanced components, each one interacting with the others, each part like a white-gold cog made by a master watchmaker. Healthy markets are resilient machines, self-healing, with their own innate brand of shock absorbers. The brilliant Nassim Nicholas Taleb, author of the international bestseller *The Black Swan,* gave a marvelous speech a few years ago on the concept of "anti-fragile." The term doesn't mean unbreakable, nor does it merely mean strong or able to withstand immense pressure. It means that every time something takes a hit, it comes back stronger. He likens it to human muscles under intense strain, how every time the fibers tear, they repair themselves with greater strength. This is the basis of all weight training, and it's probably why Taleb is such an avid dead-lifter. Years ago, we had drinks in Monaco, both of us having been flown in to a conference to speak on global macroeconomics. It was an honor to meet one of the risk-management greats, and his theory on resilience and anti-fragility remains fascinating. It's a theory in which government officials have no faith. Not anymore. They coddle the markets, they pamper them, they pander to their whims, leaving an economy that can no longer stand firmly without any support.

In the years of easy money following the Lehman crisis, after two rounds of QE, the markets floundered again. They were addicted to stimulus, and we could see the resulting behavior very clearly in the early 2010s. They simply wouldn't rally without the Fed's help. And that's exactly what they received, from Operation Twist (which controlled long-term interest rates by buying long-term Treasuries and selling shorter-term T-bills and notes) to an additional $1.7 trillion in QE3, the third round of quantitative easing—the experimental drug even Ben Bernanke admits does not work in theory but by some miracle works in practice. And so, shortly after entering the second decade of the new century, the Fed kept doing what it knew how to do: suppress interest rates. This kept the markets climbing ever higher. Energy prices retraced their footsteps, too, with crude oil climbing all the way back from $35 in late 2008 to $125 per barrel in 2011, a level that could support another oil and gas boom.

U.S. Oil and Gas Capex

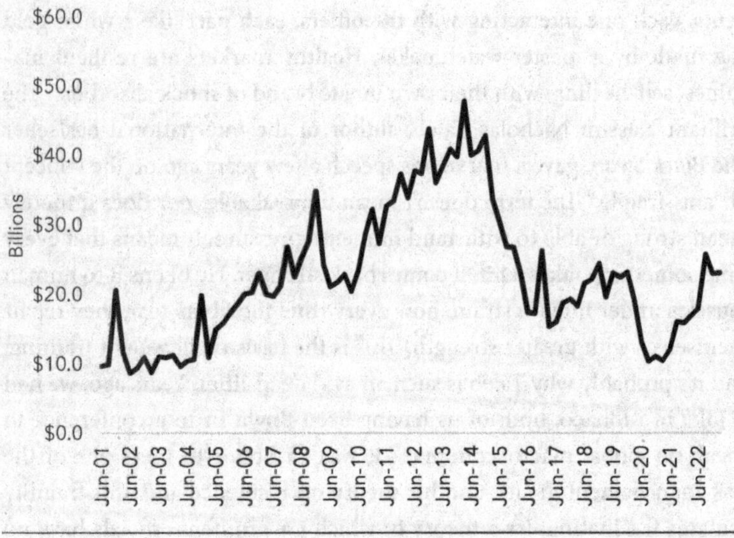

Cheap borrowing rates single-handedly created a great wave of exploration. The floodgates opened for wildcatters and rogue oil and gas explorers, and competition became ferocious. U.S. oil production doubled between 2009 and 2015 to 10 million barrels per day. Companies like Apache, Devon Energy, and Southwestern Energy were all in the mix. Exxon famously bought shale driller XTO Energy for $41 billion in 2009.

Other shale drillers, such as Range Resources, EOG Resources, Diamondback Energy, and Pioneer Natural Resources, spent billions on acreage in the Permian Basin and the 200,000-square-mile Bakken Formation in the badlands of North Dakota, tapping into billions of barrels of crude oil and natural gas.

Chesapeake was no longer the dominant force. Chief financial officers inside these energy companies charged forward like the bulls of Pamplona. And the big players racked up debt. They borrowed cheap money and piled it into drilling and exploration. The leverage in the sector was dizzying, and Chesapeake's operation was no different.

Tom Ward was long gone by then. Aubrey McClendon was all alone, in a sense, without that lifelong friend by his side. And that's when he crossed the ethical line, bidding on land with staged auctions, having planned the winning bid weeks beforehand. His edge was gone, swallowed by the vast army of rivals chipping away at his bottom line. He could compete only with better deals on land leases, or else he'd be finished. And in those desperate times, with so much leverage on the books and the multitude of other drillers, the boom in oil and gas production created a supply glut that eventually cratered energy prices.

There is always a moment that defines a market bottom. It is usually handed to us by a price that scares everyone to death. But something in addition to the price often accompanies this moment. It could be a big fund going down. A bank collapsing. A large company throwing in the towel, the top executives getting carted out, and the bankruptcy lawyers arriving on the doorstep. On February 10, 2016, oil hit $27 a barrel, a new low. Less than one month later it tried to retest that level. On March 2, 2016, the oil and gas markets were heading south again, and all over the news the next day was the story of how Aubrey McClendon had taken his own life by crashing his truck into a brick wall. That day oil hit $34 a barrel, and the big celebrity in the energy sector had been taken to a morgue. The bottom was in.

Purse strings tightened across the energy sector, with oil companies hesitant to invest, especially as government regulation and red tape increased. And as stockpiles dwindled, the price crept northward. In 2018, oil hit $77.41 for a barrel of Texas light sweet.

. . .

Speculators' Positioning in WTI Futures

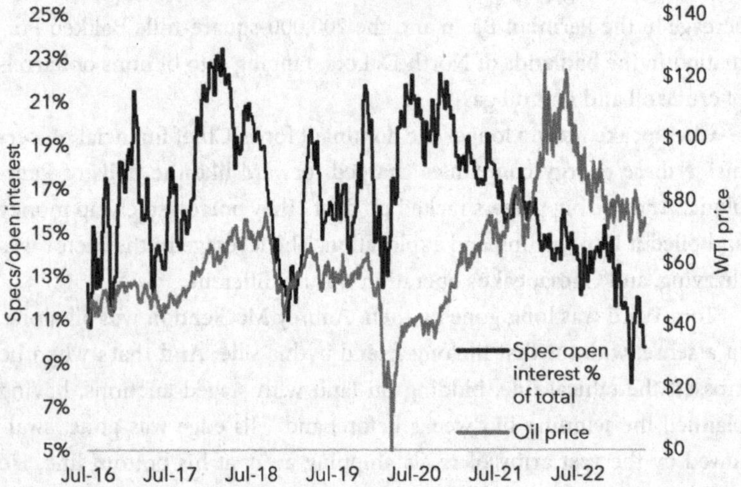

With the global population on an upward trajectory, planet Earth will have an *unstoppable demand* for energy in the coming years. Meanwhile, supply growth is under arrest, a problem we'll explore in the pages ahead. This has left a gaping chasm between the amount of energy and critical resources needed to continue raising our global standard of living and the amount on tap. This chasm will only widen in the coming decades.

Western politicians are driving hard for alternative energies and run the other way if someone suggests a continuation of drilling, fracking, and mining. And I largely support the push to adopt green energy, but we're about twenty years too early. I grew up going to Cape Cod, sailing on Nantucket Sound, breathing that pristine air, walking on the immaculate beaches, and eating raw scallops right out of Barnstable Harbor. My respect for nature and the natural world is part of my soul, but I'm also an economist who understands what it takes to feed, clothe, transport, and provide living quarters for about 8 billion people; the toll on our power grids is a heavy one. And it *cannot* be done with wind farms, solar panels, and hydroelectric power. Not even close.

Right now the top priority should be keeping the lights on, and keeping the gargantuan global economy rumbling forward in a responsible, low-inflationary fashion. That requires fossil fuels, and somewhat ironically, they *will* pave the way to the green-energy revolution. But knocking out oil with green energy right now is a mathematical impossibility, especially since some of the most populated countries in the world (such as India, China, and Russia) have no intention of being bound by Western emission standards—all of which we'll cover in this chapter.

The Crude Necessity

"If Trudeau was here, I'd tell him this coffee is made of oil," Rafi Tahmazian commented wryly as he poured a cup for each of us. I was meeting with Rafi, one of the world's finest energy asset managers, in his downtown office in November 2021 after I gave an afternoon speech at the Calgary Petroleum Club. "Machines to grow it and harvest it, vehicles to transport it, more machines to pack it, electricity to roast and grind the beans, heat to boil the water," he continued. "It doesn't happen with pixie dust, old pal. It happens with crude oil."

I could hear emails chiming into his inbox as he spoke. He runs the investment division at Canoe Financial, a $2 billion management firm focused on oil, mining, and natural gas. He wasn't political in his views, but he firmly maintained a single belief, one he'd held for many years: "The entire planet is run by crude oil. Everything we touch. Everything we consume. It's nothing to do with politics. It's pragmatism. This war on the supply side of oil is the dumbest thing I've ever seen. But Trudeau . . . he came into power and put the entire downtown of Calgary into meltdown in 2015. I'll never forget it. The man is a drama teacher, and he's dictating energy policy!"

Standing beside the window, he swept his hand across the panoramic view. The big cluster of skyscrapers bore the logos of the energy giants—Shell, Exxon, ConocoPhillips, Suncor. It was a striking change from the financial cathedrals of Manhattan. It was also about twice as cold. "You see all these office buildings? This is how we judge the booms and busts in our business." Back in 2014, the smartest guys he knew had quickly recognized a market top. "Up here, once New York money starts flooding in—big banks like Goldman and Morgan Stanley, along with the big energy guys—it's a sign we're in the thick of a bull market. It trickles in at first, then it's gangbusters. When they see office space double or even triple the price per square foot, that's when all the veteran, local Canadian wildcatters start to unwind positions and take down long exposure to oil and gas." But dynamics have shifted radically since then.

Energy Consumption and Population

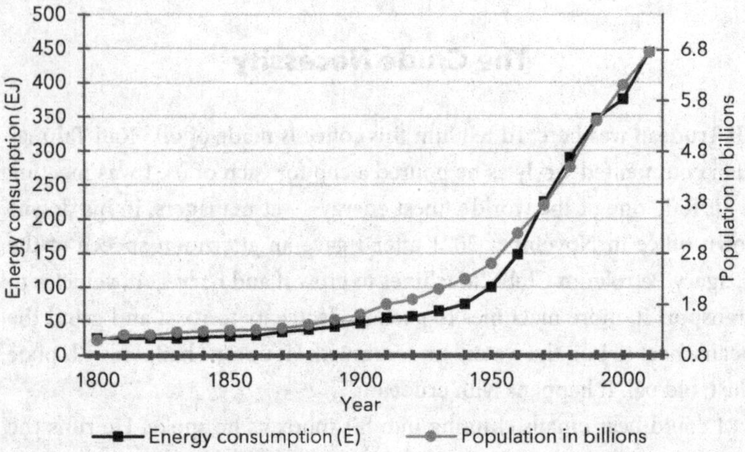

Rafi took a sip of his coffee and paused for a moment to collect his thoughts. "In 1850, before we discovered crude oil, 80 percent of the world's population made less than $1.50 a day; most people were subsistence farmers. That was still 50 percent in 1985, though, but it really started to decline from then on. Fast-forward to 2020 and it's down to just 10 percent. Almost single-handedly, oil raised billions of people out of dire poverty—especially in the past three decades as more production has moved outside the Western world. More than that, it gave most of them something resembling a middle-class existence." He then leaned back. "What that means, though, is more and more consumption in the developing world, of everything—clothes, televisions, cars, you name it! And that's going to continue, at least until they reach Western standards of living."

He leaned in intently. "Larry, think of India. Energy use has doubled there since 2000, and it's going to grow at three times the global average because they're urbanizing so fast. That's going to mean a colossal surge in air-conditioning demand from 2021 to 2031. So we are in a climate crisis, and 1.4 billion people make up the fastest-growing swath of energy demand on planet Earth. That's three to four times faster than the U.S., UK, Germany, and the rest of the developed world. India is addicted to cheap coal and fossil fuels. There is an important investment thesis brewing here. Of the roughly 320 million households in India, fewer than 22 million have air-conditioning units right now."

Rafi started gesticulating to express the gravity of the situation. "We are talking about a country with an average daytime temperature near 29 degrees Celsius—that's 84 degrees Fahrenheit. As per capita incomes rise in India, as the standard of living moves higher, the first thing a family adds to the monthly budget is AC! Carbon-neutral 2050 is a fantasy; it's more like 2100 or 2125 for the 4 billion human beings in the developing world, and oil, gas, and nuclear will be needed to fill this void. Exporting higher-paying jobs around planet Earth comes with a price—it's *not* free."

Rafi had grown up in Calgary, had been around energy investments all his life, and now he held a big seat in a huge investment fund right in the action. He was born to trade the energy booms and busts. His analysis and his worldview were direct, were logical, and, above all, revolved around a central thesis of such staggering simplicity that it almost evaded modern governments altogether.

"When you get right down to it, Larry, an energy shortage in the West means a cold shower. Maybe not such good coffee. But in emerging markets, you've got carnage, chaos . . . perhaps a civil war on your hands." He looked at me with a wry smile. "Can someone tell me why we don't have a pipeline sending our oil to eastern Canada? It's because the Quebec government blocked it! Can you imagine? They'd rather buy Saudi oil than pipe it across a green field!"

Rafi stood there in mock amazement.

As I traveled back home to New York, I couldn't stop thinking about the supply of energy in the foreseeable future or, rather, the lack of it. By my estimate, $2.4 trillion was cut from the fossil fuels and metals capex between 2014 and 2020. "Capex" is short for "capital expenditure," and it's a word that's thrown around in the energy markets all day long. Energy is one of the most capital-intensive businesses on the planet. Think sophisticated drilling rigs, extensive pipeline systems, advanced refining technology, processing plants, and much more. Sometimes, especially in the mining business, companies have to build railroads to cart the commodity away from the origination point. Building railroads is not cheap.

Anyway, the $2.4 trillion cut was due to a combination of bad capital

Commonly Accepted Projections of Global Energy Demand May Be Flat-Out Wrong

The International Energy Agency's (IEA) vision of a sustainable-growth scenario that cuts global CO_2 emissions in half in twenty years? Unlikely. Its projection that per capita energy demand will decline by 25 percent by 2040? Breathtaking. The IEA assumes demand will decline even in emerging-market economies, which is simply insane. Leigh Goehring and Adam Rozencwajg's research in this area is a must-read. A good rule of thumb from Goehring and Rozencwajg is that once a country's per capita GDP exceeds $2,500 a year, commodity consumption begins to increase exponentially. Once per capita GDP crosses $20,000 per year, consumption can level off. But first, transportation preferences will shift from bicycle to scooter to car. As urbanization boosts productivity and income, people will want air-conditioning, heating, lighting, and power. They'll also eat more meat, which requires more energy to produce than vegetables. A reasonable estimate is a 10 percent increase in per capita global energy demand over the next twenty years.

According to OPEC, the world consumed around 102 million barrels of oil per day in 2023. If we assume flat oil demand in the developed economies (the United States, Western Europe, developed Asia, etc.) for the next five to ten years, as population and GDP discipline after the 2014 bust, which led to many bankruptcies and asset sales, and to government regulation. In other words, there have not been nearly enough good old-fashioned investments in coal, oil, gas, uranium, and metals exploration and production, especially in North America. Over the same period, the global population grew by 800 million. Today, we might need $3 trillion in additional capital expenditure just to play catch-up.

The COVID-19 pandemic changed the oil sector, perhaps for a decade. Right after COVID hit, demand for all oil dried up like a drop of

growth are offset by a continued reduction in per capita energy consumption, then the growth in oil demand must come from the emerging markets. Assuming trend demand growth in those countries from the last five years, we estimate that oil demand will increase from 56 million barrels per day in 2023 to 65 million barrels in 2028 and 77 million barrels in 2033. This means that the world will consume 123 million barrels in that ten-year period. All that extra demand is coming from the emerging economies, and this doesn't even account for a potential acceleration of demand from regions such as Africa and India when per capita income reaches levels that drive exponential oil demand growth. On the supply side, U.S. production has been stagnant since 2019, with around 12 million barrels produced in 2022. Production capacity in Venezuela, Iran, and Russia—each subject to international sanctions—is suffering from a lack of access to advanced drilling technology and Western capital. In other words, production in these countries continues to stagnate as well. Saudi Arabia and the United Arab Emirates are the OPEC members with the most excess capacity, but this is about 4 million barrels at present and far below the 21 million extra barrels needed. Without a massive ramp-up in investments in new production capacity, there is simply no way the oil industry can meet this expected demand growth.

Oil and Gas Sector Total Debt

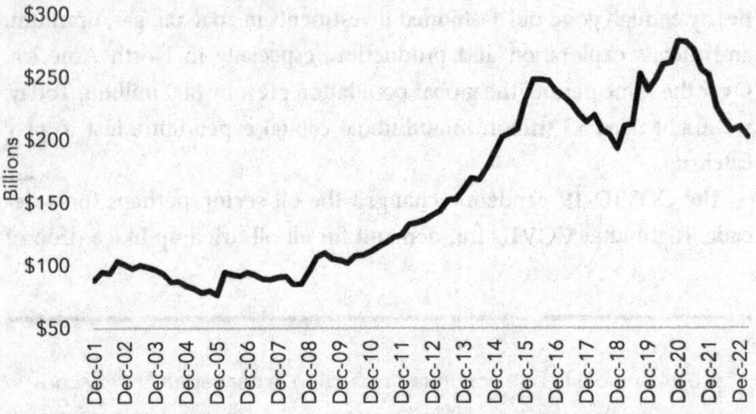

Oil Reserves: Majors vs. Independent E&Ps

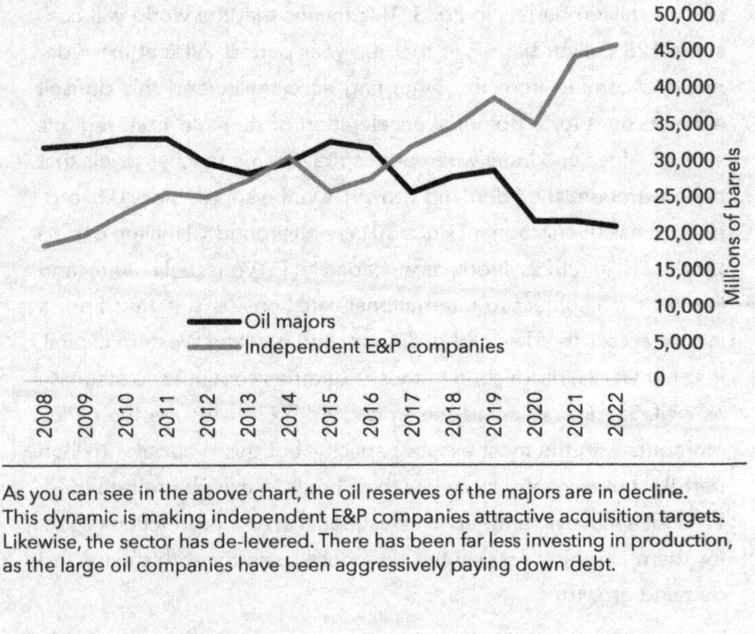

As you can see in the above chart, the oil reserves of the majors are in decline. This dynamic is making independent E&P companies attractive acquisition targets. Likewise, the sector has de-levered. There has been far less investing in production, as the large oil companies have been aggressively paying down debt.

INVESTORS TAKE NOTE:

Could Nuclear Bridge the Gap?

More and more green activists globally have finally acknowledged that the only path to the green meadow and carbon neutrality runs through a heavy nuclear component. Yet it's not a simple solution. In the wake of the Chernobyl disaster in the USSR in 1986 and then Fukushima in Japan in 2011, the media hammered everything to do with nuclear reactors and nuclear energy. Germany led the charge out of the sector, closing most of its nuclear plants and transitioning to wind farms and solar energy. There has been a terrible underinvestment in nuclear, leaving the state of the uranium market as bleak as an empty parking lot in the rain. The United States has only two years of uranium supply for its fleet of fifty-four commercially operating nuclear power plants.

Reactors take years to build. Reversing this course would be like turning around three aircraft carriers. Hiring new minds, finding the correct PhD brains to oversee operations—all this will be a long, drawn-out process that could take nearly a decade—five to seven years at a minimum. Meanwhile, the sector is suffering from brain drain, losing significant talent to industries such as crypto.

In Washington, there is now bipartisan, hand-in-hand support for the sector, unthinkable five to ten years ago. Above all, the global supply-versus-demand backdrop is very bullish for the commodity and the equities as a whole. In Canada, Europe, and Asia there is a significant trend shift fueling meaningful higher future demand. Per Bloomberg, unit production costs of nuclear power ranked the cheapest among all energy sources, just 90 percent of the cost of hydropower, 46 percent of wind power, 40 percent of solar power, and 27 percent of oil.

According to Bill Gates, "Modern nuclear energy, in terms of an overall safety record, is better than other energy." We love this sector as an investment. The global population has grown by 800 million since 2014. It grows by that margin every ten years. This naturally increases demand for fossil fuels, energy, and electricity. Right now, there is a giant disconnect between the energy demands and the nuclear capacity of the world's largest economies—namely, the United States and China. Nuclear power supplies upward of 30 percent of the electricity for titans like France, Hungary, and Sweden. In bigger countries like the United States, China, Brazil, India, and the United Kingdom, that figure is even below 20 percent—just 5 percent in China.

Elon Musk recently came out in wholehearted support of expanding nuclear capacity. He said, "Germany should not only not shut down the nuclear power plants, it should reopen the ones that are shut down. . . . Total madness. The world should increase the use of nuclear power!" People on the demand side of the equation are starting to call for an increase in generation capacity. They see shortages looming. Because if all this demand eventually arrives at the doorstep of a horribly undersupplied nuclear-energy sector, it could cause a super spike in the price of uranium.

Our longtime consultant John Quakes, an expert in the uranium sector and an earth sciences researcher, has told us about dozens of developments in the sector in the past couple of months. "It has been mind-blowing," he said, "to see how the nuclear energy narrative has snowballed, with announcements of new reactors being

water on a hot copper pan. The oil markets crashed, sending West Texas Intermediate oil to $0 a barrel. Companies right across the industry switched off their wells, turned off their equipment, and sent their employees home to collect unemployment checks. Everybody remembers the monumental economic shutdown. Even the highways emptied, and Manhattan on a Saturday night didn't have a car horn within earshot. The wide, ghostly avenues of Midtown were like something from a dystopian film. The new world was pushing ahead with a future based in the metaverse, or an augmented reality. The Gen Zers and millennials were convinced that the energy future was not in the dirty oil patch anymore, that built, planned, extended, and restarted like never before. Germany seems to have been the flashpoint. Their catastrophic nuclear exit, which made them reliant on Russian gas and overpriced wind farms, is now acting as a catalyst for other nations to do the exact opposite."

Because on almost every metric, nuclear energy beats every other source of energy hands down. Carbon emissions, costs, safety, waste . . . the list goes on. But all we hear about in the papers is nuclear waste and the leftover pain from Fukushima and Chernobyl. Rarely does anybody talk about waste from solar. According to BloombergNEF, "The global volume of solar-panel waste generated annually will rise from 30,000 metric tonnes in 2021 to more than 1 million tonnes in 2035, and more than 10 million tonnes in 2050." Junk panels, discarded in a decaying heap of rust and plastic. Neither do we read much about the mountains of toxic waste created by the refining of rare earths, an essential raw material that goes into wind turbines.

Surprisingly, a few years ago, the uranium sector was already heading toward a massive supply deficit just keeping the current global reactor fleet up and running. But then a new resurgence took hold in late 2022. The COVID-19 pandemic hit supply chains on the chin, but demand is back and is about to skyrocket.

In chapter 9, we'll show you how to get ahead of this coming trend.

---

it would be different somehow, free of carbon emissions in a new electrified world, and the gas-guzzling cars of the last hundred years would be towed, finally, to the junkyard of history. But this was a terrible misjudgment.

When the world reopened in 2021 after the COVID lockdowns, OPEC imposed a firm limit on supply, while U.S. production was slow to recover. Rhetoric about "killing shale" dominated Democratic Party debates in 2020, too, which scared a lot of participants away from the space, especially after Biden won the election. Why invest in a kill zone? Capital didn't just walk; it ran away from the sector.

INVESTORS TAKE NOTE:

The Coming Wave of Mergers and Acquisitions in the Oil Industry

There were three major M&A waves in the oil and gas space: one in the late 1990s, when Exxon and Mobil merged amid historically low oil prices; one between 2004 and 2007, when oil prices were surging and the shale revolution was just starting in natural gas; and one between 2015 and 2019, after the big-oil investment boom, when weak players were scooped up.

Today, the industry is poised to go through another period of consolidation. Much of the most lucrative shale acreage has already been bought up, and the ESG, a type of investing that screens where companies can borrow capital based on "environmental, social, and governance" criteria, restrictions on drilling and capital make it attractive for the oil majors to acquire rather than develop acreage. In a multipolar world, fossil fuel reserves are more valuable when closer to home, as those in faraway places could get caught up in geopolitical turmoil or be repatriated by foreign governments. For instance, all the joint ventures between global oil majors and the Russian government were dissolved when the United States and Europe slapped sanctions on Russia in 2022. BP had to take a $25 billion hit when it abandoned its 20 percent stake in the Russian company Rosneft, which represented about half of BP's reserves. Shell also took a loss when it backed out of its joint venture with Russia's Gazprom to finance the Nord Stream 2 pipeline.

In 2020, ExxonMobil had $4 billion of cash. By 2023, this number had surged to $33 billion, while the company's free cash flow annually grew from –$2 billion to more than $58 billion. The majors have a lot of greenbacks burning a hole in their pockets, most in need of a new home, and nowadays an acquisition is one of the easiest ways to add reserves.

Unsurprisingly, oil prices climbed higher and higher. There simply wasn't enough. Demand quickly outstripped supply, and inflation started to roll through markets as fleets of airlines turned on their massive kerosene-powered turbofans, diesel cruise ships for three thousand people cast off their lines, and highways steadily reloaded with gasoline-powered cars, buses, and trucks. And this was occurring not just in America but all over the world.

The last three years have seen the West escalate its battle on fossil fuels into a full-blown war. ESG restrictions are on the rise. The West wants to encourage companies to act responsibly, but that's just a euphemism for "Stay the hell away from anyone trying to pollute planet Earth—especially fossil fuels." You can see it in the news, you can see it in campaign promises, and you can see it in the boardrooms. This killed investment in the traditional energy sector including oil, natural gas, and coal and is an important reason why supplies are down across the board.

And an increase in oil supply doesn't just happen with a snap of the fingers. It takes many years to bring big production back online. First, there are multiyear regulatory loopholes to jump through. Then governments need to incentivize the companies to do it. But many governments slapped windfall taxes on big oil companies instead. And that's the wrong approach. Taxes stop production. Period. Next, the exploration phase has to be carried out, finding the most oil-rich patches of land to drill. That's an expensive game. Phase four is moving the equipment, a multimillion-dollar problem. Then comes the hiring of qualified people, and then the drilling, infrastructure, transportation, and logistics. And on and on. It will take about seven to ten years to flood the market once again with oil and gas after the ESG drive eventually fails. And it will. All one has to do is study the numbers.

If governments really wanted to replace oil as a source of energy on planet Earth, it would currently take a wind farm a little bigger than France, 134 million acres of land. A solar field to replace oil would need to be the size of Spain, at 120 million acres, not to mention that it would need to experience at least 70 percent sunshine for eight hours a day, *every day, every year.* Now think about the amount of plastic that would be used, the fiberglass, the steel shafts and turbines, the endless maintenance, the millions of batteries and cabling. It simply cannot be done without bankrupting the planet. Maybe one day, over the course of many decades, but not today.

ESG investing's red tape is mired in unintended consequences, quite separate from the financial markets. Behind the scenes, it is wreaking havoc. California has seen multiple devastating fires in the last few years;

Africa Petroleum Demand

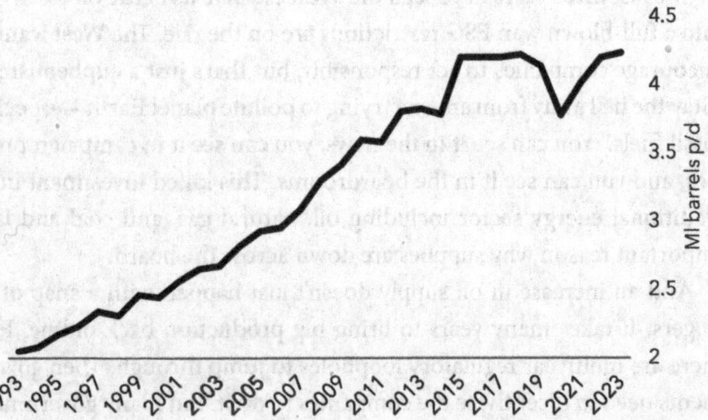

China Petroleum Demand

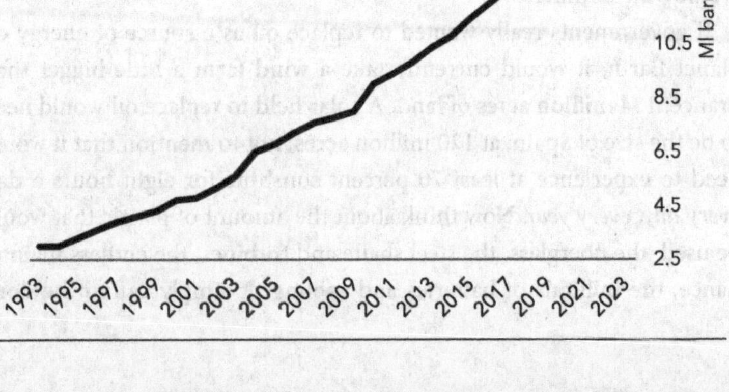

more than sixty thousand structures have burned to the ground. Miley Cyrus, Neil Young, and Gerard Butler lost their homes. In total, California's forest fires have burned down 22 million acres of woods and grassland since the turn of the century, the equivalent of the entire state of Maine. All these fires have produced CO_2 pollution equal to running 120 million cars for one year straight.

It's easy to blame climate change, but that is far from the whole story. In fact, much of the cause comes down to California's zeal to use renewable energy without considering all the possible consequences, and the mismanagement of its utility, Pacific Gas & Electric (PG&E). This company and its haphazard transmission infrastructure maintenance practices have been responsible for starting dozens of major wildfires since 2000, causing hundreds of deaths and billions of dollars in damage. Part of the problem is that onerous regulation has mandated utilities like PG&E to get renewable energy from faraway places, such as hydroelectricity from Washington State and solar power from Nevada. The required connections between PG&E's grid and these distant renewable sources cost PG&E a fortune in building long-distance high-voltage lines to out-of-state locations. The regulator approving these investments was the Federal Energy Regulatory Commission (FERC).

California's state regulator, the California Public Utilities Commission (CPUC), and FERC oversee the rates that PG&E charged the consumer for electricity. Like most utilities, PG&E must get regulator approval for any rate increases, and these are based on the investments the company makes. Because of all these renewable mandates and the expensive infrastructure necessary to meet them, California ended up with the highest electricity rates in the country. For that reason, CPUC often rejected requests for rate increases based on other expenditures that PG&E was proposing to make, such as simple maintenance spending on its local distribution lines into towns and cities. In other words, the utility regulators, and not PG&E, decide what maintenance plans PG&E should carry out. Therefore, the funding to maintain local lines, poles, and transmission stations didn't exist, and eventually the lines started to fall apart—and subsequently set the state on fire.

Juicing Inflation

Energy prices are the root cause of inflation, when you get right down to it. Think of every drop of gasoline and energy used in something simple like our Calgary cup of coffee. Add high oil prices to that, and suddenly that $4 cup of coffee at Starbucks costs $6.

Mergers and Acquisitions in U.S. Oil and Gas

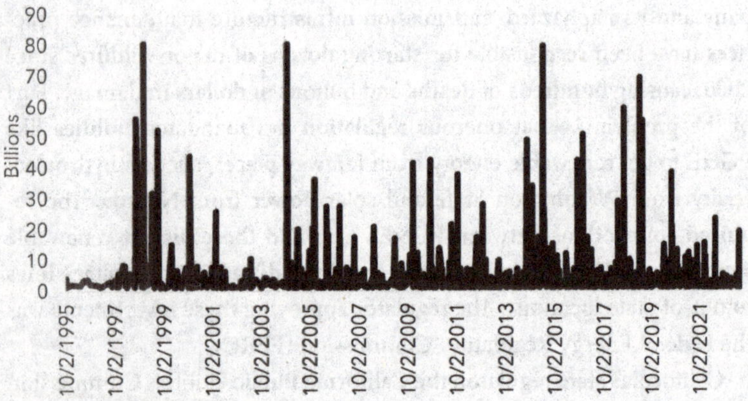

But there's a second layer to the relationship between energy and inflation. Not only will higher energy costs drive other costs up along with it, but it will make inflation harder to fight. The following may be the most important sentence in this book: If inflation normalizes in this cycle at 3 to 4 percent instead of 1 to 2 percent as in previous decades, trillions of dollars are misallocated across the investment asset ecosystem, as most portfolios are still massively overweight growth stocks.

Usually, during a time of recession, the prices of energy and oil drop dramatically due to lower demand, which acts as a major deflationary force. But going forward, the price of energy will likely stay relatively high even during recessions. Through chronic underinvestment in the oil and gas industries, the United States and Canada handed over valuable market share to the Saudis, the Russians, and OPEC, giving them way more control over the global price of oil. In a multipolar world, these not-so-friendly players can now coordinate supply cuts during recessions to keep the price high.

If the U.S. had eight thousand drilled but uncompleted wells (DUCs), we could just ramp up production and steal market share back from them. But we don't. DUCs are at a ten-year low, and this dynamic sets us up for a longer-term battle with higher and stickier inflation. We saw this during the minor energy crisis in 2022, and it is going to be the norm in the years ahead.

In the year 2020, BlackRock CEO Larry Fink wrote a lengthy letter to all the CEOs and board members of the companies in which BlackRock's ETFs were heavily invested. This gave Fink a commanding presence in every boardroom. In that letter, he outlined his stance on climate policies and a decarbonized future. It was a matter-of-fact essay on the importance of a carbon-free world. In 2022, he sat down once more and penned a follow-up letter. In it, he made a case that leaves little room for negotiation. As the most powerful shareholder in most of these companies, he is brazen enough to write, "The tectonic shift towards sustainable investing is still accelerating. . . . Every company and every industry will be transformed by the transition to a net zero world. The question is, will you lead, or will you be led?"

The entire global conversation, from Davos to political campaigns to climatologists to journalists—the entire dialogue from top to bottom—is basically around carbon dioxide and companies that are responsible for big CO_2 emissions. It's basically an attack on fossil fuels—coal, oil, and natural gas—and they can't wait to replace it all with wind, solar, hydrogen, and whatever else they can muster up that doesn't emit CO_2, even if it makes little sense mathematically. It's about supply, *not* demand.

Given that the mathematics of green energy is unrealistic, forcing this path toward a net-zero-carbon world will risk a global economic reversal. In Fink's view, "Every sector will be transformed by new, sustainable technology." Has the goal of carbon-free energy now morphed into a fanaticism, or do they still have our best interests at heart? An electric future is an impossibility at the moment, based on the amount of available copper in the world.

INVESTORS BEWARE:

More Causes of Sticky Inflation

Setting aside sociopolitical considerations, from a purely economic perspective, the broadening of the social safety net post-COVID has likely built the foundation for a much higher normalized rate of inflation, relative to previous decades. Econ 101: What happens when you subsidize demand and arrest supply? Beyond the newly strengthened role of Saudi Arabia, Russia, and OPEC, there are internal political factors that raise the likelihood of high energy prices causing sticky inflation or even an inflationary price spiral. In 2022, governments around the Western world made the unorthodox move of subsidizing energy demand during an inflationary crisis. California spent $23 billion on "inflation relief" checks, which were largely issued to cover increased energy costs. Italy spent $14 billion to do the same thing. The biggest of all these energy-demand-subsidization payments was the cost-of-living adjustment (COLA) tacked onto U.S. Social Security and government retiree checks. The year 2023 saw the highest COLA increase in forty years, clocking in at 8.7 percent. The COLA is calculated using CPI figures, which themselves largely come down to the cost of energy (since crude is in everything). Through Social Security alone, the federal government sent an extra $207 billion to retirees to offset the decline in purchasing power in 2022 and 2023. COLA capital oozes through the economy, buying food and clothing off the shelves, and keeps inflation sticky.

We saw this in the 1970s: Even if prices normalize, they are supported on a higher-inflation-rate trajectory. Since the adjustment

For copper, 40 percent of the future demand growth is expected to come from electrical applications in green technologies, such as electric vehicles (EVs), wind turbines, and solar panels. According to the research and consultancy firm Wood Mackenzie, this demand growth will create a ten-year supply gap of up to 5 million tons due to the lack of new lags the true cost of living by a year, it also projects the previous year's inflation forward. The direct and indirect demand-subsidizing measures will probably also pop up in the next energy crisis, which will add to the global inflationary burden.

In the post-COVID world, the broader social safety net has also been made meaningfully larger. There is no more telling look at sustained inflation than Supplemental Nutrition Assistance Program (SNAP) benefits. During the pandemic years, the number of recipients rose 25 percent to hit 42 million across the country. In 2001, this number was 16 million, or 5.6 percent of the U.S. population. Per Pew Research, by April 2023, 41.9 million people received SNAP benefits. That translates to 12.5 percent of the total U.S. population.

In 2020, Walmart captured nearly 26 percent of SNAP grocery dollars. SNAP payment cycles now have a large impact on Walmart's earnings, as cited on company conference calls. Per the Department of Agriculture, federal spending on the USDA's food and nutrition assistance programs totaled $182.5 billion in fiscal year (FY) 2021, 49 percent more than the previous high of $122.8 in FY 2020.

And this is a U.S. economy that is near "full employment." In other words, almost anyone who wants a job can find one. Heading into the next recession, the United States will be running at least 5 to 7 percent annual budget deficits, with social welfare spending already 20 percent higher than the twenty-year average. Fighting inflation with Federal Reserve rate hikes and then juicing inflation with much higher deficit spending during COVID-19 likely built the foundation for a much higher normalized rate of inflation going forward, relative to previous decades.

copper mining projects. According to the Edison Electric Institute, the U.S. electric transmission network consists of more than 600,000 circuit miles of lines, 240,000 of which are considered high-voltage lines (230 kilovolts and greater). Copper is a key material component of transmission, which consists of structural frames, conductor lines, cables, transformers, circuit breakers, switches, and substations. A global electricity grid of 152 million kilometers (the distance from here to the sun) is needed to meet net-zero targets by 2050—double the size of the grid today. And according to the Oregon Group, an investment research team, 427 metric tons of copper will be needed by 2050. To meet this target, $21 trillion will need to be spent, with annual investment increasing from $274 billion in 2022 to $1 trillion by 2050. We are talking about the capital expenditures required to find the copper and rebuild the grid and the logistics needed to get all the materials in the right place.

Lithium is another vital mineral for the green transition. Expected global demand for lithium for EVs in 2030 is estimated to be twenty-three times what was produced in 2021. The supply deficit of lithium is therefore expected to persist until at least 2030 as demand continues to outstrip supply. Nickel is another green metal because lithium batteries almost always use nickel, since that metal can easily absorb and release lithium ions as they are pushed back and forth to release or charge energy. Demand is expected to double by 2040, thanks to the growth of nickel-based batteries in EVs and power walls. Demand for cobalt, a mineral we go deeper into in chapter 9, is forecast to double by 2030, with an estimated supply deficit of 32 percent.

Putting another 10 million electric vehicles on American roads will put significant stress on an entire electrical grid infrastructure well-known to be failing in some spots. We've seen countless tragic lessons over the past few years, from devastating outages in Texas to the rampant fires in California. The American electrical power grid is more than half a century old and increasingly unstable, underfunded, and, most of all, incapable of taking on millions of EVs. And it will cost as much as $7 trillion in the United States alone to upgrade that infrastructure to support a decarbonized U.S. transport sector.

Our team recently heard a bizarre story from across the Atlantic Ocean. In Germany, headlines were dominated by the country's failed wind-power sector. Having shut down their coal and natural gas, limited their oil power, and plowed billions into solar and wind, the Germans were faced with a real crisis. The operator of the grid in the southwestern state of Baden-Württemberg sent a warning to clients for the first time ever: It was going to lose power for one hour that afternoon and was asking clients to ease up on their energy consumption. This was *Germany,*

Europe's number one economy, and it was suddenly beholden to the elements. A weather pattern known as a *Dunkelflaute* (literally "dark calm," or, more loosely, "no wind") was causing havoc. For the first time, the grid operator admitted that the increasing share of renewables such as wind and solar was making the German energy grid "a challenge." How's that for German understatement?

E&P Valuation

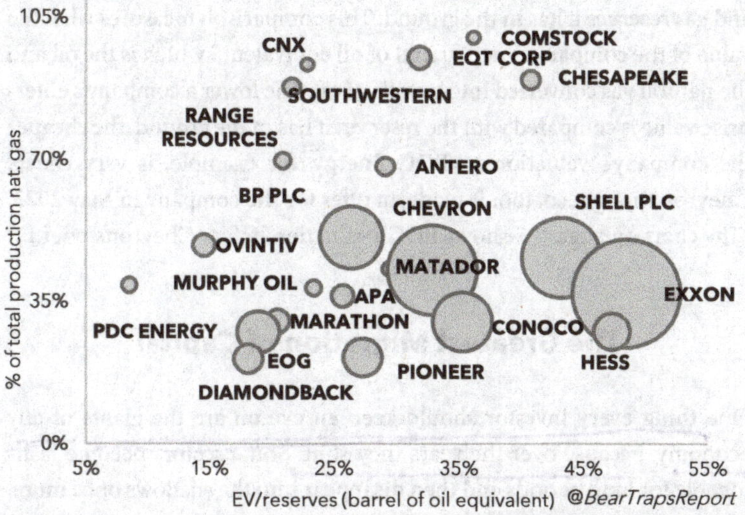

With the endless issues hanging over the global energy markets, you might be asking how an investor can capitalize on this knowledge. And our advice is simple: *Get long oil.* You need solid exposure to these markets. We love this sector for the next decade. The energy ETFs XLE and XOP are great places to start, along with Chevron, Shell, and ExxonMobil. In particular, Exxon is interesting because of its massive new reserves in Guyana, right on the northeastern tip of South America. The company has an operating office in Guyana's capital, Georgetown, with numerous ongoing exploration and development operations offshore. At its Stabroek oil field, in operation since May 2015, it has made significant discoveries, and the company expects production capacity to reach 1.2 million barrels per day in 2027, up from 375,000 barrels in 2022. This implies that in four years Guyana will represent approximately 25 percent of Exxon's worldwide production. It is a solid place to park capital. We are buyers of ExxonMobil (XOM) on dips. In the preceding chart, we highlight several smaller oil and gas producers with an attractive valuation and the potential to be acquired by one of the oil majors.

How does Wall Street value oil and gas companies, and what can investors glean from big business's approach for their own profit? One way to value a company in the energy sector is to compare its enterprise value (the sum of its debt and its market capitalization) with the value of the oil and gas reserves it has in the ground. This comparison measures what the value of the company is per "barrel of oil equivalent," which is the oil and the natural gas converted into barrels of oil. The lower a company's enterprise value is compared with the reserves it has in the ground, the cheaper the company's valuation is. PDC Energy, for example, is very cheap. Chevron thought so, too: It made an offer for the company in May 2023. (The chart on page 107 shows PDC's valuation before Chevron's offer.)

The Greatest Migration of Capital

One thing every investor should keep an eye on are the giants of any economy, because over the years they shift. Some sectors become fashionable for long periods and then disappear into the shadows once more. If you can stay ahead of these trends, and learn how to spot them, your portfolio will be in a far better place. For instance, the oil, gas, industrials, and materials sectors accounted for 49 percent of the S&P 500 in 1981. This percentage plummeted to just 12 percent by 2021—a real shocker, after a decade of deflation. The composition of the S&P 500 has changed in other ways. Over the next forty years, up until 2020–2021, we saw an overdose in financial assets, long-duration assets that are best represented by growth stocks and bonds. This stampede climaxed in January 2022, when technology stocks represented 43 percent of the S&P 500. This moment was the turning point for the markets, and the beginning of a seismic shift, one that happens every decade, and it is a shift that will prevail, we forecast, until possibly 2030.

We have moved from a highly certain *deflationary* regime to an *infla-*

tionary one, and that's when the components of asset allocation change across all portfolio construction. We believe higher energy and metals prices will be sustained for the next decade, and they're already forging the greatest migration of capital we have seen in our lifetime. In 2022, investors were flocking away from technology and growth stocks, and they're moving to harder assets, constructing portfolios that are better able to handle sustained higher energy prices and sustained inflation. From the COVID lows to the end of 2022, as inflation raged higher, the Energy Select Sector SPDR ETF (XLE) was up 325 percent, the Sprott Uranium Miners ETF (URNM) was up 318 percent, the Global X Copper Miners ETF (COPX) was up 260 percent, and the SPDR S&P Metals and Mining ETF (XME) was up 260 percent. As we moved from the certain-deflation era of 2010–2020 to a sustained-inflation regime, hard assets flourished over long-duration financial assets.

The oil stocks are still in the early innings, and we predict that in the next few years billions of dollars will flow into these companies; valuations are cheap. Warren Buffett, the Oracle of Omaha, sees these megatrends clearly. Most of Buffett's new capital put to work in recent years has been in the energy patch. Berkshire Hathaway now owns close to 25 percent of Occidental Petroleum (OXY) and 7 percent of Chevron (CVX). U.S. oil production has been in decline. Just before the pandemic, the United States was producing 13.1 million barrels a day. Three years later we are still at 13.3 million barrels a day. In the three years from 2016 to the end of 2019, U.S. production surged from 8.4 to 12.9 million barrels a day. Many argue this pace is needed, given the expected demand growth of 20 million barrels per day in the next ten years. The population is growing, demand is surging, and supply growth is under arrest.

Larry Fink wrote in his investment letter about the dodo, the flightless bird that went extinct in the seventeenth century, and the phoenix, the immortal bird from Greek mythology that rises from the ashes of its predecessor. The dodos of the future will be those who cling to their ailing growth stocks. The phoenixes will be invested in hard assets and the still-unloved energy stocks. Borrowing costs will be high, the $2 trillion capex hole will take years to plug, and low prices for fossil fuels—oil, gas, and coal—will soon be a distant memory.

MASTERS OF INVESTING WEIGH IN

An Interview with David Tepper

In the winter of 2013, I found myself heading west, the highway's light gray asphalt stained by road salt. In the rearview mirror were the asymmetrical peaks of the Manhattan skyline. But they were getting smaller as I headed down I-78, the fast highway that sweeps through New Jersey, passing Weequahic Park with its two-mile rubberized jogging path, an eighty-acre lake filled by a natural spring, and the oldest public golf course in the United States. A few miles on, I banked right onto Millburn Avenue and drove my way through the tony suburbs on the commuter belt. To the north was Millburn, and to the southwest was Summit, one of the wealthiest towns in the state. Summit was just a cozy farming community in the mid-1800s, but after the Civil War it became a gentrified summer resort, with its clean mountain air and easy firing distance to the Big Apple. The next town on was Chatham, just beyond the private Canoe Brook Country Club, home to two of the finest championship golf courses in the country. Back in the day, when I had the time, I'd have damn near parred them both, but I never had the swing to make it to the majors. Not in that world, anyway.

Three minutes later I parked outside my destination. It had taken seventeen emails and twelve phone calls to land this appointment, but in a sense, it had taken me all my life, and now I was ten feet from the door. Appaloosa Management is a hedge fund that specializes in distressed debt, run by David Tepper, a Pittsburgh native with a photographic memory. In 1987, Tepper was the only trader at Goldman Sachs who didn't lose money. In fact, he shorted that crash and made a fortune for the firm on the way down. At the market bottom in 2009, he famously purchased blocks of many of the U.S. banks. While they were in flames, there was Tepper, buying with both hands.

"Buying right never, ever feels good, Larry," he told me.

He is a priceless piece of work.

Appaloosa Management made a $7.5 billion profit when the U.S. financial sector recovered. Tepper was one of us, buying intense fear when the world was running scared. Capitulation is your friend, far more often than not. But no one did it like Tepper. Junk bond trading legend Larry McCarthy used to say, "Higher prices bring out buyers. Lower prices bring out sellers. Size opens eyes. Time kills trades. When they're cryin', you should be buyin'. When they're yellin', you should be sellin'. Takes years for people to learn those basics, if they ever learn them at all." Tepper has unshakable nerves, and his career embodies McCarthy's words. And when he speaks, there is a familiar toughness to his voice, the kind you often hear when you're in the presence of greatness. But in Tepper's case, "greatness" is not a word I use lightly, because if anyone had invested $1 million in Appaloosa Management in 1993, by 2013 they would have had $149 million. By any standard, that is sensational.

In the conference room was an encased helmet from the Pittsburgh Steelers, Tepper's hometown football team. I had never seen something like that before at a hedge fund, so we chatted for a while about the NFL and Tepper's excitement about owning a minority share in the team. (In 2018, Tepper bought the Carolina Panthers in a $2.3 billion transaction.)

"All the colors in the famous logo," he told me, "represent three different materials used in the making of steel. The yellow is for coal. Orange for iron ore, and the blue is steel scrap." Back in the early 1960s, the Steelers had to petition the American Iron and Steel Institute in order to change the word "Steel" inside the Steelmark (the trademarked circle with the yellow, orange, and blue starlike symbols) to "Steelers" for the team's logo.

Tepper could've chatted about football for hours. But we could have discussed distressed debt just as easily. We were both vulture traders at heart, always looking for the obfuscation, always looking for the lie hiding somewhere in the balance sheet or a phantom in the markets—the bear trap, as it's known on the Street. But Tepper has an elevated level of character. One of the most highly respected names across the asset-management industry, he even left Goldman Sachs after he was asked to compromise his integrity—not so much Goldman's integrity but his own. He walked out the door in the early nineties and started Appaloosa Management. His investors are grateful to this day.

INVESTORS TAKE NOTE:

Importance of Fifty-Two-Week Highs / Fifty-Two-Week Lows

High numbers of stocks trading at fifty-two-week lows and low numbers of stocks closing above their two-hundred-day moving average (a statistic that captures the average change in a data series over the last two hundred days) are very bullish setups that signal a selling climax, something known as a capitulation. There are 2,800 stocks listed on the NYSE. The chart on page 113 shows that days with extreme numbers of fifty-two-week lows, such as in October 2008, March 2020, January 2016, and August of both 1998 and 2015, would have been great times to buy just about any stock.

The same signal can be derived from the NYSE stocks closing above their two-hundred-day moving average. The lowest percentage of stocks closing above this key benchmark came in March 2009 at 1.1 percent. After that was March 2020 with 3.8 percent, August 2011 with 6.7 percent, December 2018 with 7.9 percent, January 2016 with 12.1 percent, and August 1998 with 15.2 percent. If you bought only when more than 1,200 stocks were trading at fifty-two-week lows, you'd easily return two or more times the market. Likewise, if you only ever invested when fewer than 5 percent of stocks

"David," I said, "I'm fascinated by how you run so much money and take on so much risk. But how do you know when to go long in the market and when to go short? What does your risk-management system look like?"

Tepper sat there and thought about his answer for a beat. "Well, Larry, I like to keep things simple. Why overcomplicate things, right?"

I looked at him and smiled; the tone of his voice had a frankness that was refreshing.

"So the way I see it," he continued, "if you have one or two things in the market that are concerning—and that could be anything from a rate traded above their two-hundred-day moving average, your returns would be outstanding.

This is far easier said than done. David Tepper has a talent for keeping his powder dry. Like a lion patiently waiting for that moment to pounce, Tepper made a large bet in Q1 2009. When a record number of stocks were making fifty-two-week lows, Tepper and his team were deploying capital, in size, into the ugliest sector of all, the U.S. banks.

NYSE 52-Week Lows

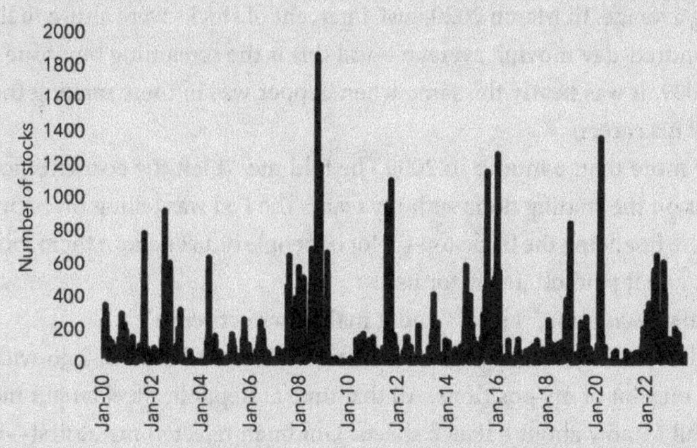

hike to a dangerous earnings patch, maybe a small conflict in the Middle East, whatever it is—with just one or two of those, I keep my long positions on. But when that number gets higher than four, I start cutting bait. That's when I shift from mostly long to adding to my shorts. That's how I stay out of trouble."

Tepper picked up a pen from his desk and started playfully turning it over in his left hand. "It's usually the best move to be long, since the market goes up far more often than not. The best time to buy in is when the market bottoms. Of course, timing is everything."

Tepper is a master at measuring pain and capitulation. There are a couple of signals we use that are fairly dependable. One of those is the number of stocks trading at fifty-two-week lows. Looking back forty years, when you get more than eight hundred new lows, especially more than a thousand, it's marked just about every local bottom. Now, central bank accommodation has a lot to do with bottoms, indeed. Over the years most reversals coming out of extreme capitulation selling involve some kind of policy reversal by the Fed. We must listen when markets speak. Another solid buy signal is the number of stocks closing above their two-hundred-day moving average. The lower that is, the better the buying opportunity. Since the 1990s, all the great tradable bottoms came with fewer than 17 percent of NYSE stocks above their two-hundred-day moving average. In March 2020, just 4 percent of stocks were above their two-hundred-day moving average—and this is the screaming buy zone.

In 2009, it was nearly the same when Tepper was in there making the trade of his career.

"For more than a month in 2009," he told me, "I left the corner office and was on the trading floor with my team. The Fed was telling investors they were financing the backstop—a lot of people didn't believe them, but we did, and it paid off nicely for us."

"That's fascinating," I said. "And it makes perfect sense."

"Well, I don't get too hung up with algorithms and quants. I go with my gut on a lot of my positions. All that time at Republic Steel taught me nearly all I know about balance sheets. Goldman rejected me at first—it took a few more years and an MBA to land a job there—and so I wound up in Ohio after my bachelor's."

"Didn't McDonald's reject you in college?" I asked with a mischievous smile. I couldn't resist the question.

"You've done your research! But I took it on the chin. How about you?"

"My roots? I was in pork chops. Then I somehow got to Merrill Lynch, then Lehman Brothers as a distressed-bond trader."

"So you took a more traditional path?" asked Tepper sarcastically.

We laughed.

Then I said, quoting the poker great Doyle Brunson, "David, when luck shuts the door, you have to come in through the window."

It's that burning desire to break through those walls of resistance we all face in life. Both Tepper and I had fought our way onto Wall Street from the sidelines. Tepper was big on experience, especially for college graduates. He thought learning was the most important thing, especially when you're starting out.

"Never chase after the money. That comes later. What you should chase is experience and knowledge," he said.

"So what do you think of these oil markets?" I asked, getting us back on track. "They're completely gangbusters."

"This will end in tears. By the end of this year"—remember, this conversation took place in 2013—"the U.S. oil-and-gas-rig count is up near eighteen hundred, double 2009 levels. This number could be under a thousand in a few years. Overnight hotel rates in the Permian, in Texas and southeast New Mexico, are up nearly 75 percent the last few years as labor demand in the oil and gas sector exploded. Oil-and-gas-industry capex plans for next year are near $800 billion—that's $300 billion more than 2010 levels. They are digging holes everywhere. This is a sell signal if I ever saw one. At Appaloosa, we like to be first movers. The first ones out of the grass, leading the pack. When we turn around and see followers, that's a good thing. But these oil markets are out of control. Too many people are chasing the action. It will most likely drive down the cost of oil and will wipe out a lot of players."

"Do you think the CFOs are under a lot of pressure to spend?"

"I do. They're not allowed to hoard cash. If they do any more capex, it's just setting it on fire."

It's important to remember one thing about David Tepper: He is an expert at spotting bubbles, and he is also an expert at avoiding them. What he was saying about the oil markets proved to be pinpoint accurate.

Tepper touched his brow briefly and looked at me quizzically for a moment. "If we cool off production in the United States, it will end up in OPEC's hands. If we turn on the taps too aggressively, it will crash the price of energy. And that could blow up the markets. It's a tough balance. We'll have to see. But one thing I know: Those CFOs are a little out of control today. I'm far from confident."

"I agree. Those are my thoughts exactly. I've been speaking to a lot of guys in the energy sector, and they all kind of feel that way."

"It's one of those stories that'll have to play out. I don't like the energy markets in the short time horizon. But one thing I know about oil, and natural gas: You can get a president who doesn't like fossil fuels, or you can get a president who loves them. But one thing I know is this: Fossil fuels aren't going anywhere. If anything, we're gonna need more and more as the world demands stable electric grids in every corner of the globe."

Half an hour later I stood up and shook David Tepper's hand. He walked me downstairs and across the parking lot. He was endlessly cheerful, and there were a couple of things in life that he had obviously done right, things that made him sleep well at night. And that was down to his inner compass, the one that guided his morals. He was a great father, and he gave a lot back to the community, to places he owed so much.

"Remember one thing, Larry: Stay alert to the risks in the market. Watch for the noise—that's always a key indicator. It was great to meet you. Thanks for coming out."

We shook hands again, and I climbed into the car. He waved me off, and all the way back to the city, I was still a little starstruck. I had just met with one of the greatest hedge fund managers in the world.

6

The Dark Side of Passive Investing

Not only our faults, but our most involuntary misfortunes, tend to corrupt our morals.

—HENRY JAMES

Market crashes are caused by forced selling. Period. Economic weakness is never the cause of a panicked stampede for the exits. Economic weakness moves markets much slower, more like a parked bus with a weak hand brake grinding to the bottom of Fillmore Street in San Francisco, until it's smack-bang in the middle of Marina Green, staring at the Golden Gate Bridge. Forced selling is more like an elevator with snapped cables, hurtling straight down at two hundred miles per hour. This happened at Lehman Brothers when the prime brokerage division was forced to auction off the stocks every afternoon, and it's how Volmageddon happened in February 2018.

It's also how Black Friday happened in 1929, when the bottom of the market fell out and stayed there for a decade, and Black Monday on October 19, 1987, by far the worst selling day in Wall Street history. I was in the trenches that fateful day, working for my dad's brokerage firm. Around midday, I called a trader.

"I need to sell a hundred shares of IBM," I said.

"$98 bid," he responded tersely.

"But, but, but . . . my machine says $119," I protested.

"Well, sell it to your machine, then," he shot back without missing a beat.

That's what it was like. Markets were dropping so quickly that bid and ask prices became wildly untethered from each other amid all the chaos.

The usual suspects were behind that forced selling: Margin. Leverage. And misunderstood technological advances in trading. Today, computer-driven trading poses a similar threat to 401(k)s and IRAs. Over the past decade, passive investors have come to dominate Wall Street and are now projected to have $36.6 trillion of assets under management (AuM) by 2025. These are immense pools of capital that are run without active managers. The most well-known examples are ETFs, which mechanically invest in indexes or sectors in the markets. Other passive investor groups use sophisticated computer models that allocate capital based on reams of data and algorithms. What few realize is that the dominance of all these passive investors has created a terrifying misrepresentation of risk in the market, and one day this could lead to a catastrophic drawdown similar to what happened during COVID, Lehman, and Volmageddon, as we'll unpack in this chapter.

Bumped around by news cycles, Main Street investors tend to invest inside their comfort zones. When markets tank, those investors hide under the bed in case the roof falls in, and when markets explode to the upside, they chase them, often with unabashed fervor. A Lehman trader on our desk would have been fired for that kind of behavior. We bought only when Main Street portfolios were in flames (fear) and shorted companies only when excessive exuberance was steering the ship (greed). Our analysts were constantly scouring markets for undiscovered value and beaten-up blue chips as we looked for the next Black Swan moment.

The Black Swan was lurking in the real estate markets in 2008. It caused the near collapse of the financial system. But that isn't the interesting part. In the wake of all that toxic leverage, the investing public was scared to death of financial markets; many would practically turn white at the thought of buying equities again. Their 401(k)s and IRAs had been destroyed, and as they saw it, none of the perpetrators had gone to jail. Looking for low-risk strategies, they turned in droves to passive investing, and to the financial product that's turned dangerous in recent years, the ETF.

ETFs were the successor to something created in the seventies by a legend of modern investing. His name was John "Jack" Bogle, and he was born in Montclair, New Jersey, in 1929, to parents who were wiped out by the Great Depression.

In 1976, two years after he had founded the Vanguard Group, Jack Bogle and his giant analytical brain created the first index fund. Like most brilliant inventions, it was simple. The Vanguard First Index Investment Trust simply tracked the performance of the S&P 500. It was the first U.S. index fund available to retail investors for very low management fees; up until then, index funds had been reserved for the well-to-do. Bogle's timing was also impeccable. In 1976, the oldest baby boomers—soon to be amassing substantial wealth—were turning thirty-one.

It was a marvelous, game-changing idea. For the first time, ordinary Americans could simply buy the market, return to their hammocks, open the pages of a beach-read thriller, and let their money grow. This method of investing lasted for close to twenty years. Vanguard's assets exploded as Bogle sucked millions of investors into his ever-growing selection of index funds.

The business model of mutual funds was simple. Find a team of professional money managers—stock pickers—put them in charge of a pile of money, and try to outperform a benchmark, which could be the S&P 500 or a specific country or sector index. The investors' fees pay the salaries of the stock pickers and the marketing team that tries to ensure assets keep growing. Clean and simple.

The funds typically focused on an investing style, not exact stock or commodity allocations. If it was a blue-chip mutual fund, for example, it wouldn't buy stock in ZZ Carpets, Inc., but it didn't have to stick to a particular group of blue-chip equities. The managers were allowed to sell Boeing after a big rally, for example, and transfer the proceeds into Apple, if it seemed like Apple had more upside. You could have mutual funds that focused on energy giants that paid high dividends, or riskier small-cap companies in the biotech space, or American value stocks, and so on. But the public never knew exactly what the fund managers had put into the mutual fund until the end of the quarter, when the quarterly statements arrived in the mail. Another very important feature of the mutual fund was how investors bought and sold. They couldn't call up their broker and immediately sell all their holdings. Notice was required. Typically, the fund would agree to unwind the sellers' positions throughout the day and give them the price at the close of trading. The money was handled by professionals, and capital was also allocated within the fund according to their discretion.

But in 1993, the ETF arrived. It was a lot like what happened in the Caribbean in 1985 with the arrival of the lionfish, a beautiful striped fish with almost floral fins. The lionfish, however, turned out to be invasive, feeding on ecologically important native fish. Today, the lionfish threatens the health of whole reef systems. While ETFs claim to do exactly what mutual funds do, they are different and potentially very harmful.*

The first major difference between a mutual fund and an ETF is the way investors buy or sell the funds. ETFs trade on the exchange like a stock, and anyone can buy or sell them in a nanosecond via an online brokerage account. The ease of getting in and getting out of ETFs without significant fees is one feature that makes them so attractive. But the more wealth that piles up inside them, the more they look like cobra lilies, carnivorous plants that secrete an intoxicating scent to lure their prey into a deadly trap.

The second difference is that 95 percent of the world's ETFs are not actively managed; the funds strictly track an index or portfolio of publicly reported holdings. Main Street investors can open a brokerage account, buy one or many ETFs, and know precisely what their money is invested in to the dime. On the surface, this *seems* like a great advantage—but as we'll see in this chapter, it's a source of risk.

The New York Stock Exchange, built in 1903 with a grand facade of white Georgia marble and Corinthian columns, is America's greatest financial relic, a monument to a bygone era. I have fond memories of the NYSE between 2013 and 2020. Many afternoons, I was on the floor as a CNBC contributor joining the *Closing Bell* program with Maria Bartiromo, Sara Eisen, and Kelly Evans. But in recent years, the place has become more and more quiet, even museum-like.

The few specialists who remain are there for emergencies only; they often watch movies all day long! Market making has morphed into something quite different, which looks more like nuclear physics than what those tigers of the floor used to do. The world of market making is governed by high-frequency trading algorithms that allow for tremendous speed—milliseconds and nanoseconds. In this lightning-fast underworld,

* See our interview with David Einhorn at the end of this chapter for a closer look at the mispricing and misallocation of capital in ETFs.

INVESTORS TAKE NOTE:
How Does an ETF Work?

A fascinating feature of the ETF is the unlimited number of shares the manager can sell. That's because ETFs are not businesses. Their stock ticker is simply the front door into the fund. It doesn't matter how many people walk through it; the ETF is immune to dilution. If Apple suddenly issued a trillion new shares, the company would still be worth the same amount, but its stock would be so diluted it would be worth a fraction of its former price. It's like giving your daughter and her friend $10 to visit the candy store. They would have $5 each. But if she brought ninety-nine friends with her, they would have only ten cents each.

Sudden, massive dilution would cause shareholders to revolt, so companies can't and don't behave like that. But in ETF land, new shares are being issued almost every day, because the price of the ETF follows the underlying value of the index and is not driven by demand and supply of the fund. For example, the S&P ETF, which carries the symbol SPY and is commonly known as the Spider, follows the S&P 500 index. If the S&P 500 trades at 4,000, the Spider trades at $400 (exactly one-tenth the price of the index). If the index plunges to 3,000, the Spider follows in lockstep, trading at $300. There could be $100 billion of buying in the fund, but its price doesn't change; it's affected only by the price of the S&P 500. Needless to say, the same applies the other way. If people sell the ETF, it will also not affect the price of the ETF directly. It leads to a reduction in the shares of the fund.

there is a never-ending race to outgun rivals; companies spend billions for that extra seven thousandths of a second. Anything to stay one step ahead of a vast field of ruthless competitors.

But in reality, market making is just a small part of what the new generation of traders does. The new market makers are high-frequency traders who constantly arbitrage tiny price discrepancies. It's similar to what LTCM was doing, but these traders have no interest in almost anything that lasts more than about a second.

It's hard to believe, isn't it? How can a trade be one second long? And it's sometimes much less—sometimes only half a second, maybe one tenth of a second. Markets are no longer made by humans; transactions are handled by preprogrammed systems. Every morning, after the opening bell rings for old times' sake, millions of trades feed through those algorithms.

Now let's look at our modern investment vehicle, the ETF. All the holdings within it—whether they are stocks, bonds, derivative-like options, or credit default swaps—have value. For now, let's focus on stocks, because that's the easiest way to get a grip on this complex subject. Let's say the ETF holds a basket of twenty stocks, weighted from the biggest to the smallest. With a calculator, you could easily figure out their exact worth. In Wall Street jargon, that's called the net asset value (NAV).

The price of that ETF trades in tandem with the NAV. But does it really trade *exactly* in tandem? For every millisecond of the day? It never deviates? Well, it turns out that it does deviate, most often only for an infinitesimal amount of time. These are sometimes differences that no ordinary person would actually notice. But high-frequency traders have found a way not only to see these momentary differences in price—some lasting for just a fraction of a second—but also to make billions of dollars from them.

To understand this better, let's lay two railway tracks, each a mile long, side by side. One represents the price of the ETF and the other the NAV. You're in a helicopter hovering five thousand feet above them. Now let's remove five crossties from one end, and then a split second later, let's put them back into position. Would you notice that? Five crossties disappearing, then reappearing half a second later? Of course not. But an analogous process is constantly happening with the prices of ETFs and the NAV. Fractional discrepancies, the most unnoticeable, microscopic discrepancies, for a mere millisecond at a time.

Just as the pages of this book appear smooth to the naked eye but look like a maelstrom of atomic activity when seen through an electron microscope, traders using quantitative methods (or quants, for short) zoom in close enough to see the differences between ETF prices and the NAV. They place arbitrage bets, knowing that those bets will inevitably even out. It's like the ocean tides. If you knew it was low tide, would you place a billion-dollar bet that the water would rise again? Of course you would. These algorithms, these ingenious scrolls of code, do just that all day long, mining for potential arbitrage trades. They bet on the one certainty that can never fail, which is that the ETF can be sold to—or received from—the ETF sponsor at the NAV price.

What role do these newfangled market makers play in helping passive investors dominate the markets? A toxic cocktail is forming, and your portfolio construction needs attention.

As they execute millions of trades between the underlying NAV of the ETF and the ETF's price, volumes surge. You'd think all this activity would provide an immense amount of liquidity to the markets. But the volume is concentrated mostly in the megacap stocks, because the twenty largest stocks in the S&P 500 are responsible for more than 40 percent of the average daily value traded in the index. Its four hundred smallest stocks together represent barely 30 percent of the average daily volume. In other words, the bulk of the volume is in the big stocks, such as Apple, Microsoft, Amazon, Google, Meta (Facebook), Nvidia, and especially Tesla.

Why do market makers concentrate on these names? One reason is that they are overrepresented in so many ETFs. They make up about 50 percent of the Nasdaq ETFs, such as the QQQ, and 30 percent of the S&P ETFs, such as the SPY and the Vanguard S&P ETF (VOO). Amazon and Tesla together make up 40 percent of the consumer discretionary ETF (XLY), and Meta and Google account for more than 50 percent of the communications ETF (XLC). There are plenty of other examples, but you get the drift. Equally important, a market maker can go to the ETF sponsor, such as iShares or State Street, or banks such as Bank of New York, and create or redeem shares of an ETF. For example, a market maker can buy a handful of big stocks, fill it out with a few smaller ones, based on the requirements of the creation desk at the bank, and then exchange that basket for shares of an ETF at the NAV price. They can also do the opposite, exchanging the ETF for a handful of those stocks in the ETF. That permanent exchangeability is key for the functioning of an ETF, because it keeps the ETF's price more or less in line with its NAV. Without the ability to convert a basket of stocks into an ETF, the fund could trade for a long time at a wide discount to the NAV. This is what sets ETFs apart from open-ended funds such as mutual funds. They often trade at significant discounts for long periods of time.

For market makers to win, they need to be the fastest. Their algorithm has to receive the price data first so the trade gets placed first and sells out first. But doesn't all information arrive at the same time? And the answer is yes, it basically does arrive at the same time, but in this game, time is not what we know it as, divided into hours, minutes, and seconds. We're dealing with microscopic time. And in that context, information arrives at vastly different times. Some of it takes nine tenths of a second. Some of it takes half a second. Even a difference of mere milliseconds can trigger an arbitrage trade.

High-frequency traders will spend lavishly to gain an edge of a millisecond or even a few nanoseconds (billionths of a second) over the competition. Take Dan Spivey, a hotshot trader from the Chicago Board Options Exchange. A Mississippi native, Spivey was built like a man who'd spent his life hauling fishing nets out of that big ol' river, with broad shoulders, a mop of dark brown hair, and a jawline that could withstand a punch from Sugar Ray Leonard. In 2009, he hatched an ingenious plan to arbitrage stocks against their futures contracts, making tiny profits on exactly the same type of discrepancies as those between ETFs and their NAVs. The trouble was, futures contracts traded in Chicago, and the Spider ETF traded in New York City. The two cities were connected by a fiber-optic cable, but it took a meandering path through the Allegheny Mountains. Spivey knew there was an inefficiency there, one that could make him a killing. He built a more direct cable in a straight line between the Chicago Mercantile Exchange and the Nasdaq data center in Carteret, New Jersey, shaving off three milliseconds. In quant land, that's the equivalent of about five hours. The 827-mile fiber-optic cable made Spivey hundreds of millions of dollars after he rented it out to a variety of arbitrage trading firms.

This was the new mindset of Wall Street trading firms, and it's why the corporate earnings calls, those quarterly conversations that force CEOs and CFOs to answer tough questions about their earnings, are becoming like empty waiting rooms. The traders don't need fundamentals anymore, like profits and losses or two-year projections. For all they care, a company could be on the road to bankruptcy. What consumes them today is the arbitrage opportunities that can be wrung out of a nanosecond. It's not earnings, because whatever those are, there will still be little differences in price that can be arbitraged. And if the lifetime of the trade is infinitesimally small, the profits can be unlimited. *Fundamentals? To hell with those. This is the game for me!*

. . .

As explained in previous chapters, from the start of the Lehman crisis until the end of 2021, the Fed pumped $9 trillion of capital into the markets, inflating the asset values of everything from stocks to real estate. The visionary Josh Brown, who goes by the alias "the Reformed Broker," described a phenomenon called the "endless bid" in his groundbreaking 2012 blog. He was describing a situation whereby institutions were constantly buying and holding stocks. And with the Fed drowning the market with excess liquidity, those institutions were the ones ultimately providing the "endless bid" for financial assets. Money from 401(k)s flocked to ETFs and other passive investment products. Individual investors figured, if the market was constantly being inflated by the Fed, then why bother picking stocks? Most stock pickers can't outperform the S&P anyway, and passives allow you to own the market in the cheapest way possible.

Wave after wave of money poured into passive investment products, and this is how they came to dominate the investing world. The man or woman on the street has no idea that their 401(k)s are being hijacked by the largest fifteen stocks on the S&P, the stocks all the passives own.

At what juncture, at what percentage, does the market share of passive investing tip into hazardous territory? Passive investors now control at least 50 percent of all the fund assets in America. This is up from just 25 percent in 2012 and from single digits at the start of the twenty-first century. And their dominance poses a poorly understood but extremely serious risk for investors. Few are paying attention to the warnings from people like David Einhorn. Too many investors are asleep at the wheel.

The core group of passive investors, who tend to just buy the index, whether it is the S&P or the Nasdaq, buy with a volume-weighted average price (VWAP) over the day. Since most of the volume occurs in the first and last hours of trading, the passive equity flows are also concentrated in those hours. Liquidity is essential for these mammoth investors because they need liquidity to lower both transaction costs and their risk profiles. On a given day, Tesla trades $28 billion worth of stock and Apple $10 billion of stock. Compare that with a stock like Las Vegas Sands, which trades a paltry $268 million. Even the stock of Walmart trades just about $1 billion daily. To compare, the daily value traded for the largest stocks in Europe, such as software bellwether SAP in Germany or the energy giant TotalEnergies in France, is also just $300 million. This shows how much liquidity there is in these megacap stocks. And it is that liquidity that pas-

LIQUIDITY = SELL / BUY EZ.

sive investors yearn for. If they need to sell, they can get out of Apple or Microsoft in minutes, while it takes days to get out of a large position in, say, Las Vegas Sands.

Passive as Percent of Total ETF and Mutual Fund AuM

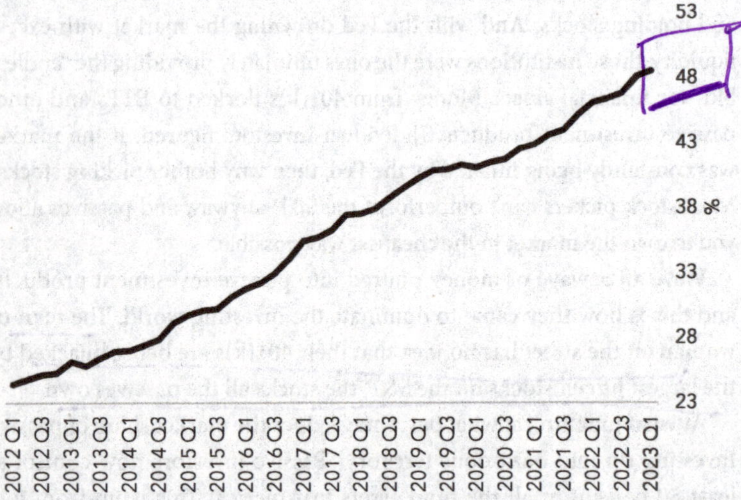

Most days the flows are net buys, which tend to suppress volatility. When a fund comes in at the last hour and buys up the market, volatility measures, better known as the VIX, decline. If this happens day in and day out, it dampens realized volatility. This attracts another group of passive investors, known as volatility-targeting and risk-parity funds (these buy a mix of stocks, usually an index, and Treasury bonds), which mechanically increase their exposure as the level of realized volatility decreases. With central banks buying hundreds of billions of dollars in assets and keeping rates at zero for years, volatility gets completely crushed. Then those index-tracking passive investors come in with their mechanical buying.

This lures in yet another batch of passive investors called commodity trading advisers (CTAs) and others with trend-following strategies. CTAs mostly trade on technical indicators, buying when markets breach certain thresholds, such as volatility levels or moving averages. For example, if the S&P breaks through the two-hundred-day moving average, CTAs mechanically increase their exposure. If the VIX falls through a certain threshold, let's say 15, CTAs deploy more leverage and buy more stocks. The opposite is true as well. If the S&P drops below the fifty-day moving average, for example, CTA algorithms lower their exposure. But during periods when an "endless bid" is in the market, CTAs and trend followers are overwhelmingly buyers.

Continue this self-reinforcing process for an extended period, and it opens a floodgate of option sellers who want to collect premium. They sell calls or puts that are far out of the money (options whose strike price is far away from the current price of the stock or index), hoping they don't get exercised. All they want to do is collect the premium (the price at which the option trades) and then wait for the option to expire, worthless, and pocket the proceeds. This option activity adds even more pressure on volatility, as dealers end up selling volatility in the underlying stocks or index to hedge.

It is a perverse, self-enhancing process that ultimately creates a terrifying misrepresentation of risk. Active investors, whether they are individual investors or portfolio managers, look at the low-volatility indicators and the market rally and have an acute fear of missing out (FOMO), the most deadly financial disease of the twenty-first century. They jump in and buy more stocks, convinced they can afford to take the risk. But passive investors have not adequately measured the full scope of market risks; they buy mechanically based on quantitative models.

Over time, this leads to large buildups of speculative capital, with hordes of active investors buying on top of multiple layers of passive investors. It leads to all kinds of speculative bubbles in stocks and other assets. This is how investors end up buying meme stocks or chasing tech stocks to stratospheric multiples. This is how GameStop surged 2,400 percent in the span of a month in early 2021 and how Rivian had a market value of $86 billion at the IPO, even though it had yet to produce one car. This is how people end up in things like Dogecoin or nonfungible tokens (NFTs) like Bored Ape, which is just a $70,000 drawing of an ape.

Over time, speculative capital builds up, feeding on this perverse loop that relentlessly suppresses volatility. All goes well until something breaks. In 2018, the speculative positioning caused the VIX to surge violently, triggering a tsunami of sell programs. The same passive investors who had continuously piled into stocks for months became indiscriminate sellers at the flip of a switch. The problem is that all the apparent liquidity evaporates as well. All those market makers who frantically arbitrage minuscule ETF deviations from NAV disappear when volatility spikes like that. Once markets go into free fall, the liquidity underneath the so-called top of the book becomes as dry as the Atacama Desert in Chile (its annual rainfall is a paltry 0.03 inches). There is a serpent forming inside the market that investors need to see for what it is.

Nothing exemplifies the dangers of this better than the COVID-19 sell-off in March 2020. According to Chicago's CME Group, home of the mighty S&P future, order-book depth (the number of price levels available at a particular time in the order book) collapsed by 90 percent that month. The S&P E-mini futures market is a $200 billion market, but liquidity was vaporized when investors needed it most. There were no more buyers. The VIX jumped from 12 to 85 in less than a month, a more than 600 percent jump. From top to bottom, the S&P declined by 35 percent in just thirty days. March alone had two black Mondays and one black Thursday. Even during the Lehman crisis, it took three months for the market to drop the same amount.

Even the U.S. Treasury market, which is normally as liquid as the ocean, was disrupted. There was talk that some of the industry's largest relative-value hedge funds, those that deploy large amounts of leverage to trade yield differentials in the Treasury market, were on the verge of blowing up. Apparently, they directly pressed the Fed's chairman, Jerome Powell, to act quickly unless he wanted ten LTCMs on his hands. This is one important reason why the deterioration in Treasury liquidity, as measured by the bid-ask spread, was so much more pronounced for U.S. Treasuries than for German, UK, or Japanese sovereign bonds, where the presence of relative-value hedge funds was a lot smaller. To stop the plunge, the Fed cut rates to zero, but this did little to stem the tide. Only when it announced open-ended QE and a $1 trillion alphabet soup of credit facilities to unfreeze the financial markets did the market find its bottom.

Although the COVID-19 crisis illustrates what happens when passive investors all try to rush out the same door, the problem has potentially gotten even worse. In the spring of 2022, the Chicago Board Options Exchange introduced zero-days-to-expiration (0DTE) options (options that are introduced and expire on the same day) on stock market indexes. This has caused option volumes to explode. In industry jargon, 0DTEs are called "dailies," and on many days they account for close to 50 percent of all the volume traded.

Imagine you have a toy car. You can park the car anywhere you want. If you choose to park it on a hill, it will—lacking brakes—start to roll back down. The steeper the hill, the faster the car will roll. Options gamma is akin to the steepness of this hill. The higher the gamma, the more sensitive the option price is to changes in the underlying asset price. Dealers use gamma to manage the risk in their options book. When dealers' gamma is positive, their delta increases when the underlying asset increases.

Remember, option delta is a measure of how much the price of an option is expected to change for every $1 change in the price of the underlying asset. For example, if I have an option with a 0.7 delta, and the stock goes up by $1, the price of my option goes up by $0.70. The major gamma hedgers in the market are the option dealers who act as counterparties for all the options traded by large institutions and retail traders. When dealers delta hedge, their goal is to be directionally neutral by offsetting long and short positions.

So, when the S&P rises, the delta of the dealers' book increases, and their hedging strategy requires them to sell more of the underlying asset—in this case, S&P futures or perhaps the S&P ETF (SPY). But when the S&P goes down, their negative delta increases, so they buy more of the index to remain delta neutral. As such, dealers' order flow acts as a contrarian force, limiting the magnitude of initial price movements. When gamma is negative, dealers do the exact opposite. They sell when the market goes down and buy when the market goes up. This creates a reinforcing trend that can compound volatility.

Most of the time—though not always—options gamma tends to be positive, often to the tune of multiple billions of dollars. With the explosion in option volume, thanks to the introduction of dailies, gamma size has increased dramatically. Gamma size tells us how much dealers must sell if the market goes up and how much they must buy when the market goes down. This activity has had an enormous impact on realized volatility. Every time the market jumps, dealers come in and sell billions of dollars' worth of stocks, and when the market slumps, dealers buy it up. Because of this contrarian force of dealer hedging, volatility has melted like ice cubes on a hot summer day. As we've seen, this has lured in all sorts of passive investors, who mechanically increase their exposure based on where realized volatility is.

What they don't realize is that volatility is low not because macro risks have disappeared but because armies of option investors are selling dailies to pocket a little premium. A large, one-sided speculative asset bubble builds over time, with multiple groups of passive investors layering long positions on top of one another and active investors also in the mix. But one ill-timed event, small or large, can trigger a sudden, uncontrolled sell-off. Since financial markets have become the linchpin that drives the U.S. economy, the Fed and public policymakers are forced to step in almost immediately to "rescue the market," lest there be another depression. Ben Bernanke said so himself in the congressional hearings after Lehman.

But we have seen that policymakers are forced to come in with bigger and bigger rescue packages. What will happen if the Fed cannot come in with open-ended QE, because inflation is still way too high? What will happen if Congress cannot authorize another multitrillion-dollar fiscal

Massive Distortion of Capital in Financial Markets

In late 2021, $20 trillion was locked up in Nasdaq 100 stocks alone through the massive QQQ ETF, which tracks these names. In the Nasdaq 100 itself, 48 percent is concentrated in its top eight holdings. Through passive investing, America has overdosed on financial assets: bonds and growth stocks. These are just pieces of paper; they're promissory notes from companies predicated on mostly unrealized future profitability. Meanwhile, the stocks in the XLE energy ETF have a market cap of just $1.6 trillion. The constituents of the global metals and miners ETF have a combined market cap of $1.8 trillion. So there was little more than $3 trillion invested in hard assets and more than $20 trillion in growth stocks. The trouble is, when you go into a high-inflation regime like we saw between 1968 and 1980, markets tend to rotate meaningfully into hard assets and value stocks and away from growth. Because of how growth-heavy the average American's portfolio has become, a similar rotation during the inflationary coming period could inflict devastating financial carnage.

stimulus package because the debt is already unaffordable and foreigners are no longer willing to buy U.S. Treasury bonds?

The Demographic Time Bomb

One of the most well-worn adages in investing is "Take your age, and that's the percentage you should have invested in bonds." In essence, the older you get, the fewer stocks you should own.

This leads us to the final point on the subject of passive investing, and it brings into focus the changing demography of America. The oldest baby boomers entered their seventy-eighth year in 2022, and with modern medicine, new technology, and nutritional advances, many will live into their nineties. But from a financial standpoint, they're battle-scarred. There was Lehman Brothers, then the COVID lockdowns, and now the 2022 crash in the technology sector. Inflation is rampant, there's a war in Ukraine, China is ramping up pressure on Taiwan, and the European Union is grappling with a catastrophic energy crisis. The world is volatile, and stock markets have proven themselves to be a dangerous bet—at least for the shorter term. If there's another big market drawdown, many boomers couldn't take the hit.

In the past two to three decades, a wall of money has come into stocks every year as baby boomers entered their peak earning years. Together, boomers control $78 trillion of wealth, while millennials have only $7 trillion. But now boomers are exiting stocks and placing their capital in bond funds. They've had enough. They want a steady income stream with less risk, just as Martin Zweig advised, and as we would, too. So that wall of money flowing into the market through passive investment vehicles is going to end, or at least dissipate dramatically.

We think that $10 trillion will move out of stocks and into bonds and hard assets (commodities) over the next decade. Ten years from now, the oldest boomer will be eighty-eight and even the youngest boomers will be retired. If the Fed isn't accommodating and instead fights inflation, there will be even more pressure to move wealth into fixed income. The bloodcurdling thought that keeps me up at night is that nobody in the financial press is looking at equity market returns in a world without low interest rates and quantitative easing.

These days, we're not dealing with a stock market that Zweig would recognize. With the big shift to passive investing, more and more laypeople are controlling their own portfolios. And there are no limits on the amount of capital that can flow into ETFs. But what will happen when another really big shock hits the markets? When $25 trillion unwinds in a reckless panic, without any professional portfolio managers to guide us through the chaos? It could cause a cascade of uncontrolled selling of proportions that have never been seen before.

This leads us to one of the most important statistics in this book for investors to understand. Think of U.S. household wealth and allocation of investors' capital. According to Goldman Sachs, stocks have surged to nearly 40 percent of household financial assets in this decade, a significant increase compared to 28 percent in the 2010s, 18 percent in the 2000s, 33 percent in the 1990s, 17 percent in the 1980s, and 11 percent during the inflation-ridden 1970s. Groupthink has taken over.

By effectively promising to save the day and provide accommodation every time markets took a plunge, the Fed has kept money flowing into stocks. Look at its responses over the past thirty years, from the bailout of LTCM and the dot-com crash to the collapse of Lehman and COVID-19. There's one problem, though. Accommodation works only when inflation is low and the Fed can open the floodgates without immediately damaging the rest of the economy. When there's inflation, or the risk of it, the Fed couldn't dream of bailing out a market crash. That would send inflation roaring to 20 percent, which would impose an unbearable burden on the American people. The American economy is built on credit, and total debt in the country is now $101 trillion, and most of it is floating debt, which means interest rates go up if the rate of inflation increases. The consequences would be unthinkable.

In previous crises, inflation was in the 0 to 2 percent range and the risk of a price spiral was low. When inflation is sticky and remains around 5 percent or more, that risk is there, and the Fed knows it.

In an unfriendly multipolar world, with the baby boomers approaching eighty and government bonds paying a lot more than they did in the last decade, Josh Brown's "endless bid" is about to become an "endless offer."

A violent white current of capital is likely moving into a demographic reversal.

MASTERS OF INVESTING WEIGH IN

An Interview with David Einhorn

"Let's take Twenty-Fourth Street. . . . We have to take Twenty-Fourth," I said to the cabdriver.

"Twenty-four? You want Twenty-four?" He squinted at me in the rear-view mirror.

"Yes, please take Twenty-four. This is a disaster."

It was early February 2022, and I was headed to a two-thirty meeting with Greenlight Capital's David Einhorn, perhaps the sharpest trader of them all. The first time Einhorn crossed my path was in 2008, he was on Bloomberg News, discussing the freight train of debt parked on Lehman Brothers' balance sheet and why he was going to short it. I'll never forget it. He was more than prescient, and he made a fortune when the company collapsed. His book *Fooling Some of the People All of the Time* is an investing classic and one of our all-time favorites at *The Bear Traps Report*.

Einhorn's days were scheduled to the minute, and he was notoriously prompt. I had allowed an hour for the two-mile journey from the New York Stock Exchange to Grand Central, which would have taken a total of seven minutes anywhere else in the world.

As the traffic light changed to green, the cabbie gunned the engine and cut across three lanes of buses, taxis, and delivery vans, all of them honking their horns in a pandemonium of road rage while he continued to talk on his cellphone in Farsi, as nonchalant as if he were strolling down a country lane. A few minutes later, he dropped me off outside Grand Central Tower.

At 2:25, I stepped off the elevator and into the offices of one of America's most impressive hedge funds. Its reception area was immaculate, with pristine carpeting and fresh bouquets of flowers in what I assumed were Lalique vases. I was ushered into a conference room and brought a cup of tea. Nestled in the bookshelves were various trophies from the

IPOs and capital market transactions, otherwise known as equity and debt offerings, that Greenlight had helped shepherd through to completion, along with other testaments to David Einhorn's lifetime of high achievement, starting at Cornell, where he had majored in government. He later gave his alma mater $50 million to launch the Engaged Cornell initiative.

Einhorn had been in business since 1996, and he'd well and truly beaten the odds. According to a Capco study, fifty percent of new hedge funds fail, and the survivors face a minefield of obstacles. Front and center is always performance; if it's lackluster or you're taking on losses, you'll soon be out of business. Greenlight had exemplary performance and impeccable ethics; in its first ten years, it pulled in annual returns of between 20 and 30 percent. Warren Buffett once posed the question "When you make an investment decision, would you be happy to have it on the front page of *The New York Times*?" Einhorn could answer him with a resounding "yes."

But I wasn't there to talk about his investments. We had a much more pressing subject on our agenda, one we'd been discussing over the last couple of years. It was the business of passive investing and ETFs, and how they were creating seismic shifts across the entire market structure. Those shifts may have been invisible to Main Street investors, but their implications were eye-opening.

At exactly 2:30 P.M., David Einhorn walked into the room. His black hair was neatly trimmed and he was wearing his usual immaculately pressed slacks and crisp button-down shirt. He was still quintessentially the man I'd always known, even though I hadn't seen him since before the lockdowns of 2020.

We shook hands and sat down. "Larry, what do you call a stock that's down 90 percent?" He waited a beat. "A stock that used to be down 80 percent, then got cut in half."

I laughed at first but then realized he wasn't joking. His expression is sometimes hard to read, like that of all world-class poker players. Einhorn's game is no-limit hold 'em, and he once ranked eighteenth in the world.

"Twice the price isn't always twice as silly," he continued, "but when the price goes down, nobody knows the value. We know it's dropped from an unrealistic valuation, but is it still unrealistic? Is the price-to-earnings ratio low enough, or could it go lower? Nobody knows the answer to this question anymore, and if value investors start buying, how long will they have to wait for the market to notice the dislocation?"

He was referring to the endless ways the investing world had changed since Lehman—and the huge proliferation of ETFs. There were 102 of them in 2002 and more than a thousand in the immediate wake of the Lehman collapse. By 2022, there were 7,100 of them. The SPY ETF had almost enough wealth in it—$328 billion—to run the U.S. Navy. In fact, there are more ETFs than stocks these days. Large-caps, small-caps, tech, industrials, transports, emerging markets, big banks, risk on, risk off . . . The menu is limitless, and they rule the markets with their $25 trillion pile of cash.

"There's nothing wrong with passive investing per se," he continued, "but when you have $4 to $5 trillion come in over a decade, the BlackRocks and the Vanguards of the world end up with much bigger seats at the table. The sun has largely set on the activist fund manager, hounding companies to improve share values using corporate due diligence. On earnings conference calls, it's now very rare for anybody on the buy side to ask a question." He paused for a moment. "The largest shareholders in most companies are passives. If you own the whole market and you don't really care how any particular stock does, you can subvert yourself to other agendas: ESG, diversity, or other kinds of check-the-box types of agendas that don't have to do with making good capital allocation decisions for corporations."

I jumped back in. "And how has this affected the way stocks and markets behave?"

Einhorn chuckled. "One of the main problems with passive funds is that they don't even fulfill their own logic anymore. It only makes sense if you have the philosophy that 'the market is smarter than I am, and I don't want to try to out-think all those thinking people.' In other words, if I buy an index of stocks and they're weighted by market cap, I can be a price taker and I can therefore participate in the market without determining the price. But when such a high percentage of the trading and investing flows becomes passive, the passive funds shift from being price *takers* to price *makers*. If you're the one making the price, you can no longer make the argument that the market is efficient and everybody else has already figured it out, because you've just run over all that analysis with a steamroller. The result is, you very likely wind up with a substantial mispricing and misallocation of capital, and investors in these passive funds ultimately bear the burden."

"Jesus Christ," I said to nobody in particular. My head spun with visions of all the potential bubbles and the catastrophes that could happen if they were to pop. How much of the trillions of dollars in ETFs was just a function of a self-fulfilling cycle, in which certain assets were bid up just because they happened to be included in a particular ETF? "I can't believe where we've come since Long-Term Capital was bailed out," I said. "We should have let them implode."

Einhorn stood up, walked over to the window, and looked out across the city. We could still hear the car horns, even twenty-four stories above the street behind double-glazed windows.

"It's almost incredible," he said. "There's been such a bifurcation in where investors want to put their money. Whatever money hasn't gone into index funds is going into big tech stocks, big growth stories, or big disruptive companies, and there's been very little investment or interest in traditional industry. That means those traditional companies—even though they have very good borrowing costs—end up with very high costs of equity (the cost of issuing new stock to raise capital). The result is that shareholders basically say, 'Your cost of equity is so high, if you have free cash flow, you should give it to us rather than make more of whatever it is that you're making.' And so there's been an ongoing underinvestment in the real economy because that part of the market hasn't attracted capital."

I was astounded. Einhorn was echoing the sentiments that Rafi Tahmazian had expressed in Calgary, but he saw the trends causing underinvestment in hard assets emerging from within the financial sector, too. I pressed him further: "I take it this applies to the oil industry especially, right?"

"Exactly, Larry. You can see it now, even though oil prices are pretty high. Historically, this would spur lots of capex and exploration, but you don't really see it. What you're seeing is shareholders saying, 'Don't do that and instead do big dividends and big buybacks.' They don't even want to find more oil because of the political pressures—Big Oil is working as hard as it can to become Small Oil! But you're not getting the capital investment you need to bring supply onto the market, so you might end up with even higher prices for a long time, which is part of what I see happening with inflation." Einhorn was making the point that the boring yet important businesses, from cement to shipping, have been starved of capital relative to crowded tech sector investing.

One take on Einhorn's message is clear. If capital is misdirected and a country like the United States is producing less and less at home, in a unipolar world with perfect trade and supply chain efficiency, this is not necessarily inflationary. On the other hand, in a multipolar world this dynamic can fuel long-term inflationary trends. Especially when many of the most important resources are in politically unattractive locations around the planet.

I paused to take it all in as I finished my tea. "Let me walk you down," he said. "I have to get moving for my three-thirty meeting."

I stood up, Einhorn held the door for me, and we walked back out into the foyer. This was a totally separate part of the offices, a long way from the trading floor, a long way from all the closely guarded secrets of a hedge fund. Their offices all followed the same format. Clients and guests never stray onto a trading floor or see any of the daily activity behind the billions of dollars under the fund's control. There was an air of great mystery and unmistakable respect about the place. I felt I had to know how the spectacular minds at Greenlight—David Einhorn and his team—were positioning themselves for the future. So as he pushed the button for the elevator, I asked him, "Besides maybe some energy-sector exposure, what are your analysts pitching these days? What assets might benefit from certain trends in passive investing but also be shielded if the whole thing blows up?"

"I think copper and silver are interesting," he said. "Money is going to go in a green direction, and if we're going to go electric vehicle, we're going to need a lot of copper—for car engines, car chargers, and to deal with the added strain on the electric grid. And there's been such an aversion to mining that the amount of copper mines scheduled to come online over the next decade is probably less than half what it was ten or fifteen years ago, maybe just two or three. And to bring a new copper mine online can take a decade. Unless you're planning to do that soon, it's going to take a while to change things."

The elevator chimed and the doors opened. It was empty, so Einhorn could continue speaking as we rode down to the lobby.

"This will all help keep the price of copper high. Same story with silver, which is increasingly being used as an industrial metal, with surging demand coming from solar panel construction. In the intermediate term, it's much more sensible to invest in copper or companies that mine it than to try and find which electric vehicle company is going to win out in what has become a very crowded sector."

"It's like the old adage: 'If you want to get rich during a gold rush, sell the shovels,'" I quipped.

"Same as it ever was."

The elevator doors opened, and we walked through the large atrium and out onto the sidewalk.

"That was an education," I said as we shook hands. "And it all hearkens back to the offshoring of our manufacturing, and the financial markets that are so myopically focused on a handful of winners."

"And the ETFs are only exacerbating this trend," he agreed. "In these markets, it's winner takes all. Safe travels home, old pal."

I turned to flag a cab, and when I looked back, Einhorn was gone, back to his kingdom. Every time we talk, I am left with the feeling that he might be the smartest person I've ever met. The rest of 2022 would bear that feeling out. As winter turned into spring and summer, inflation surged, driven by high energy costs stemming from super-tight oil supply. To prevent an inflationary spiral, the Fed had to turn very hawkish (threatening interest-rate hikes) in a flash, killing stocks, especially those most vulnerable to higher interest rates. Overall, the S&P 500 fell 19.6 percent, the worst market performance since Lehman went bust in 2008. It was the opposite for David Einhorn's Greenlight Capital, though. Instead of following the lemmings into the massively top-heavy tech, financial, and growth sectors, Greenlight went its own way. Its positioning proved not merely inflation-proof but also able to thrive in the new paradigm. The fund's overall returns in 2022 clocked in at 36.6 percent—an unbelievable 56.2 percent alpha (the excess return of a stock or a fund above the return of the market) against the S&P.

Going your own way is all well and good, but there's a reason, of course, why a lot of fund managers and market participants pile into the same trades. At a given moment, that's probably what's making money. It probably won't be at some point in the future, though, whether that's two months, a year, or five years. One of the greatest lessons I've learned in all my time in finance has been about precisely this. Say you see an investor whom you really respect, whose philosophy you really know, stake out a strong position in something, perhaps double down on it. It might be kind of languishing for the time being, trading sideways or even trending down. These almost always turn out to be great investments. Usually that investor has a brilliant insight or idea that just hasn't fully played out yet. I've seen this happen countless times with the greatest fund managers I've known.

One of my favorite examples of this happening is David Einhorn and his multiyear faith in GRBK, the stock for the American home-building company Green Brick Partners. You see, Einhorn correctly identified the groundwork for a long-term secular shortage in U.S. housing supply all the way back in 2014. This was mostly due to the economic devastation that beset the construction industry after the 2008 housing crash, difficulty in mortgage financing, and building overregulation by municipal governments. This would increase prices and help companies in the space. He took a huge 24-million-share position in GRBK all the way back in the fall of 2014, immediately making it the second-largest component of his fund. The stock saw great gains, rising 900 percent by late 2015 and 2,450 percent by 2021. Einhorn held the stock all the way through and made great profits for Greenlight Capital. He kept it as one of his top, if not the top, positions through all the choppiness. From the 2021 high to the 2022 low, GRBK shares lost nearly 40 percent. Sensing an opportunity, we sent out trade alerts to clients, recommending GRBK shares. Bottom line, when you see a position of a Hall of Famer like Einhorn or Buffett for sale, it can be an attractive entry point.

7

The Psychology of Bubbles and the Mania of Crypto

When first I see a bubble, I rush in to buy it.

—GEORGE SOROS

In Manhattan, there is a rather unusual trading shop called Jane Street Group. This is one of those elusive market makers in ETFs we talked about in chapter 6. It employs two thousand computer scientists and is a huge player in the world of quantitative trading firms. In fact, by 2022, its market cap and profits rivaled those of Citadel Securities, trading close to $17 trillion worth of securities a year. At Jane Street, it's not unheard of for first-year hires to earn $425,000 per year. It is unusual in that sense, and also in that it lacks any board of directors. It doesn't even have an executive suite, just a kind of thirty-member leadership team, where the lines of authority are blurred, which bears almost no resemblance to Wall Street traditions.

Company-wide lectures are often about computer programming and how different languages and paradigms differ from one another. Computer scientists from a diversity of backgrounds fill the room, with expertise in classic scripting languages like Perl, Haskell, and JavaScript, as well as high-speed compiling languages such as C++. But the one they use almost exclusively at Jane Street is called OCaml—industrial strength, with an emphasis on expressiveness and safety. To run arbitrage trades at this level, they need every edge they can get.

There is a culture of great secrecy in this downtown Manhattan ivory tower, which is complete with a brand-new gym, cafés, rooms to take a nap, Ping-Pong and chess tables, screening rooms, and lecture halls. But it's not really a culture. It's a cult. And in 2014, a twenty-two-year-old with dark curly hair, dressed for a day at the beach, walked into Jane Street's offices on Vesey Street to start his career. He had just graduated from the Massachusetts Institute of Technology and had an IQ that rivaled Albert Einstein's. He was born on the campus of Stanford University to two parents who are both law professors there. This new kid wasn't planning to stay in New York for long. He was obsessed with making money and had much bigger ambitions than working for somebody else. In fact, his ambitions were so big, eight years later he would be responsible for losing $40 billion in the greatest cryptocurrency crash the world had ever seen. His name was Sam Bankman-Fried.

The Psychology of Bubbles

Professor Sigmund Freud sat quietly in his favorite café, tucked into a booth with the afternoon light on his notebook, wisps of white smoke in the backlight of the window. He puffed the cigar again, the smoke encircling his entire head in a bright, sunlit fog. He continued writing in his notebook, deep in thought. On the table were a cup of coffee and an ashtray. A waiter approached, and Freud paid the bill, put on his overcoat, and walked out of the café with his ivory-handled walking stick in his left hand. Above the entrance, the black lettering read "Café Landtmann." Freud spent most afternoons there, thinking quietly or playing chess, but that day in December 1920 he was in the trenches of writing a new book, *Group Psychology and the Analysis of the Ego.*

Back in his office, sitting at his desk, Freud picked up his fountain pen, dipped it into the black ink, and started to write in his rich, complex handwriting. "This is an aptitude very contrary to his nature," he began, "and of which a man is scarcely capable, except when he makes part of a group." His eyes scanned the page, turned it over, and stopped halfway down the text. The professor dipped his pen once more and made an addition. "The conscious personality has entirely vanished; will and discernment are lost. All feelings and thoughts are bent in the direction determined by the hypnotizer."

He looked at the page. The ink began to dry. Freud read the words once more, placed his pen on the desk, and reached for another cigar. He walked to the window and looked at the quiet street below. The trees swayed in the wind. As he lit the cigar, creating another cloud of smoke that surrounded his entire torso, the first snowflakes of winter began to fall on Vienna. Despite his brilliance and his endlessly inquisitive mind, what Freud couldn't have known at that moment was that the pile of loose papers on his desk would one day explain the giant real estate bubble in Japan in the 1980s. It would shed light on the frenzy behind the dot-com bubble of 2000. And in 2022, it would tell us why a secretive digital currency born out of blockchain technology would create an asset bubble exceeding $2 trillion—the largest hot-air bubble there has ever been.

There's an adage on Wall Street that is really more of a cliché at this point: "The market can stay irrational longer than you can stay solvent." While it's overused, it also couldn't be truer. A human being is a creature of two natures: a rational ego, which tends to dominate conscious thought, and a prerational or even irrational so-called id lurking beneath, which controls the subconscious mind. Every asset price bubble—whether in stocks, bonds, commodities, currencies, or something else—depends on this latter phenomenon. At some point, market participants let pure greed, ecstasy, and hypnosis take over their financial behavior. They become willing to pay almost anything to own the object of their desire, leading to a climactic explosion, a jouissance, in market price, followed by an equally dramatic comedown.

The annals of economic history are littered with asset price bubbles. Some of the most famous are the Dutch tulip bubble of the seventeenth century, the South Sea Company bubble in 1720, and the Japanese real estate and stock market bubble of the late 1980s, which we discussed in chapter 2. We've also seen several major bubbles in the United States over the past thirty years, which we mentioned in previous chapters. These are the dot-com bubble, the housing bubble that led to the Great Recession, the commodities bubble of the 2000s, and the tech and crypto bubble right after COVID-19.

Each of these had some sort of compelling story that made the asset price appreciation initially plausible. Conventional oil production was peaking, and China was fully industrializing its economy—the commodity bubble. Cryptocurrency was digital gold and offered an alternative to fiat currency (currency not backed by a commodity such as gold but used as legal tender—the dollar, the euro, the yen, etc.) and the government transaction system—the crypto bubble. The internet was taking over the world and everyone needed a new PC ahead of the year 2000—the dot-com bubble. At some point in each, however, investors became speculators and the prices assigned to the given asset became wildly detached from economic reality. When bubbles are just about to climax, market participants enter cloud-cuckoo-land. Blinded by how rich they're getting on paper, they confuse temporary blips driven by innate human irrationality for new paradigms. And then everything comes crashing down.

The formation of asset price bubbles doesn't just rely on the irrationality of the subconscious mind; it also depends on the available capital for that mind to direct. Without any money, eighteenth-century Englishmen wouldn't have been able to bid up the price of the South Sea Company into the stratosphere. Human greed is innate and basically unchanging. It's a force that's part of our biology; it's always been with us, and it always will be there. What can change are the conditions that determine how capital is directed and how much capital is sloshing around in financial markets. When the supply of money increases suddenly, bubbles form more easily. This is especially true when the money supply grows not through an increase in actual economic productivity but rather through government fiat: extreme central bank accommodation or fiscal stimulus. It's like air-dropping a box of knives into a prison full of hardened, violent criminals. Now instead of just their fists, the prisoners have knives at their disposal to maim and kill one another. This "stimulus" has both a real and a psychological effect: It will raise the severity of violence between the prisoners as well as their propensity for it. The more weapons, the more this is the case.

This is what happens whenever the Fed pumps trillions into the markets or Congress authorizes massive fiscal stimulus. When governments use a fire hose to douse financial meltdowns with artificially cheap capital and easy money, it intensifies the extent to which people's irrational nature can affect and interfere with market economics. As we saw in the example of how public policy fueled an explosion of great white sharks off Cape Cod, which we mentioned in chapter 4, when big governments start meddling with markets and nature, either existing problems are exacerbated or new ones are created. In the end, however, the problems are rarely solved. There are always unintended consequences. We must never forget that inflation comes in different flavors. Over the past thirty years, when governments have tried to use policy to address disinflation, they have generally ended up fostering inflation. Not in the real economy of businesses and consumers. Rather, they created almost unbelievable inflation in financial assets, over and over again.

When the Fed bailed out LTCM, the dot-com bubble appeared almost immediately. When it cut rates after 9/11, it fueled the speculative housing bubble that eventually brought down Lehman Brothers and caused the Great Recession. When it held rates at zero and initiated QE in the 2010s, it enabled the most crowded trade of epic proportions in tech and growth stocks through passive investing. The rate cuts and unprecedented level and manner of fiscal stimulus during the COVID-19 pandemic represented the granddaddy of them all in terms of accommodation. This gave rise to unprecedented bubbles in cryptocurrency, meme stocks, and unprofitable tech companies.

One of the Biggest Bubbles in History

We first heard about Bitcoin in 2009. It was created because the public had lost trust in the banking system and was more skeptical than ever about central governments and their handling of the public purse. After the Lehman crisis, after the breathtaking loss of wealth throughout the world, people wanted another way, another form of payment, and another store of value (an asset that can retain its purchasing power into the future) outside traditional, regulated currencies. The origins of Bitcoin are still a mystery to this day. It was created by the enigmatic "Satoshi Nakamoto," which may have been one person or a group of computer scientists, mining encrypted currency on a huge network of computers known as the "blockchain." Explaining this in simple terms is actually a challenge, because there is nothing simple about how it works. It involves reams of code, multiple computer systems, public keys, private keys, and quite a few algorithms. Throw a dusting of quantum physics on top, and you wind up with something called Bitcoin—a word that is a compound of "bit" (in computer terms, a "binary digit," the most basic unit of information) and "coin." And it is impossible to hack; the "keys" are twenty-six alphanumeric integers long, which produce more combinations than there are grains of sand on earth. With this unimaginable level of encryption, blockchain technology started to be rolled out across the world, into many business verticals, and what it essentially did was *decentralize* transactions.

A Great Breeding Ground for Fraudsters

The world of business and money became divided very acutely after the Lehman crisis. Think once more of the Berlin Wall cleaving Germany in half. Now imagine a line etched right across cyberspace and the entire world of transactions. The two sides in this new world are called *centralized* and *decentralized.* In 2009, the West had reached peak centralization—right here we're talking about big government, big regulation, and big control over taxpayer dollars. And there was a litany of proven problems, or externalities, as a result of centralization. Society had lost trust in the financial industry. The arrival of blockchain was almost like Saint George drawing his sword and slaying the marauding dragon. Transactions could now take place outside of banking systems or established online retailers or even institutions with long histories of settling trade between two parties. The heavily encrypted, unduplicable blockchain technology could create an entirely new world, and perhaps a brand-new currency. But could the blockchain really rescue the world from centralized-government overreach and give birth to an entire network of *peer-to-peer decentralization*?

The short answer was yes. But beneath the promise of a decentralized financial future stood a fragile ecosystem in the hands of young cowboy entrepreneurs from Silicon Valley. Cryptocurrency had a sexy investment

INVESTORS TAKE NOTE:

What Makes Bitcoin So Special—and How Investors Can Profit

If the price of a car goes up, automakers will—over time—make more cars to take advantage of the higher price. There are plenty of carmakers in the world, and if each one makes more cars, the increased supply will eventually bring prices down. If the price of a precious metal such as platinum goes down, miners will mine less of that metal so that—over time—the price goes back up.

Bitcoin doesn't work like that. Bitcoin is mined on the network. The network will release a bitcoin block to the "ledger," which records all transactions involving bitcoins using blocks secured by cryptography, roughly every ten minutes no matter what. Whether there is one person on the network mining or 7 billion people, the ten-minute release is fixed.

Mining a bitcoin is a process of validating the information in a blockchain block by generating a cryptographic solution that matches certain criteria. The reward is a bitcoin that is given to the miner. The level of mining difficulty is therefore constantly adjusting to keep the average time between block releases more or less constant at ten minutes. Which means that the more computing power is dedicated to mining bitcoins (in total), the more computing power you will need to mine the next block.

There is a hard limit on the total number of bitcoins that can ever be created. The Bitcoin protocol specifies that the reward for adding a block is halved every 210,000 blocks (approximately every four years). Initially, every block contained 50 coins, but ultimately, the reward will decrease to zero, and the limit of 21 million bitcoins will be reached. As of mid-2023, there are 19 million bitcoins outstanding, and the rate of reward has dropped to 6.25 coins per block. As the protocol cuts the reward in half every couple of years, bitcoin mining won't reach the 21-million-coin limit until the next century, but the required energy consumption will make mining prohibitively expensive much earlier than that.

Here is the key issue: If the price of Bitcoin goes up, more people jump on the network to mine coins. In order to stick to the ten-minute release interval, the algorithm adjusts so that it becomes more difficult to mine a coin. "More difficult" means more energy intensive, which pushes up the cost of mining a coin. When the cost goes up, it means that the break-even price for a bitcoin goes up. In other words, Bitcoin must increase in value to keep it profitable to mine. And the higher price lures in even more miners, making mining more expensive still. This creates a self-reinforcing run-up in price that can go on for many months. However, the same holds true on the way down. If Bitcoin goes down in price (which it eventually always does, mostly due to a reversal of the excess liquidity that is sloshing around in the financial system), people stop mining and the break-even price of mining a coin declines as well. The lower break-even price leads to a lower Bitcoin price and more people stop mining. This explains the extreme price volatility in Bitcoin, and this makes Bitcoin unique.

Almost all other cryptos have an infinite supply, although daily production may be capped. Nevertheless, almost all cryptos are highly correlated with Bitcoin, so even if they have an infinite supply, their price tends to go up and down with Bitcoin. Investors need to be aware of the process of self-reinforcing run-ups and sell-offs in Bitcoin and other crypto. When they see the formation of a big run-up or sell-off, investors should not be afraid to participate, because the momentum of these moves can be very powerful and last for weeks or months.

thesis around the demise of fiat currencies—citing the 93 percent drop in the value of the U.S. dollar since 1900—and the outrageous debt being racked up by Western governments. And this thesis made digital currencies the hottest investment in the world, with the Bitcoin bubble well and truly underway by 2017. But every bubble brings out a group of shrewd, immoral characters who take advantage of investors and their ignorance about the technologies that drive the boom. In the 1990s, it was companies like Enron, WorldCom, and Adelphia that committed accounting malfeasance to inflate profits; in the 2000s, it was people like Bernie Madoff and Allan Stanford or companies like Countrywide and Lehman that misled investors. The crypto bubble, too, had its fair share of malicious characters.

Sam Bankman-Fried was the CEO of an upstart cryptocurrency arbitrage trading fund named after an island near the shore of San Francisco Bay. But Alameda Research had an investment strategy that was supposedly almost immune to the price decline of cryptocurrencies. Like the quant traders at Citadel and Jane Street, the traders at Alameda Research wanted price volatility—*big arbitrage opportunities and big bucks.* They had no interest in holding anything for longer than an hour or two. And the price differences between American crypto exchanges and those in Asia were perhaps the most exciting Bankman-Fried had ever seen. Right out of the gate, the company made close to $20 million.

Despite Sam's early success with Alameda Research and the great arbitrage trades it did, the price swings in Bitcoin damaged the status as a currency. What originally set Bitcoin apart from the rest of the cryptocurrencies was its limited supply. There would only ever be 21 million coins, no more. This was its store of value, and the value proposition for investors. But by mid-2018, it was proven susceptible to wild price swings, which blew the "store of value" theory clean out the window. And that, above all things, changed the game. Hence, Bitcoin became speculative, with all the risks that come with that category of investment. That made Bitcoin a medium of exchange—not a currency—and mediums of exchange are evaluated according to a different set of parameters. The great seal of the United States of America, with the bald eagle clutching an olive branch in one claw and arrows in the other, symbolizes war and peace, and it's stamped on every banknote issued by the United States. This is the power behind the American dollar. A power greater than any other nation has ever dreamed of—twelve aircraft carrier battle groups and *five thousand* nuclear warheads. That's what you need to back a *real* currency. Maybe not so much firepower, but a currency must be a government-mandated, government-regulated, government-enforced legal tender. By these parameters, cryptocurrencies were doomed from the beginning. But the dream of decentralized finance didn't die in 2018. Not even close.

In the spring of 2019, Sam Bankman-Fried launched FTX, which became the fastest-growing digital asset exchange in the world, trading Bitcoin, other cryptocurrencies, and nonfungible tokens (NFTs). As a marketplace for crypto traders, FTX made money by charging trading fees, as every other exchange did, but it undercut everyone and in the process raised millions for advertising. It ran aggressive ad campaigns with its logo all over the place, including at a Formula One race in Miami, along with giant images of the founder wearing an FTX T-shirt and his signature shaggy hair. Soon he became the poster boy of crypto, and the institutions loved it. The exchange raised capital from a venture capital fund out of Menlo Park, California, called Sequoia Capital. Sequoia is a specialist in seed-stage, early-stage, and growth-stage investments across the technology sector and has one of the best reputations in the business. And it took a chance on FTX, giving the exchange immediate credibility.

With the Sequoia brand in its sales pitch, it wasn't long before a wave of big hitters stampeded to this new hotshot company in the hottest sector of the market. Not even Sam Bankman-Fried would have believed the pile of money he was about to make. Nobody could have predicted it, because what happened next was like something out of the Old Testament. The entire world went into lockdown as COVID-19 leaped from one person to the next until every town on earth was affected. And suddenly all the e-commerce companies, all the videoconferencing companies, all the software and hardware makers became the new lords of commerce. When the U.S. government tried to fight off the virus with more than $10 trillion of monetary and fiscal stimulus, everyone in America was suddenly flush with cash. Crypto ripped out of the two-year valley it was stuck in between 2018 and 2020 and rocketed higher. Cryptocurrencies didn't just become the hot new sector. They became a religion, and Freud's theory of group psychology, the one he had written about decades ago in his smoke-filled Viennese office, could be seen once again. This time it grabbed hold of the hungry mob—which was hypnotized by a common belief that a new monetary era had dawned—and led them into the greatest asset bubble since tulip fever in the seventeenth century. To some people, it seemed that Bankman-Fried, who had ostensibly predicted the entire market, could be the new Warren Buffett. And over the next eighteen months, his personal wealth grew to nearly $30 billion, which solidified this belief.

But there was one man who didn't believe one word of it.

"Who the fuck is this goofball?" he muttered, glaring at his computer, right into the eyes of Sam Bankman-Fried's LinkedIn profile picture.

The Hard-Eyed Sniper

Marc Cohodes is a brilliant Wall Street skeptic, especially when he sees things that don't add up or make sense—things that make you go Hmmm. Most important, things that can help you protect your portfolio.

A year before the crypto giant FTX collapsed, Marc was there, a lone voice calling out all the failures of his smell test. What kinds of things tip off Marc? Dozens, but often it's the little things most people don't notice. One of our favorites is the Cohodes "Wig" Indicator. Marc said, "I have a very good batting average betting against wigs, Larry." Hilarious, but wigs in the C-suite do smell to high heaven. If CEOs can't come clean on their hairstyle or lack thereof, what else are they covering up? In the years before Lehman went down into bankruptcy, guys like Marc were counting all the footnotes in the SEC filings, the 10-Ks and 10-Qs that must be filed with the regulators in Washington. "Larry," Marc once told me, "always beware of a sequential (quarter over quarter) surge in the footnotes; it's a high-probability sign of obfuscation."

---

ob·fus·ca·tion (noun): the action of making something obscure, unclear, or unintelligible.

When confronted with sharp questions, they resort to obfuscation.

Marc is as rare a breed as the Marsican brown bear. There are only a few dozen of them alive today, living deep in the Apennine Mountains of

Italy on a diet of mainly apples, pears, prunes, fungi, and berries. But Marc is no vegetarian. He feeds on crooks, villains, and fraudsters. Not literally, of course. He does it by shorting their companies, and when he sets his sights on someone, he latches on to them like a pit bull terrier and doesn't relent until the market chews them up and spits them out. That's when Marc cashes in. Sometimes the journey is a light tussle, but most of the time it's a bare-knuckle fight, the kind that was often on display in Renaissance Venice on the Ponte dei Pugni, where two men would beat each other for more than ninety rounds.

Cohodes is a graduate of Babson College, located outside Boston, where he studied finance, but he didn't fall in love with short selling until the mid-eighties. After his first trade, he knew it was what he was born to do. He became a bounty hunter in the financial markets, shooting down anyone he could find who was cooking the books or pulling the wool over the eyes of Main Street investors. His mission was to unearth slick-talking balance sheet manipulators, and he would stop at nothing to hunt them down. He spotted Crazy Eddie's Sam Antar, who eventually went to prison, and he blew the whistle on Valeant Pharmaceuticals, which imploded under a multibillion-dollar scandal, and NovaStar, one of the great real estate optical illusions, which collapsed right before Lehman Brothers went down.

And in January 2022, thirty-five years after his first successful short trade, Marc stared down the barrel of his fearsome rifle and found himself looking at the biggest bounty he would ever see. Beneath a mop of floppy black hair stood that strange, geeky kid from Stanford—Sam Bankman-Fried. Not a good place to be. The hard-eyed sniper used only high-velocity, self-exploding bullets that were apt to blow the target asunder. Marc Cohodes carefully adjusted his telescopic sight, and at last the founder of the doomed FTX came into sharp focus.

Marc was immediately confused by how this young man had parachuted onto Wall Street as a billionaire, as the founder of the second-largest cryptocurrency exchange in the world, from nowhere. He was confused because he had never known anything like it.

Marc once said to me over the phone, "Larry, if you think about it, we both know nobody arrives on Wall Street out of the blue like that. Everybody who was anybody in finance came from somewhere. But not Sam Bankman-Fried. It was like the guy popped in from Mars. Who taught him? Who did he work under prior to FTX? Who could I speak to, to have him checked out? Late last year, every call I made and asked the right questions, I got crickets on the other end of the phone. It was like peeling back an onion and getting to the middle staring at a skull and crossbones."

It was all baffling to the financial sniper. He looked once more at his computer screen, at SBF's LinkedIn profile. All he could find beyond his education was the three-year stint at Jane Street trading emerging-market stocks. Marc knew in his soul that nobody could become this great without something called the "it factor." Simon Cowell calls it the "X factor." You can see it more obviously in rising stars on the ball field—kids who run, throw, and hit better than anyone else on the team. You know they're destined for the big leagues. But this Bankman-Fried guy was confusing the life out of Marc. He had no background, no experience, and no secret sauce. In Marc's mind, that could mean only one thing. Fraud.

He delved a little deeper into FTX and the other people on the team. The most talented person he could find had reached the dizzying heights of intern at a real estate company. Other than that, it was a wasteland of credibility. As far as he could tell, even the so-called kimchi trade, which had made Alameda Research its first big stack of cash, was a physical impossibility. The kimchi trade was an arbitrage opportunity that took advantage of the structural premium in the Bitcoin price primarily in South Korea, hence the nickname "kimchi." But Asian exchanges demand that the person be there, in the flesh and with the cash, for any crypto arbitrage. Bankman-Fried could not have pulled this off unless he had also graduated from Hogwarts School of Witchcraft and Wizardry. Which he hadn't. Not according to his LinkedIn.

A surge of major FTX logo placements had started. Tom Brady became a brand ambassador, tennis stars wore the logo on their shirts, and the Miami Heat stadium even had it in giant lettering right across the roof. Paradigm had given FTX $238 million, SoftBank $100 million. Sino Global Capital was in for $50 million. The mainstream media was pumping up Sam and FTX to look like the Second Coming, but Marc was increasingly disgusted by the entire outfit.

It was obvious that FTX had somehow duped the entire mainstream media. Bankman-Fried had duped investors. He had duped the regulators. And to Marc, the entire company was nothing more than a $40 billion scam. He was left believing that, in 2022, the markets had been rallying for so long that there had been a death of thinking, one of the hallmarks of a true bubble. People had lost the ability to think critically and ask the right questions about investments. If they saw big celebrities and sports stars jump into something, that was all the research they needed. Nobody was checking the facts anymore. The whole investing landscape had become a "monkey see, monkey do" environment. Nobody had FTX under the microscope. And Marc believed that Sam Bankman-Fried was keenly aware of this as he set out to con the entire world. He knew that people researched more about the next restaurant they would visit than they did about their investments.

"Isn't it sad," Marc said to no one in particular, "how hard people work for their money, and then they lose it all in the fucking scams where no one is thinking."

When Bubbles Burst

In the year 2020, right after the COVID-19 lockdowns began, Bitcoin started its monumental rally. Three days earlier, on March 12, 2020, Bitcoin had hit its lowest point since its 2017 rally: $4,826. One and a half years later, it hit the spectacular high of $68,789.63, achieved on November 8, 2021. Much of that was due to the free money from the federal government, the endless stack of stimulus checks mailed to every household in the country. This was what initiated the mania during the lockdown. Was it really a new world, a new digital age, or was the Freudian phenomenon of group psychology at work once more? Cryptocurrencies attracted billions of dollars, and the bubble sucked in just about everyone who believed the world was fundamentally changing as a result of the pandemic.

But there was another market also skyrocketing right alongside the digital currencies. And that was growth stocks—the ones that would surely lead the migration to the new nirvana, new earth, new dimension—pick whatever lingo you like. Half the country was under a kind of hypnosis, and they piled on their money accordingly, backing the common new belief that the digital world would be our future. No two ways about it.

The most prominent figure and latter-day heroine in this movement was Cathie Wood, a dark-haired Wall Street investor from Los Angeles. After earning a bachelor's in economics at the University of Southern California, she had a classic career path from Jennison to the hedge fund Tupelo Capital Management and then to AllianceBernstein. She worked there for fourteen years in a fund with nearly $800 billion in assets under management by 2007, $5 billion of which was managed by Cathie. In 2014, she wanted to start an actively managed ETF focusing on disruptive innovation, but AllianceBernstein deemed it too risky. That's when Cathie Wood jumped ship, right into a fund of her own. She called it ARK Invest. The first four ETFs at ARK were a rare breed of actively managed ETFs funded by Bill Hwang at Archegos Capital Management, a firm that blew up in March 2021; Bill himself was arrested on federal charges of fraud and racketeering. He's currently out on bail—a $100 million bond.

Cathie grew from strength to strength, but she hit a grand-slam home run during the pandemic lockdowns. She was the flavor of the month throughout 2020 as growth stocks kept right on climbing with all the post-COVID stimulus sloshing around in the economy. Her company's flagship ETF, ARKK, was experiencing a rally that seemed destined to break all records. It surged 150 percent in 2020 and had appreciated another 24 percent by mid-February 2021. Total assets under management were close to $27 billion. In fact, Bloomberg named Cathie Wood "Stock Picker of the Year" for 2020, and in March 2021 two of her funds hit a list of "10 largest female-run funds by total net assets." Even permanently skeptical *Barron's* was bragging about her, with headlines like "Red-Hot ARK ETFs Add $12.5 Billion in New Cash in 2021."

ARKK basically took the stocks of the most speculative tech or "innovation" companies and threw them all into a single investment product. I'm talking about Tesla, Coinbase, CRISPR Therapeutics, Robinhood, Roblox—you name it. Perhaps the most bizarre example of all was Teladoc Health, which trades under the ticker symbol TDOC. This company was connecting physicians to patients over video chat. It never made a profit and maybe never will. It's purely a play on future expectations—and hopes that the company's debt doesn't do it in before it can reach profitability. None of this stopped the company's stock from surging amid all the Fed accommodation in 2020 and 2021; it went from a $3 billion to a $42 billion market cap company in a year's time. It reached a point where it even became the third-largest holding in the massive ARKK ETF.

Of course, a lot of that gets back to the danger of ETF investing that we discussed in chapter 6. As more money poured into ARKK, it purchased more shares in Teladoc and its other holdings, increasing their prices and, in a self-reinforcing feedback loop, attracting more buyers to the ETF. In any case, the stock has since crashed 90 percent from its 2021 high. The average stock in the ARKK ETF is down 60 percent from the February 2021 highs. Even now, after the spectacular crash of all these highfliers, some of ARK Invest's largest holdings, such as Roku, are still down 80 percent. The lesson here is that when so much liquidity enters the market, it fuels such immense bubbles that assets of various kinds start to behave like crypto. Valuations assigned by the market become untethered from reality—there's nothing there behind the stock. It's just pure hopes and dreams.

This was the height of the bull frenzy in the tech-heavy Nasdaq. And those heights change the mindset of investors. Especially when everyone is getting rich. As J. P. Morgan said more than a century ago, "Nothing so undermines your financial judgment as the sight of your neighbor getting rich." Reasoning is cast aside, and the merest indications of logic replace full-blown, properly thought-out investment decisions. This is the time when the worst bond deals are created, covenants fall by the wayside, and companies that are financially stretched start issuing convertible debt—what we on Wall Street call the "last-chance saloon." One of the best risk management strategies comes down to wariness of "serial issuers" of convertible bonds. Companies habitually coming back to the convertible bond market for financing are not long for this world.

All this is a hallmark of real trouble ahead. Classic examples are SunEdison, Chesapeake Energy, Molycorp, and Lehman Brothers in this century and, in the 1990s, Enron, Tyco, Adelphia, and WorldCom. Most of them went belly-up. But that's not all. Tremendous pressure also falls onto the shoulders of financial professionals and Main Street investors to participate in the bubble. A crypto exchange having celebrity brand ambassadors seems a good enough reason to jump in. That's also how Theranos, run by the crooked Elizabeth Holmes, attracted so much capital between 2014 and 2017. The whole board was chock-full of credible names, guys like former secretaries of state Henry Kissinger and George Schultz and the four-star general Jim Mattis. There was the beady-eyed Richard Kovacevich, former CEO of Wells Fargo, and William Perry, who served under President Clinton as secretary of defense. But the entire company was an illusion; it was nothing more than a lie. Investors must always delve into the books and take nothing at face value. The market is a minefield of devious operators. Bright, shiny objects, slick-talking CEOs, convoluted earnings calls, and celebrity endorsements should all be red flags. Especially in bull markets. That's when people get careless.

Somewhat ironically, February 2021 was the top of the market for the ARKK ETFs. Nobody quite knows why tops or bottoms happen in February and March, but they do. Great turning points seem to always land on the second and third month of the year. March was the beginning of the end for the dot-com bubble in 2000. March was also the bottom of the market in 2009 and in 2020. It's a strange month. In March 2021, there was a sudden flight out of the ARKK ETF, away from risky electric vehicle stocks, away from wildly overpriced Zoom and Roku. Investors wanted solid growth names, stocks that had worked well for a decade. They jumped deeper into the FAANGs—Facebook, Amazon, Apple, Netflix, and Google—real companies with immense cash flows and great track records. The world was also opening back up, and it seemed like the great dream of an all-digital future was fading by the day. But that wasn't the only reason. Inflation was rising, and when inflation rears its head, rates *must* go up to cool things off. That's when the net present value of all future cash flows crumbles. It tends to eat valuation for breakfast, and when stocks like Zoom and Roku were trading at a price-to-earnings multiple of five hundred, the smartest investors got cold feet about future valuations. That's when they abandoned the ARKKs of this world and romped further into the FAANGs, which were perceived to be a safe haven. By December 2021, Cathie Wood's once-heroic funds were listed as one of the top ten ways to destroy capital.

The sell-off was brutal, but the stalwarts of technology kept performing very well. In the crypto space, Dogecoin, Litecoin, XRP, and Tron were taken to the woodshed and turned into kindling, but Bitcoin powered ahead undeterred. It reached its all-time high in November 2021. That's when President Biden reappointed Jerome Powell as the chief man at the Eccles Building in Washington, D.C. And the markets reacted overnight, suspecting that this dashing figure from Princeton University would pivot dramatically and become a hawkish (threatening interest-rate hikes) inflation fighter now that he ruled the markets once more. As a result, Bitcoin started a long, drawn-out sell-off. In January 2022, the entire technology sector followed suit, and by the end of the year, most growth stocks had dropped by more than 50 percent, some by more than 75 percent. The total loss of wealth in 2022 between the crypto bubble and growth stock markets alone totaled $9 trillion.

The sales pitch was so sexy, the narratives filled with enticing hot air. At the end of the day, investors in ARK Innovation, crypto, and NFTs were all long central bank accommodation the whole time. They all prospered from the wall of money the Fed poured into the market starting in 2020. Many failed crypto coins had charts highly correlated with the amount of stimulus money the federal government was mailing to U.S. households. In a low-inflationary world, these types of speculative trades do very well, because money is so cheap, and huge asset bubbles are created. In the words of the great Robert Shiller, "We are irrationally exuberant beings." It's human nature to be optimistic, as beautifully explored in Tali Sharot's 2011 book, *The Optimism Bias.* That's what made the housing market go bananas at the turn of the century. Cheap rates and unbridled optimism made the market explode to the upside, creating yet another huge bubble on the back of cheap money.

A classic adage is "Time is money." Every investor, business owner, or worker knows that it's better to have a million dollars in your pocket today than even a sure promise of a million dollars in ten years. But how much more valuable is it? What if it were half a million dollars today versus the full million in ten years? To solve this question, analysts and investors use discounted cash flow (DCF). This is a formula that estimates the net present value (NPV) of future cash flows, discounted to account for time, risk, opportunity cost, and inflation. Inflation expectations play a crucial role in the model because they directly impact the discount rate used in the calculations. The discount rate is basically how much the government bond yields (the "risk-free" rate) plus a risk premium. When inflation expectations rise, the risk-free rate increases, too. A higher inflation rate therefore means a higher discount rate. In other words, rising inflation expectations decrease the NPV of future cash flows, so stock prices fall and multiples contract.

INVESTORS TAKE NOTE:
Understanding (and Profiting from) DCF Models

One of our core missions in this book is helping you hear, evaluate, and profit from all the noise coming at us from the markets and analysts. Markets are always speaking, but what are the most telling signals for you and your portfolio?

Over the years, much of Wall Street equity research has become the gang that can't shoot straight. Analysts hide out in packs to avoid sticking their necks out. After all, those hefty mortgage payments and private schools in Connecticut need a steady, secure income at a high level. God help the analyst if a divorce enters the picture. The sad facts are right there for all to see. Groupthink takes over, with analysts constantly upgrading stocks near the highs and downgrading them on the lows. The 2021 to 2023 equity market research landscape was littered with this charade.

At *The Bear Traps Report,* one of our favorite shell games is what we call the "DCF mirage." In a world where deflation certainty is high, an equity analyst has the luxury of valuing a growth stock in a very wide range. In the 2020 to 2021 regime, when interest rates looked like they would be near zero forever, analysts were upgrading software companies at 30x earnings, hoping for that greater fool to come along and pay 40x. In a world of highly certain deflation, it maximizes the NPV of all future cash flows. But in a world of rising inflation expectations, the NPV of all future cash flows can be worth a lot less, and this favors value stocks over growth.

Let me explain. The DCF model is the most common model portfolio managers use to value companies, especially those that generate a lot of free cash flow. The formula calculates the sum of the cash flow in each period into the future. The basic premise of the DCF analysis is that a dollar ten years from now, or five years from now, is not as valuable as a dollar today. For example, a dollar five years from now discounted at a 10 percent discount rate is worth 62 cents. And the dollar ten years from today is worth only 40 cents.

This is because the value of money constantly erodes due to inflation, a principle known as the time value of money. Future cash flow dollars therefore need to be discounted to the present. So the model discounts the future cash flows by using a discount rate. The main component of this discount rate is the risk-free rate, such as the U.S. Treasury bond yield, but there are other factors as well, such as how risky the company is. The discount rate used to value a company via the DCF method is therefore the weighted average cost of capital (WACC). The WACC discount rate includes the risk-free rate and the additional interest rate a company needs to pay to raise capital, whether that is via issuing debt or equity. A top company like Apple or Microsoft clearly has a much lower weighted cost of capital than, for example, Roku or GameStop.

By adding the stream of cash flows from each year, discounted to the future, analysts get a total sum of discounted cash flows. The analyst then adds to that sum the terminal value of the company, which is the firm's value beyond the forecast period when future cash flows can be estimated. This terminal value is also years into the future and also has to be discounted to the present. The grand sum of these is considered the fair value of the company, or DCF value. If this value is more than what the company is worth today, analysts and investors deem it undervalued.

The key component of the cost of capital is the risk-free rate, which is the yield on the U.S. Treasury bond. The lower the discount rate, the higher the NPV of a dollar in the future. To exemplify, when the discount rate is 5 percent, five years in the future our dollar from the first example would be worth 78 cents, and ten years in the future it is worth 61 cents. At a discount rate of 15 percent, those future dollars are worth only 50 cents and 25 cents, respectively. So the discount rate has a strong influence on the NPV of a stream of cash flows. If the risk-free rate increases, because inflation increases, the future stream of cash flows and the terminal value become less. Using our previous example, the sum of these cash flows with an interest rate of 5 percent is $8.7, but at 10 percent the sum is only $7.1, or 18 percent less. In other words, if inflation expectations go up, future cash flow streams are worth less and the value of these companies goes down.

Let's take the price-to-earnings (P/E) ratio—a company's stock price divided by its earnings. This is a simple window into how the market is valuing a stock at any given time. A higher P/E usually means that investors anticipate much greater earnings in the future, so they're willing to pay up now to own the stock. Of course, not every stock trades at the same multiple. As a rule, "value" stocks tend to trade at a lower multiple of their current earnings than "growth" stocks, for which hope of future earnings plays a bigger part. Companies in the "real" economy have seen their cost of equity rise (i.e., their share prices lag) because of overinvestment in speculative growth stocks. This is part of that whole equation. We've seen thirty years of relatively consistent deflationary pressure, which has let stocks, particularly in the growth bucket, enjoy high multiples. However, when a deflationary regime turns into an inflationary regime, multiples contract across the board. But because value stocks were already trading at lower multiples, they end up much less affected than growth stocks, which are assessed more on the basis of future earnings and have much farther to fall. Always remember that in an inflationary regime, value stocks in the commodity space are meaningfully long assets (oil, gas, uranium, coal, aluminum, copper, etc.) that tend to appreciate. These assets can provide a natural inflation hedge.

We've been talking about how accommodation by the Fed has led to money piling up over and over again in more speculative investments. In a deflationary regime, the Fed can drop interest rates to zero and buy bonds endlessly. This makes investors more confident that their speculative investments will get bailed out if all goes awry. Once the trajectory starts to shift toward a more inflationary future, the speculative assets lose their luster because the Fed becomes not a friend but a foe. Amid inflation, it's going to be hiking rates, thereby tightening credit conditions. Most high-growth-stock companies rely on relatively cheap debt to finance themselves until they reach profitability. In a world where this debt becomes more expensive or harder to come by, many of them will inevitably go belly-up.

Style	1968–1970	1972–1976	1983–1986	1988–1990	2000–2001	2004–2006	2007–2008	2011	2021–2022
Value	-15.5%	10.8%	39.5%	47%	-4%	11%	-33%	-2%	-2%
Growth	-15.5%	8.1%	38.7%	42%	-12%	18%	-37%	-6%	-8%
Value/Growth	0%	3%	1%	5%	8%	-7%	4%	4%	6%

Let's think of tradable assets as a spectrum for a moment, ranging from utter value to pure growth. Utter value would be something immediately tangible, like a bar of gold, a shipment of lumber, or an airline's planes. Pure growth, on the other hand, would be something completely ephemeral, like altcoins (alternative cryptocurrencies, i.e., any cryptocurrency aside from Bitcoin) or NFTs. Most assets fall somewhere in the middle, though they might lean toward one side or the other. For example, a share of stock in an established steel company is more on the value

INVESTORS TAKE NOTE:

Value Outperforms Growth When Inflation Is Above 3 Percent

Historically, "value" has outperformed "growth" during inflationary times. In periods when the CPI inflation rose at a rate of 3 percent or more on a year-over-year basis, value stocks have almost always outperformed growth stocks. We do note that the outperformance occurred primarily in the phase where CPI inflation was accelerating. Once inflation reached its peak and started to slow down, even when remaining at a rate above 3 percent, growth stocks began to recover vis-à-vis value stocks.

side than one in a new software firm. Alternatively, an ETF like Pacer US Cash Cows 100 (COWZ) represents a passive product strongly on the side of value, whereas ARKK is strongly on the side of growth.

Remember, 44 percent of all U.S. dollars ever created were created in 2020 and 2021. The Fed increased its balance sheet by $5 trillion and cut rates all the way to zero. As a result, we saw massive bubble formation in the most speculative assets possible. We're talking about stock in an effectively bankrupt company like GameStop shooting up 3,000 percent in 2021. An off-brand cryptocurrency like Dogecoin appreciated by almost 23,000 percent the same year, and Bored Ape NFTs—those collectible pictures of morose monkeys—sold for nearly $1 million each. These are some of the most extreme examples, beyond growth and clearly in the realm of fairy dust.

Still, whether it was Ethereum or Goblintown NFTs, Fed accommodation drastically inflated market values across the decentralized finance (DeFi) space into a furious bubble. It opened up a Pandora's box of all sorts of different currencies, tokens, and straight-up scams, all fueled by the easy money and cheap credit. In March 2022, the total market cap of all cryptocurrencies even jumped above $2 trillion. It's certainly very possible that in the long term, crypto aficionados will be proved right about their digital gold's value in helping to escape the centralized, state-controlled financial system. But for now, the irony is that their key to financial freedom is just another play on government largesse and monetary dovishness. Given its detachment from hard assets, it may even be more sensitive to Fed action than stocks or bonds are.

One key lesson to take away is that for investors, bubbles are an incredible opportunity to make money—as long as you recognize when the sell-off is no longer a buying opportunity. Of course, this is one of the hardest things to recognize, but the Fed is a great indicator here. Since the Fed has been responsible for inflating these bubbles in the last thirty years, we need to listen to the Fed and how markets react to the Fed's signals. The Fed took the punch bowl away in 2000, and this sealed the fate of the dot-com bubble. The Fed kept hiking rates between 2004 and 2006 until the housing bubble popped, which ultimately led to the Lehman crisis.

In November 2021 the Fed, after Powell was reappointed, made it very clear that the days of easy Fed money were coming to an end. The stock market started its bear market a month later. But do not be afraid of bubbles. George Soros said he runs to them when he spots them (but he makes sure to get out of them before they pop). Needless to say, guys like Soros often identify the bubble far before the average investor. Investors who bought Tesla in 2019, which was seven years after the Model S debuted, would have made 2,600 percent to the top. Even if they bought the stock in 2020, the return would have been a still-amazing 180 percent. Even if they bought Bitcoin at the 2017 peak, they would have made 255 percent if they held it until the end of 2021. Of course, that was after an 83 percent drawdown, and few human beings can withstand that kind of volatility. If you bought it any time before late 2020, you would have made 630 percent at the top. The key for investors is to listen to the market. When does the asset stop going up on good news? What is the driver of the bubble (the Fed), and is it about to change its stance?

Nasdaq vs. Bitcoin

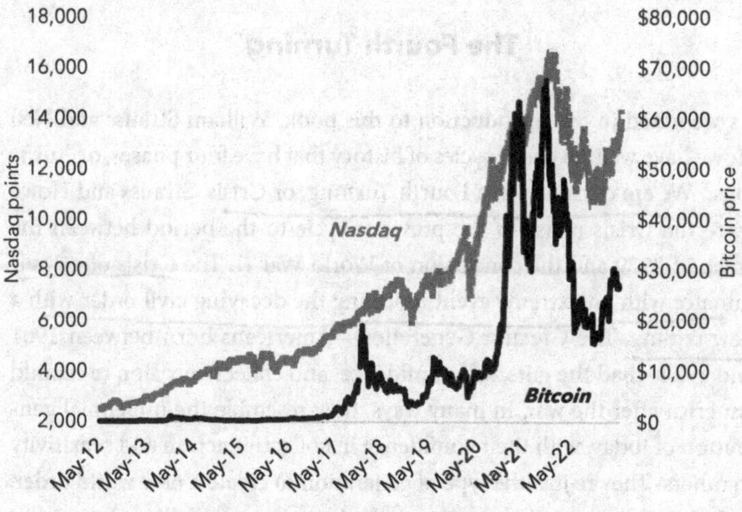

One thing bubbles are not good for is the long-term health of an economy. At the most basic level, they temporarily create jobs in overinflated sectors, and financial markets start buzzing with mergers and acquisitions and capital raises, and certain stocks tend to do very well for a while because all the money is pouring into that sector. But bubbles are responsible for colossal distortions of capital, and that leaves other sectors starved for capital. This ultimately leads to a decline in the population's purchasing power, widespread layoffs when the bubble bursts, and a loss of competitive position. Money often chases financial assets that have little benefit to the larger economy. Take, for example, real estate. Soaring property values are great for landlords and real estate investors, but then everyone has to pay a premium for homeownership and rent, and when the bubble pops, many are left with high-interest mortgages and home values that are below the purchase price. The capital that was poured into crypto, with no discernible benefit to the real economy, leaves other businesses starving for capital. Capital is a scarce commodity, and if one sector of the economy sucks up an excessive amount of it, other sectors are deprived of it. The bubble in the U.S. oil-and-gas sector in the 2000s eventually led to years of overcapacity, bankruptcies, and job losses.

The Fourth Turning

As we noted in the introduction to this book, William Strauss and Neil Howe have written about cycles of history that have four phases, or "turnings." We are currently in a Fourth Turning, or Crisis. Strauss and Howe trace the Crisis phase of the previous cycle to the period between the crash of 1929 and the conclusion of World War II. The Crisis often culminates with an extreme event replacing the decaying civil order with a new regime. The Greatest Generation—Americans born between 1901 and 1924—had the guts, self-confidence, and collective vision to rebuild America after the war. In many ways, they resemble the millennial generation of today, with their confidence in collective action and sensitivity to others. They're just the type of generation to create a new world order.

In our current cycle, crypto was the first sign of rebellion. It was a financial rebellion waged by millennials against regulated finance. This generation will be handed a bill for $33 trillion in national debt and almost $200 trillion in unfunded entitlements, once the baby boomers are gone. And cryptocurrency, at its very essence, was the embodiment of the new rebel class. We can begin to see why it was so attractive. This debt, now dumped onto the sovereign balance sheet, is a mountain of IOUs that could carpet the earth. In the long run, the only way out of this mess is a wholesale debasement of the dollar. But how can we blame millennials for charging into a new sector, a revolutionary technology, and a currency that didn't have to answer to any government, or any bank, or any foreign exchange, one that promised a store of value like gold?

As mentioned earlier, more than 40 percent of all dollars ever created were printed between the years 2020 and 2021 in response to COVID-19. How can anyone have any faith in that fiscal infrastructure? Millennials are scared to death of inheriting this. They have been dealt a rotten hand. From Lehman Brothers and the Great Recession to the latest growth-stock and crypto implosion, this somewhat wayward group is still prepared to risk everything to escape the grip of Capitol Hill. The failed deregulated-finance bubble may have just placed the dream into the first stages of government control, but their battle isn't over yet. It's only just begun.

8

The Decline of the U.S. Dollar

Cherish public credit. . . . Use it as sparingly as possible . . . avoiding likewise the accumulation of debt, not only by shunning occasions of expense, but by vigorous exertions in time of peace to discharge the debts.

—GEORGE WASHINGTON, FAREWELL ADDRESS, SEPTEMBER 17, 1796

This is the story of an empire in decline. A quote often attributed to the eighteenth-century Scottish historian Alexander Fraser Tytler says, "A democracy is always temporary in nature; it simply cannot exist as a permanent form of government. A democracy will continue to exist up until the time that voters discover that they can vote themselves generous gifts from the public treasury. From that moment on, the majority always votes for the candidates who promise the most benefits from the public treasury, with the result that every democracy will finally collapse due to generous fiscal policy, which is always followed by a dictatorship." Although there is no evidence that the words are actually Tytler's (and no consensus on who actually said or wrote them or when), they certainly ring true.

Tytler is said to have been the originator of a theory about the life cycles of nations and empires. The United States is clearly in the later stage of the cycle—just before the whole house of cards comes crashing to the ground. The upward path begins from subjugation: Think of the American colonies in 1770 in the grip of the king of England. Next comes spiritual faith and great courage, on to liberty, then abundance. If only empires could stay right there, they would last forever. But each generation becomes weaker, born into increasingly comfortable times. That eventually breeds complacency, apathy, and a nation of dependents on the federal government. And that's what the United States is moving toward today. In the final stage, the entire society is thrown back into subjugation. The bottom line is that a well-functioning society must have a robust and secure middle class. Looking back more than one thousand years, this segment of the population has been repeatedly destabilized. Today, we can see the impact of high inflation rates on the financial security and purchasing power of people in countries like Argentina, Turkey, and Venezuela.

A group gathered in the Oval Office shortly after 9:00 A.M. on February 28, 2022. Vladimir Putin's war against Ukraine had been raging for four days, slamming Kyiv with long-range artillery fire, ballistic missiles, and 3M-14 Kalibrs—Russia's land-attack cruise missiles. The assault stretched right across the perimeter of eastern and central Ukraine, blasting several cities and bases with air raids and shelling—Luhansk, Donetsk, Kharkiv. The Russian president was after a quick victory, and he was hitting Ukraine right between the eyes with the best right hook he could muster, in flagrant violation of international law. And on that mild late-winter morning, the top brass at the White House were royally fed up with this former KGB thug from Saint Petersburg.

One by one they filed into the room: Jake Sullivan, the national security adviser; Janet Yellen, secretary of the Treasury; Tony Blinken, secretary of state; and Susan Rice, director of the Domestic Policy Council and former national security adviser under Barack Obama. Finally, President Biden entered and asked everyone to be seated on the wide, cream-colored sofas. He was on edge, consumed by Putin's actions and his disregard for any semblance of diplomacy.

The meeting proceeded with a rapid-fire discussion of how the United States and its allies could hold Putin hostage financially and watch him bleed dry. The group hatched plans to block Russia completely from international financial systems and impose restrictive measures against

Russia's central bank, banning any Russian banks from the global SWIFT financial messaging system, which would essentially place a padlock and chain on Russian money in the international market. There was a debilitating plan to create a joint task force to freeze the assets of sanctioned Russian companies and oligarchs, as well as the Kremlin.

But that wasn't all. They wanted to shut down Russia's war machine totally, using the most brutal program of sanctions since the Cold War. Many people in the room had been there when Obama faced a similar crisis in 2014, when the Russia-Ukraine conflict began. And they had all learned from their mistakes—too soft, too passive, too hopeful for diplomatic solutions. It had to be different in this second phase of Putin's aggression, and the plan was to stun Moscow with total isolation from the global financial system—the government, the banks, and the oligarchs.

There was a huge amount of international and economic experience in the room. Degrees from top-class universities, lifelong operators in geopolitical negotiations and overseas diplomacy. Brian Deese, Biden's director of the National Economic Council, didn't see a risk in such brutal sanctions. He believed to his core that there was no capital market on earth quite like America's, with its staggering wealth, liquidity, and ability to withstand economic shocks. Any nation on earth that fled these markets, this level of safety for their foreign reserves, must be insane. And among that tight cabal seated in the Oval Office, it was unanimously agreed there was little alternative to the U.S. dollar. Even if the sanctions spooked the markets, cast doubt among the giant holders of greenback reserves—countries such as China, Saudi Arabia, Brazil, and India—they couldn't run far. And if they did, they couldn't run for long.

But Janet Yellen's face was etched with doubt. The dollar had been the global reserve currency for almost eighty years, and it had always stood for a gold standard of diplomacy and goodwill, exemplary legal systems, and the protection of human rights. But could these punishing sanctions lead to an eventual flight of capital from U.S. Treasuries? Would China still want 50 percent of its foreign reserves in U.S. dollars? And since Russia was the supplier of China's production machine, wouldn't the Red Dragon prop up Russia's oil markets? It didn't matter a jot to the Treasury secretary that the sanctions were now backed by America's Western allies. In the end, big economies that don't agree with American foreign policy might grab hold of a Hammacher Schlemmer felling axe, with its alloy-steel edge and flexible hickory handle, and chop down their dollar reserves.

But the group brushed aside Yellen's concerns. That night, at the State of the Union address, President Biden announced new sanctions that were to be leveled on Russia's economy.

Dollar in the Last 55 Years

Dollar MACD (Moving Average Convergence/Divergence)

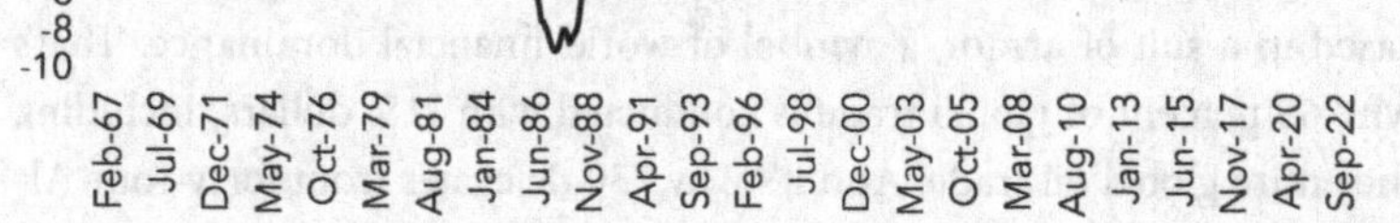

What Biden and his advisers didn't know was that the devilish Putin had been planning the war for years. In 2016, he started to unwind his U.S. Treasury bond holdings, and by the middle of July 2018 he had sold the entire position—all $120 billion of it. Vladimir Putin may have looked like a madman in the eyes of the media, an unhinged despot, but this latest attack on Ukraine was well planned. His dollar-denominated financial assets had been sold down, and he had stampeded into hard assets with that money. In 2018, his gold holdings increased by $30 billion—a 60 percent increase, ramping them up to $80 billion. And amid his invasion of Crimea in 2014, Putin shook hands with China on a gigantic thirty-year gas deal worth $400 billion known as the Power of Siberia. It connected the gas fields of central Russia via a pipeline, with the capacity to move 61 billion cubic meters a year, to Shanghai and Beijing. This Russian pipeline was launched in October 2019, and that's when Russian gas started flowing into China, the Middle Kingdom. Putin was preparing, ultimately, to disconnect Europe from Russian gas, and was hedging against the strong possibility of Western sanctions. But despite Putin's effort to decouple from U.S. government debt, he still had $625 billion in foreign currency and precious-metal reserves scattered in banks around the world, and the sanctions froze half of it. But he wasn't knocked out of the game. And through the blood and violence of his latest war, nasty ramifications emerged for the greenback, ramifications every investor should know about. Because there has been a huge shift in the global currency ecosystem, and for the first time in history, the U.S. dollar could be in real trouble.

The United States—a Friend or a Foe?

Weaponizing the dollar is seen from inside the Beltway as an effective way of winning a conflict without firing a gun. But the weaponization must be used sparingly—treated with the utmost respect. The U.S. currency is encased in a suit of armor, a symbol of world financial dominance. That's why 65 percent of global trade is conducted with U.S. dollars, including the entire global oil trade. And it's why 730 delegates from forty-four Allied nations gathered at the Mount Washington Hotel in Bretton Woods, New Hampshire, in June 1944. It was there, in the foothills of the White Mountains, that an agreement was signed that solidified the U.S. dollar as the global reserve currency. That's not a responsibility anyone should take lightly. And it's a power that ought never to be wielded by politicians who may lack the backbone for military conflict.

But that power has been abused. Badly abused. And it has reached a tipping point. America's finances have entered a precarious chapter through years of reckless overspending and opposing bad actors on the world stage. George W. Bush invaded Iraq and Afghanistan. Obama bombed Libya and Syria and slapped sanctions on Russia. Trump sanctioned China, Iran, and Venezuela. And now Biden has brutally sanctioned the "third Rome"—the second time Moscow has borne the brunt of a weaponized U.S. dollar in the last six years. And sanctions have a checkered history. In the twentieth century alone they were enacted 110 times and seldom changed anything in the targeted foreign country. If anything, sanctions cause defiant leaders and autocrats to dig in their heels even further, to the detriment of their citizens. Reagan imposed sanctions on Argentina, but they did nothing to stop a hot war in the South Atlantic. His successor, Bill Clinton, hit India, Cuba, Pakistan, Iran, and Libya with them. Later, Clinton lamented somewhat hypocritically that America had become "sanctions happy." In the face of geopolitical tensions, especially where Washington's interests might be on the line, economic weapons are the preferred method of preserving peace.

But world leaders, both friends and adversaries, have taken note of all the times the United States has gone to economic war. They are also now waking up to the unavoidable fact that the effectiveness of sanctions is tied to how reliant their countries are on the U.S. dollar and how much of the currency they hold in reserves. The growing trepidation is that any country that doesn't fall exactly in line with America's agenda or worldview could face a fate similar to the one Russia did in 2022. In other words, having the assets of its government, companies, and citizens frozen to the tune of billions of dollars. Furthermore, although at the time of Bretton Woods the United States boasted half of total global GDP, in 2022 that figure was down to just a quarter. That means more and more ways for countries to avoid fully buying into the American-led economic system. The creeping hesitation around holding too many dollars—and the diminishing need to hold them—is about to hurt America much more than the current administration would like to admit. The debt ratcheted up by politicians who believed America's fiscal rope could stretch till the end of time has finally created the biggest bear trap on earth. And it's a bear trap every investor needs to know about.

INVESTORS BEWARE:
The Handcuffs of Financial Repression

In the summer of 2023, we hosted a client conference in London. It was great to be back in Mayfair, one of my favorite places in the world. Much like Manhattan, the financial community in this neighborhood of London is one of the crown jewels of the planet. While Europe battled a much-talked-up record heat wave, it was a cool 65 degrees Fahrenheit as I walked up Albemarle Street—umbrella in hand, of course—on my way to meet one of my favorite investors of all time.

In the late 1980s, Marc Cheval came out of the London School of Economics. Good looks, class, and brains are blessings Cheval carries with the most polite humility. After a decade at Goldman Sachs, Cheval had more lofty ambitions. In the fall of 1997, Louis Bacon's Moore Capital brought Cheval in at the highest level, and his macro trading success in the emerging-market and energy spaces became the stuff of legend. We are fortunate to call him a friend and an important mentor on our tireless mission for higher learning and understanding across asset classes. Over the years, Cheval has provided a unique piece of the puzzle or an eye-opening perspective. But today, a glass of wine at the Donovan Bar at Brown's Hotel was first on the agenda.

We sat down at the corner table, caught up on our latest family activities, and then Cheval, as he so often does, dived right in.

"Larry, we could be on the verge of one of the most significant trades of a career and a lifetime. There is close to $19 trillion in the Nasdaq 100, up from less than $12 trillion in December. Wall Street analysts are falling all over themselves to upgrade stocks they were running away from last year. If you look at the inflation picture, it looks far more like a high-inflation volatility regime is coming at us over the next three to five years, while equities are pricing in a linear, straight-shot decline back to the 2010-to-2020 era. Everyone wants a piece of last decade's darlings—hard assets are grossly under-owned relative to the risk setup looking five or ten years down the road."

"Old sport, you are in a chipper mood today," I said with a smile.

But Cheval was on to something about the tectonic plates shifting beneath our feet. Only one thing is nearly certain on Wall Street: The most deeply held consensus view is more than often wrong. When all the strategists and analysts are singing the same tune, run, do *not* walk, the other way.

"Big picture, Marc, what troubles me the most is the aging population in the developed world. The G7 is a political forum of government officials consisting of the USA, Canada, France, Germany, Italy, Japan, and the United Kingdom. What are the unfunded liabilities, those future promises made to voters in exchange for their support that have no assets set aside to pay for them without theft (confiscation of private property)? In the U.S. alone, including the national debt, estimates reach as high as $200 trillion."

"It's right up there, Larry," Cheval agreed. "The only way out of this hole is an epic debt jubilee default cycle, or the governments have to inflate their way out. Many of the deflation tailwinds are becoming inflation headwinds, and the U.S. is sitting on by far the most liabilities and the best asset profile. Bottom line is, they inflate their way out, and step one is to have their Fed pawns start pumping those white papers. In the coming years, they will start the sales pitch on a new 3 percent inflation target (currently 2 percent as part of the Fed's dual mandate). It will be gradual, but that's the plan of action in my humble opinion."

"Marc, we have heard a thousand times, the U.S. dollar is the cleanest shirt in the laundry bin and there is that never-ending greenback demand. What's your take on that line of thinking?"

"We are moving to the pig pen arena, Larry," Cheval answered. "So many shirts are very dirty, including the USA. At some point soon, this drives capital into hard assets (oil, copper, gold, platinum, silver) and things like Bitcoin. For the USA, the basic issue at work is—the side effects of debt take time to kick in. Debt takes time to roll, and therefore the negative follow-on impact of high debt levels only kicks in with a lag, like a multiyear hangover after a very big (debt) party."

"Marc, in 2011, at the top of the commodity market, at one point the MCSI World Energy Index was worth more than the Nasdaq 100. Today the NDX is $15 trillion larger; we think at least $5 trillion comes out of big tech and moves back into energy and metals."

"I don't disagree, Larry, but the biggest issue for all investors is financial repression. I won't name any names, but I know many of the key players on a very personal level. These guys would prefer to take down their debt load by massaging interest rates below inflation. The next trick up their sleeve will be to mandate the entire U.S. pension system into a higher bogey in terms of ownership of U.S. Treasuries. The UK and Japan have already walked down this road."

Cheval continued, "Another thing, they are absolutely terrified of AI (artificial intelligence) as a real threat to the middle class, adding even more entitlement receivers relative to revenue producers into the equation. We are near 3.5 percent unemployment in the USA with another $1.7 trillion deficit. The USA is on pace to spend 25 percent of federal revenue on interest by 2025, most AAA sovereign credits on the planet are around 1 to 2 percent in this department, and just under 5 percent for AA credits. The Fed will have *no* choice but to step in and support the market. Since 2013, China's stockpile of U.S. Treasuries is down by about $400 billion in the last five years, and Japan's is down by around $200 billion since 2021. This is a recipe for financial repression certainty."

Financial repression is a set of policies that place public debt with financial institutions at artificially low rates.

"There is a gentle way of doing this," Cheval explained, "which would be through regulation to mandate that private sector institutions have to hold more debt. In the worst case, Western governments can cram down their debt to financial institutions and the public via a war. In this scenario, they could suspend capital mobility similar to the suspension of the gold convertibility in 1914, and confiscate some of the $30 trillion of foreign holdings of U.S. stocks and bonds. With the risk of this kind of financial repression, we could very well be in the early innings of a multiyear run for commodities and value stocks. Add to this your observation about the lack of investment of the metals and mining sector. If capex had stayed on the 2014 trajectory, our planet would have invested another $3 trillion in oil, gas, metals, and uranium exploration, but that's *not* the case—we are way behind, and the global population is some 600 million larger than ten years ago."

"Marc, the Federal Reserve may not be the best risk managers, but they are not so stupid as to replicate the Weimar Republic's hyperinflationary monetary policy," I said.

"Agreed, Larry. They want to slow-walk financial repression, keeping the government interest rate below the rate of inflation by a modest yet significant degree, which means keeping what savers can earn, lending to the U.S. government below the rate of inflation. This isn't being done by some emerging economy as part of a plan to protect inefficient industries; it is being done by the largest economy and greatest military power the world has ever seen, by the country that has the dominant and deepest financial markets, which can be chipped away a bit but not rejected out of hand. You can't pretend America doesn't exist."

"But what the U.S. does ends up being copied by the rest of the planet?"

"Precisely, Larry. The U.S. government's financial repression is a backdoor way of lowering government debt, thereby improving the debt-to-GDP ratio to a sustainable level. Politicians are loath to outright raise taxes on the middle class, so they tax everybody via inflation. The Fed doesn't want inflation to go away. It wants inflation to stay above the rate the U.S. government pays on its debt. The secondary, but vital, concern is to do that without causing hyperinflation. Hence the slow walk. It's a fifteen-year program, not a fifteen-month program. It is no accident the Fed pauses with Fed Funds matching the inflation rate. The Fed spends more time looking at Treasury's blended average interest rate versus the inflation rate than at the inflation rate itself in isolation."

It was a fascinating look down the road ahead with one of the all-time greats in macro finance. What Marc Cheval is talking about, though, is financial repression in a high-inflation era. It's almost like something we often see in emerging economies that have lost control over inflation and national debt. This will not be the type of financial repression we saw during the secular stagnation era of deflation, when Fed funds rates were held near 0 percent and growth outperformed value.

After the implosion of Lehman Brothers, President Obama had the luxury of borrowing money at 2 percent. In fact, from 2002 to 2021, as we have already explained, rates largely trended lower. And in 2014, the near-zero interest rates allowed the United States to have a debt of $15 trillion with an annual interest payment of $440 billion. This means that the United States was paying an astonishingly low 2.6 percent interest rate on all that money.

But America is in the crisis zone now. President Joe Biden faces $11 trillion of debt maturing between 2023 and 2025, and he's in a high-interest-rate environment that is doomed to continue for several more years. That mountain of debt must be refinanced at rates near 5 percent. For every percentage point increase, the cost of interest payments goes up by $110 billion annually. The total interest payments per year for all the U.S. debt is going to reach $1.5 trillion in the next year. President Biden, and whoever walks into the Oval Office after him, will have to address the post-COVID hangover, the energy crunch, and any crises yet to materialize amid high inflation and high rates. The annual interest payments will be at least $1 trillion higher than they were under Obama. That is a big problem.

The world is now unsure about America—the country's reckless use of sanctions, its freezing of foreign reserves, and its increasingly precarious-looking mountain of debt. And what got America into this mess? One word: complacency.

As of 2023, Japan held $1.1 trillion of American debt, followed by China with $867 billion, the United Kingdom with $655 billion, Belgium with $354 billion, and Luxembourg with $329 billion. But the rosy days of America raising easy money might well be over. Global finance ministers are leery of tying up capital in dollars, ever since the latest episode of Russian sanctions. As we will explain in this chapter, the United States is now increasingly competing with Europe for global savings to finance its ballooning budget deficits and the already-existing debt it is rolling over. In years past, the United States was the only major issuer of hard-currency sovereign bonds, but because the Eurozone introduced mutualization bonds (see page 186) during the COVID-19 pandemic, there is now serious competition. And the Fed is no longer in the market buying bonds. In fact, it is selling. More important, the countries that the United States could always rely on to buy its debt—countries like China, Saudi Arabia, Brazil, and India—are all collaborating these days to develop a competing global payment system so that they are no longer dependent on the dollar. This is a game changer with enormous consequences for the dollar.

Major Central Banks' Gold Reserves (excluding U.S.)

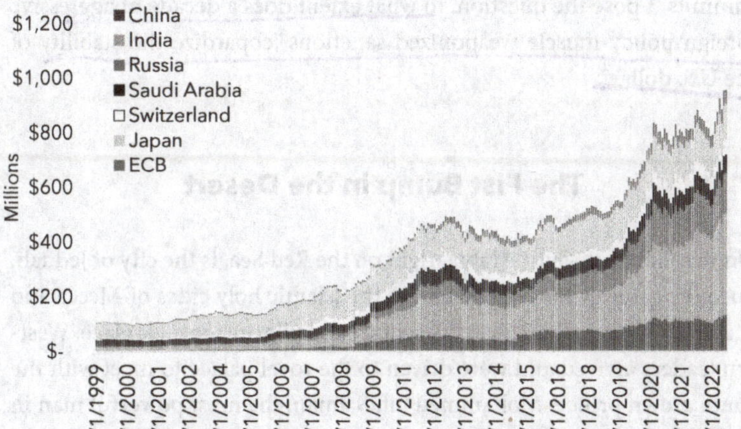

Foreign reserve managers have been motivated to look elsewhere—and not just because of U.S. sanction weapons, and not just because of the dollar's strength. We must also take into account America's unpredictable politics. Is the United States still the nation everyone visited to sign the Bretton Woods agreement in 1944—one of pragmatism, logic, and grand strategy? Or is it something quite different now? Something remarkable happened in the summer of 2023, and hardly anyone noticed. The yuan overtook the dollar as China's top cross-border currency, growing from near zero market share in 2010 to 20 percent in 2018, and touching 51 percent in July 2023. These are different days indeed.

This is the country that just five years ago threatened trade wars with the European Union over such mundane things as lobster and steel. It rushed out of Afghanistan in the dead of night without properly notifying its NATO allies ahead of time. It pressured Australia into a last-minute backroom deal to buy American military submarines, thereby killing a bona fide submarine contract signed half a decade ago between Australia and France. This is the country that was eavesdropping on the personal cellphones of Chancellor Angela Merkel and 125 other German government officials for a decade, as well as on the UN secretary-general and numerous other UN officials.

America was once known for its diplomatic high-wire acts to avoid a world war, such as the Berlin Airlift and the Camp David and Reykjavik summits. I pose the question, to what extent does a decade of aggressive foreign-policy-muscle weaponized sanctions jeopardize the stability of the U.S. dollar?

The Fist Bump in the Desert

On the shores of Saudi Arabia, right on the Red Sea, is the city of Jeddah, once the gateway for pilgrimages to the Islamic holy cities of Mecca and Medina. On July 15, 2022, a different type of pilgrimage took place. Western leaders arrived and were driven to the royal palace to meet with the Saudi crown prince, Mohammed bin Salman, the most powerful man in global oil. And, under the pitiless summer sun, President Biden stepped out of his black stretch limousine and fist-bumped the robed Bedouin ruler of the desert kingdom. Mohammed wore the formal red-and-white *shemagh* atop his head, held in place by the traditional *iqal*, a round black leather cord. His beard was clipped, and as his clenched right hand met with the president's, he stared into Biden's eyes, at the man who during his presidential campaign promised to make Saudi Arabia a pariah.

This thirty-six-year-old man, the son of the retired King Salman, had spent his life working under the wing of his father. He had learned how to control tribal wars and adversaries, how to run a government, and how to carefully lead a country with definitive action and guarded secrecy. And despite their economic power, it was Western nations that had to answer to the crown prince on the topic of oil prices. Biden was there for exactly that reason. Prices at the pump in the United States were killing his approval ratings, inflation was out of hand, and midterm elections were four months away. The U.S. president was there with his hat in his hand, and he had a tough hurdle ahead. Biden needed to walk back the insults of the campaign trail and somehow negotiate an increase in oil supply.

Arab heads of state looked forlornly at the American contingency, once their tough, reliable ally against any regional tyranny disrupting the supply of crude oil on the world market. That was the whole idea behind the creation of the petrodollar in the 1970s by Nixon and the leadership of the Treasury Department. He might have taken the dollar off the gold standard, prompting other nations to flee the American currency, but the petrodollar brought everyone back into the fold. America promised to provide unbreakable security for the kingdom's oil fields, and the Saudis agreed, in return, to accept only the greenback in exchange for their black gold, promising to invest all their dollars into U.S. Treasuries and American businesses. That saved the currency of the United States and gave it unimaginable power.

But over the next fifty years, American complacency, massive debt, and the weaponizing of the dollar against nations noncompliant with American interests rocked the foundation of the petrodollar agreement. It works if the world *wants* to own dollars, and it works if America can *comfortably* afford its vast military. The old adage comes to mind: "Don't bite the hand that feeds you." But when Joe Biden and his team sat across from representatives of the Arab states at that expansive table in the royal palace, they faced expressions of grave concern. The sanctions on Russia were frightening countries with large dollar holdings into downsizing their positions and buying gold. China and Russia had both been doing exactly that, buying large blocks of the precious metal in 2022, at levels not seen since 1967—coincidentally, one year before a decade of runaway inflation.

Global Central Bank Gold Purchases

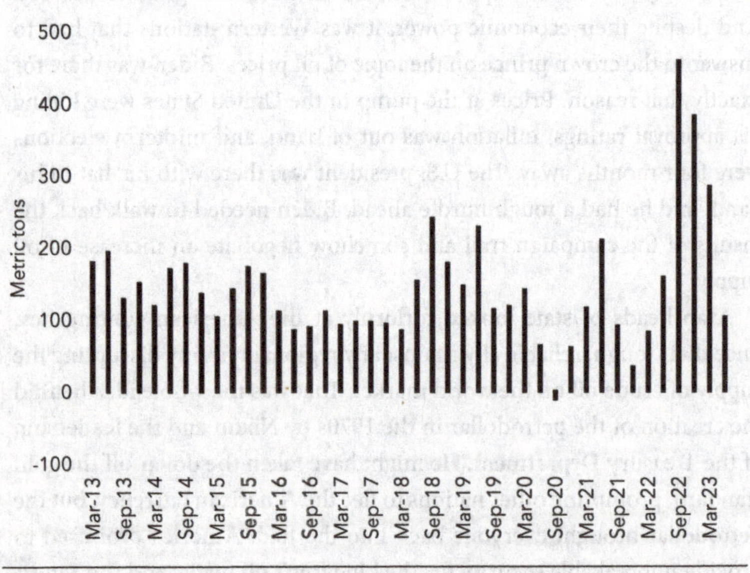

And it wasn't just Russia and China snapping up gold bars. Central banks around the world were also bingeing on the precious yellow metal, buying 1,136 tons in 2022, a volume unprecedented since at least 1950. To further clarify the picture and illustrate that the dollar is in fact losing its invulnerable status, the People's Bank of China achieved the inclusion of the yuan in the International Monetary Fund's Special Drawing Rights currency reserve basket in 2016. All of this is now paving the way for a new system of exchange in the oil markets. The petrodollar is unquestionably in decline, as Saudi Arabia is already accepting the yuan, Russian rubles, and even gold in return for its oil. On the other side of the Persian Gulf, Iran is eagerly collaborating with Russia to create a stable gold-backed coin to replace the dollar for payments in oil and gas and eventually more international trade. Russia, Iran, and Qatar together control

60 percent of the world's reserves in natural gas and are contemplating the creation of a gas cartel similar to OPEC. These are early indications that the outside world is looking very seriously for an alternative currency to the dollar. Possibly one that's backed by hard assets, like gold.

From an objective standpoint, you can't blame Saudi Arabia for diversifying. If the world fears the dollar, oil markets dependent on the petrodollar will suffer. As we speak, it is in serious discussions with the BRICS countries—Brazil, Russia, India, China, and South Africa—five nations with a combined GDP of $25 trillion. That's right in line with the GDP of the United States, but they're not saddled with crippling debt, oceans of unfunded liabilities, and ballooning trade deficits. No. These are five nations on an upward trajectory, with booming middle classes, manufacturing ambitions, or vast commodity resources. An alliance like this might be very fitting for the future king of Saudi Arabia, a leader with abundant energy and huge plans for modernizing his country, the de facto ruler with seemingly little respect for the man in the White House. Perhaps that's why, one month after the president returned home, Crown Prince Mohammed bin Salman cut oil production, raising the price per barrel once more.

The Fraying Fabric of Global Security

If the United States withdrew military protection from Saudi oil fields, any regime could gain control of the world's greatest natural resource. Saudi Arabia has a large military, with 257,000 active personnel and a budget of almost $50 billion. Nobody knows the playbook in this scenario, but it would elevate global risk, leaving control over the global price of oil at the mercy of, essentially, the highest bidder. According to Niall Ferguson, the world-famous historian who penned a biography of Henry Kissinger, America is in a cold war with communist China, and has been since 2020. He poses three questions: "Will Cold War II lead to World War III? Will the Russia-Ukraine war grow into something much larger? And if war is back, could world war also make a comeback?" These scenarios might sound far-fetched, but in actuality, war has been a great mechanism for resets throughout history. The prospect of war, a huge global conflict, is perhaps minimal, but it's worth thinking about.

INVESTORS BEWARE:
Global Efforts to Move Away from the Dollar Means a Structural Decline of the Greenback

The EU and U.S. sanctions in response to its invasion of Ukraine have driven Russia firmly into the arms of China and made it a pariah state for the West. The United States was already showing increased animus toward China in recent years, slapping tariffs on its exports and scolding it for human rights violations. Now China and Russia are spearheading the development of a system of payments that doesn't use the dollar anymore. China is actively pressuring other countries to accept bilateral yuan transactions instead of dollars, and many are all too happy to comply. In recent years China has strengthened its relationship with Saudi Arabia, and in December 2022 President Xi Jinping urged Gulf countries to use the yuan in their settlement of oil and gas purchases. This is laying the groundwork for a petroyuan system. Now the top two producers of oil in the world, Russia and Saudi Arabia, are no longer trading oil solely in dollars. Many other countries that have been sanctioned by the United States over the years are also joining an alternative global payments system; countries like Iran, Venezuela, Yemen, North Korea, and Syria are first in line. In April 2023, the BRICS indicated that they have started a project to create an alternative global payments system. Iran and Saudi Arabia have initiated the formal process to join, and ten other countries, including Mexico (a NAFTA member!), the United Arab Emirates, and Nigeria, want to join as well. In May 2023, Brazil and Argentina signed a trade agreement that excluded the dollar as payment currency. This agreement is similar to the swap agreement the countries have in place with China.

It's hard to imagine in the modern day, but the chance of one happening is not zero anymore. And the cause of most wars is money—debt, trade, and cash.

In chapter 1, we described currency pegging and trade surpluses, using sailboats to illustrate how the process works. With all this talk about energy, ETFs, and crypto, it's easy to get off track, but we need to dive back in and discuss how the United States desperately needs a steady flow of dollars back from their trading partners to finance its deficits. America operates a trade deficit every year. For most countries it's the opposite—they have a trade surplus because they export more than they import. But not the United States. And not the United Kingdom, either. These are the only two major countries with chronic trade deficits. China, as explained in great detail in chapter 1, has an enormous surplus, and it piles that money into U.S. Treasuries. And that massive amount of capital, now close to $1 trillion per year, mostly flows into the United States. Those dollars are largely used to finance the other structural deficits the United States has—namely, the gaping budget deficit. All goes well if both countries happily work together, but slap sanctions on China and threaten to decouple the two economies, and this could go sideways real fast. That's bad. Really bad. It's like an untreated wound baking in the sun. The longer it sits there, the worse it becomes.

The numbers continue to make my hair stand on end. Foreigners now collectively own more than $7.5 trillion of U.S. government debt, up from $1 trillion in 2002. (As interest rates go up, bond prices move down. The losses here are colossal.) But they're not the only ones buying the debt. In late 2008, copying Japanese monetary policy, the Federal Reserve embarked on a QE program and ended up buying as much as $5.5 trillion in Treasuries, along with $3 trillion in agency debt, over the course of about thirteen years. Social Security contributions, taken out of every American's paycheck each month, go into a trust fund that has purchased another $7.5 trillion of government debt over the years. Grand total: $20 trillion of combined government debt ownership. The Fed, Social Security, and foreigners collectively own 60 percent of the $33 trillion debt. The rest is held by domestic households and institutions. Now that Russia has invaded Ukraine, the brutal sanctions that the United States has leveled on it are starting to push foreign capital away from the dollar. In light of the inflationary environment, the timing couldn't be worse.

Because way out there on the horizon, there's a tsunami rumbling toward American shores.

The demand for U.S. Treasuries is receding—just like Lake Chad in central Africa, slowly evaporating under the equatorial sun, where the rain no longer falls as it once did. The Fed was once a trillion-dollar source of funding for the Treasury, but not anymore, as it is now—forced by inflation's sword—selling assets. The assets held by the Social Security trust fund are in decline, because more people are taking out than paying in. They, too, are gone as buyers. Foreign buyers, especially those in China and Saudi Arabia, are diversifying away from the dollar and no longer adding to their pile of U.S. debt holdings. Not even Japan, historically the largest buyer of Treasuries, buys that much anymore. Its trade surplus has all but disappeared, so it has no more need to sterilize it (recycle dollars by buying Treasuries to prevent a rise in its exchange rate, as explained in chapter 2).

So where does the demand for Treasuries come from now? They could find only a trillion dollars from domestic institutions and households, and that's not enough. Not even close. In the next two years, $11 trillion of debt comes due. That debt was borrowed at 2 percent, and it can't be paid back. Not in this life. It's money that must be borrowed again, refinanced. Rates aren't 2 percent anymore, though—they've gone up substantially. Inflation will persist this time, at least long enough to force the government to "roll over" that debt at 5 percent interest rates, possibly even more. Each percentage point of extra interest on the debt translates into $110 billion more that the government has to pay every year to service it. Three percentage points higher and the Treasury is staring down the barrel of $330 billion extra interest annually on top of the $1 trillion of yearly debt-servicing costs. When that distant tsunami comes crashing onto the shore, the government will have to make some tough choices. It can't afford higher rates, not with its current spending habits. The only option would be to cut, and to cut something big.

If households and institutions stick to their annual Treasury purchases of just $1 trillion, there will be a gap of $1.5 trillion. Markets will naturally solve this by driving up the yield on Treasuries, and that might tempt investors to pile once more into U.S. debt. But America can't afford higher yields. The $33 trillion of debt parked on the sovereign balance sheet may already cost the U.S. government close to $1 trillion in

INVESTORS BEWARE:

When Will Social Security Be Exhausted?

At the end of March 2023, the trustees who oversee the Social Security and Medicare trust funds projected that the assets in the Social Security trust fund will be depleted by 2033, one year sooner than previously anticipated. The report blamed "significant financing issues" for the shortfall. Ever since 2010, Social Security has been running at a loss, and it has worsened every year. The big drag on the fund is the number of people who must be paid, which is growing much faster than the number of people who pay into the system. The Social Security trust fund currently has $2.8 trillion in assets, but once those are exhausted, the fund will pay only 80 percent of promised benefits. At that point all the benefits will be paid directly from the revenues the government collects, but this will put an even larger drain on government expenses and leaves less money for discretionary spending, such as the military, infrastructure, education, and R&D. This could mean higher taxes or more debt issuance as the government has to pay all Social Security expenses directly from tax revenues.

2023. And that's an astronomical increase from the $500 billion it cost in 2020. It's more than the United States spends on its military budget each year.

Major foreign holders of capital can go elsewhere with their reserves. The Eurozone issued an unprecedented €550 billion of debt in 2021 and is now actively competing with the United States for funding. China is likely to convert more of its dollars into euros. It will also use some of its dollar reserves to invest and lend to emerging markets, serving two very strategic goals: to off-load dollars and to gain influence in commodity-rich countries at the same time. It could also buy more dollar-denominated commodities and products, such as Boeing and Airbus aircrafts, which cost upward of $150 million each. This would greatly reduce China's trade surplus, leaving it with far fewer dollars to recycle into American debt. China has also a grandiose policy to develop its domestic consumer market. This sounds like a noble idea, but the ulterior motive behind it is to reduce the gaping trade surplus. If the Chinese consumer spends more, it should increase demand for everything from oil to Hermès bags. This will reduce the trade surplus that China has to plow back into dollar-denominated assets. It is all part of China's strategy to diminish its exposure to the greenback.

Complacency blinded America to the external economic threats of the bond market, threats brewing miles from its shores. Sanctions obviously played a large role in tempting investors to park their money elsewhere, beyond the once-gold-plated bond market of the U.S. Treasury. Today the risks are only mounting, and one major place they are coming from is high-quality debt from Europe, which is offering a kind of bond it never has before, one considered safe enough to rival even the U.S. Treasury. It's called a *mutualization bond,* which means that all the member states of the Eurozone are collective guarantors of the bond—all eleven countries in the Eurozone backstopping one another's debt. In other words, German taxpayers are now backstopping the bonds to finance Italy's chronic budget deficits. In 2019, this would have been unthinkable—because Eurozone countries operated their own fiscal policy regimes, they issued their own debt. After COVID, though, collective debt offerings became a reality. These mutualization bonds will be issued annually for the next eight years, and each year they will raise $100 billion, for a total of $800 billion.

So each year, this European bond will take away $100 billion of potential capital from the United States. That's not to mention all the other debt the countries of the Eurozone are trying to issue in the wake of COVID. We estimate they're already taking away $300 billion per year from the U.S. Treasury market. Think of the international bond market as a group of salespeople competing for business, each one vying for the attention of buyers. Global fixed-income investors need to put their money somewhere, preferably in a safe place with an acceptable yield and sufficient liquidity. That is typically why the bonds of the Western, democratic countries are so attractive. Especially the Treasury bonds of the United States. At least, until now.

The U.S. government's endless litany of sanctions and threats has driven away the most reliable group of buyers the U.S. government ever had, and in their absence, yields need to rise further. But that's unbearable. The country could never afford that. The government is in a total bind, and spending cuts must be made. But where? Will politicians cut entitlements? No way. That would be political suicide. Will they slash defense spending? They might have to. But that would further erode America's superpower status and, in turn, risk more geopolitical turmoil and weaken the dollar. After all, it's those impregnable warships that keep the currency a tower of international strength. The government has effectively placed itself on the angry waters of ancient Greece, right between the mythological Scylla and Charybdis—the six-headed monster and the swirling torrent of ocean strong enough to swallow a hundred-thousand-ton aircraft carrier. The position will be almost impossible to navigate without creating a market rupture, without setting off a giant chain reaction.

In the long run one option might be to resort to yield curve control, which is the final stage in the QE cycle. Ironically, this would again be a policy tool that is adopted from the Bank of Japan. The Fed will have to control rates by buying more bonds, and those rates will be held at a fixed level of, say, 5 percent, or somewhere near there, inflation be damned. This means more liquidity that can inflate another bubble, but it will likely exert more downward pressure on the dollar. How do we know this? Look at Japan, where yield curve control is now a key factor in the relentless decline of the Japanese yen. As they often say in Great Britain when describing a total disaster, in typical sardonic understatement, "They've really done it this time."

As hedge fund legend Kyle Bass once told me, "Buying gold is just purchasing a put [a bet] against the idiocy of the political cycle. It's that simple." Currency is only paper, a promissory note, backed, in the case of America, by an unrivaled military—in range, surveillance, and firepower. But the U.S. government has overstepped the line. It has meddled too much in foreign affairs. And it is losing the bet on globalization. The manufacturing base is gone. Countries have become rich off American trade, and the dollar reserves, a once-unassailable tour de force of financial strength, are in decline. We have established that higher rates and inflation are largely unaffordable options for the Treasury. Any increases will be lethal additions to America's annual fiscal bill. Already in 2023

INVESTORS TAKE NOTE:

Gold Remains Deeply Undervalued Relative to the Stock of Outstanding Dollars

The best estimate of the total available gold that is above the ground is 209,000 metric tons, or 6.7 billion troy ounces. Gold theoretically never gets lost, so all the gold that has ever been mined in history is still available. Whether it is locked in an Egyptian pyramid or an Aztec temple, worn on the finger of a newlywed, within the reflective layer of a DVD player, or secured deep in the vault of Fort Knox, gold never evaporates or disappears as scrap back to the earth. This is part of the reason why gold is generally considered to be a premier store of value. Since gold is valued in U.S. dollars, what would be the equilibrium value of gold? In other words, how much would gold be worth if all the dollars in the world bought all the gold in the world? The M2 is a measure of the total U.S. money supply—currency, time deposits, and money market funds—reported on a weekly basis. The dollars outstanding as of June 2023 totaled $20.6 trillion. If we divide that by the total amount of gold aboveground, gold has an equilibrium value of $3,300 per troy ounce. Compare this with the current price of around $2,000 per troy ounce.

There is a strong relationship between gold and the dollar. Gold is priced in dollars and is also part of the capital account of each country's balance of payments. Because the dollar is still the world's global reserve currency, gold is generally accepted as a substitute for the dollar, and this is one important reason why gold is extremely negatively correlated with the dollar. Accordingly, valuing gold in terms of outstanding dollars is a common approach to derive an equilibrium value.

more than $7 trillion is maturing and will need to be refinanced at higher rates. But as investors, we want to know one thing: *What's the trade?* And we can answer that.

We've seen central governments, especially in China and Russia, increase their gold reserves in an untethered fashion over the last year. This trend is set to continue as dollar reserves get chopped down and holdings in precious metals (silver, gold, platinum, and palladium) flourish. They're a well-known hedge, the precious metals, and when the dollar declines, precious metals tend to do very well. Great places to park capital are companies like Barrick Gold, Newmont, Hecla Mining, Sibanye-Stillwater, and Impala Platinum. These are leading miners of gold, silver, palladium, and platinum. There are good ETFs such as VanEck Gold Miners ETF (GDX) and iShares Silver Trust (SLV), too. That's how to get exposed to a multitude of names.

Besides their appeal, the platinum-group metals (PGMs) could become key in the green economy transition. PGMs are used in the purification of hydrogen for use in fuel cells that can power cars, trucks, buses, and even ships or planes. Although there are other technologies to purify hydrogen, the PGMs appear to be the lowest-capital-cost option. The amount of platinum or palladium needed to run a vehicle on hydrogen fuel cells is around 30 to 60 grams, whereas a conventional catalytic converter uses only around 5 grams. In other words, a hydrogen-powered car uses between six and ten times as much palladium or platinum as a gasoline-powered car. If we take the most bullish scenario, which assumes all cars annually sold will be powered by fuel cells, global automotive demand for PGMs will increase fivefold and will far exceed the volumes of these metals being mined per year.

This is, of course, the long-term bull case for PGMs and it will take decades to play out. But fuel cells have great potential and could even be more efficient than battery-powered EVs, especially for heavy-duty transportation such as trucks and ships. Governments in Europe, the United States, and China are all investing in the technology, with billions of dollars in the United States alone from the bipartisan infrastructure and inflation reduction legislation. The West is pushing fuel cell technology and hydrogen-based storage as an essential strategy to achieve the net zero 2050 targets, and hydrogen will become an important driver for PGMs in the coming years. Global output of platinum and palladium has remained virtually unchanged since 2010. There is thirty times more gold aboveground than there is platinum. If all the platinum ever mined in the history of humanity was poured into an Olympic-size swimming pool, the level would be well below your knees; gold, in contrast, would fill more than three pools. So the world is woefully unprepared for such a demand surge, especially given that Russia is responsible for as much as 40 percent of total palladium and 15 percent of total platinum supplies. This is why we are so bullish on major PGM miners such as Sibanye-Stillwater and Impala Platinum. The world is going to need a lot more platinum and palladium in the coming years, and will increasingly rely on miners outside Russia to meet their demand. In recent years, platinum's price per ounce has ranged from $600 to $1,300; a decade from now we could see prices in a whole new neighborhood, somewhere between $1,800 and $3,900.

Gold and Silver Mining M&A

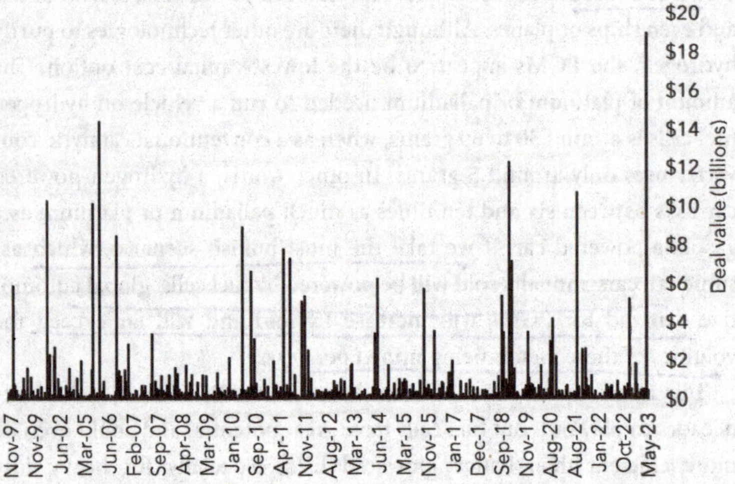

The great migration of capital, moving from growth stocks into value stocks, has only just begun. We are in the first inning. And as every rally in the growth space fails, it will bring more disappointment to those investors who are still searching for the promised land. One day they will grudgingly pack their bags and walk into the value sector. They will see the rally happening in gold, silver, platinum, and palladium. And that's where they will park their capital, occasionally looking back over their shoulders at the stocks that broke their hearts. But their investments in precious metals will drive prices up even further, as the growth sector of yesteryear stays trapped where the trade winds converge, right down near the equator, in a place famous throughout the international world of sailing, where the wind seldom blows and the rains rarely stop falling. That place is called the doldrums. The future is not growth; it's value. And it's not just precious metals. It's not just oil and gas. There will also be a big stampede for cold, hard assets, which brings us to the final chapter in this tale of global finance and investing.

INVESTORS BEWARE:
Commercial Real Estate Poses Another Major Threat to the U.S. Dollar

If an economic shock hits the United States, and the Fed is forced to reverse monetary policy quickly, that is when the dollar can weaken dramatically. This is when emerging-market equities (EEM: iShares MSCI Emerging Markets ETF), gold (GLD: SPDR Gold Shares ETF), and silver (SLV: iShares Silver Trust) can really outperform other asset classes. Look at what happened after previous rate hike cycles. In June 2000, the Fed completed its last rate hike for that cycle; gold appreciated 47 percent in the next four years. In June 2006, the Fed raised rates for the last time in that cycle, and gold was 50 percent higher by 2008. In December 2018, the Fed finished off that rate-hiking cycle; gold was 47 percent higher by the third quarter of 2020. In all three instances the central bank pushed up front-end rates and eventually broke something. In a weaker dollar regime, funds like the VanEck J. P. Morgan EM Local Currency Bond ETF (EMLC) typically flourish. The portfolio is loaded with emerging-market government bonds. The last three times the Fed was forced by the beast inside the market (an economic or credit-risk shock) to reverse course (2016, 2018, and 2020), the returns were 17 to 35 percent.

So what is the Fed breaking now, and where does the dollar go from here? As of mid-2023, the U.S. regional banking system is in intensive care, but so far it's primarily interest-rate risk. As interest rates move higher, bond prices move in the opposite direction. Apple's CFO, Luca Maestri, might be the best bond seller who's ever lived. In 2020, Luca backed up the truck and sold billions of dollars of bonds, taking advantage of rock-bottom rates and a Fed backstopping credit market. In twelve months, Apple sold nearly $28 billion worth of bonds at record-low interest rates. Some of these bonds traded as low as 54 cents on the dollar in October 2022 as the Fed had pushed interest rates to the moon. Who wants to buy a long-duration bond like that with a measly 2.4 percent coupon when a six-month Treasury bond pays 5 percent? Nobody! This is why the price went down and the losses on these $28 billion of Apple bonds would be in the neighborhood of $12 billion. This is just one example that illustrates the staggering losses across the banking system on the bond books. If the Fed keeps rates up here, the banks are sitting on hundreds of billions of dollars of losses in U.S. Treasuries, mortgage-backed securities, and commercial real estate loans. When will the banks start recognizing these losses? When do they have to?

I tweeted in March 2023: "Dear Central Banks—When you suppress the true, market-driven cost of capital for longer and longer periods of time, you incentivize the yield reach across the banking system. Then you juice rates 500bps in 13 months to 'fight' inflation and light it all on fire." The longer that central banks distort the true cost of capital, the more they incentivize bad behavior in markets and enable idiocy. When you dig beneath the surface, you find that all those years of capital misallocation created a lot of victims when the risk-free rate moves from 1 percent to 5 percent. Few know where the proverbial bodies are buried, but some investors saw the regional-bank train wreck miles away, maybe too far away.

One of those investors was Paul Hackett. In early March 2023 we

AAPL 30-Year Bond

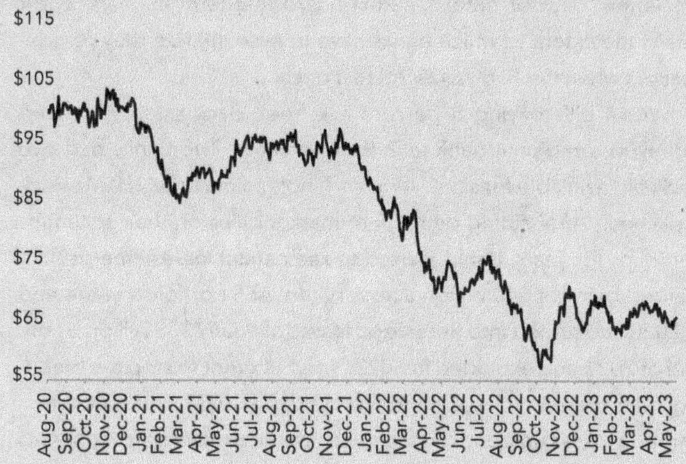

received an urgent direct message in our Bloomberg chat room with institutional investors: "Larry, we need to talk. It's urgent."

Paul "Hack" Hackett, chief investment officer at Sidus Investment Management, has been a friend of ours for years. He's a thoughtful investor with a deep skill set across credit and equities, especially the financials. Our assistant, Valentina Sanchez-Cuenca, set up a call with our team of analysts and Hack. It was an eye-opening phone call, one we had been expecting, with many of the missing pieces to the puzzle.

"Guys," Hack told us, "I think the U.S. banking system will lose $500 billion, maybe $1 trillion in deposits this year. The Lehman crisis in 2008 sowed the seeds for a widespread bank run in 2023."

Hack was short the banks—Silicon Valley Bank and First Republic for all of Q1, and was in a lot of pain because these banks kept going up. After delivering an impressive performance to its investors in 2022, Sidus was down high single digits going into March. Hack never wavered, highly confident his bearish bet on the banks was about to ring the register. He explained that once the Federal Reserve had backstopped U.S. money market funds and the too-big-to-fail banks in 2008, any credit stress in the regional banks would accelerate "deposit beta." I hadn't heard that term in years, but it means the extent to which banks have to raise the rate they pay depositors when the Fed raises interest rates.

"With T-bills paying 5 percent risk free," Hack said, "why keep money in a regional bank at 2 to 3 percent?" The banks had two pockets: "available for sale" (AFS) and "hold to maturity" (HTM), Hack explained. "After sitting on mark-to-market gains on their securities portfolios for years, banks started to see painful losses emerge. Unrealized gains of $40 billion across banks' AFS portfolios at the end of 2020 had turned into unrealized losses of nearly $33 billion by the end of 2021 and exploded in 2022." In an attempt to stop the bleeding, many banks reclassified AFS securities as HTM. This meant recognizing losses up front, but the switch would protect balance sheets from further losses as bond prices continued to fall. Hack reminded our team that the cost of credit default protection was starting to diverge between large money-center banks and small regional players.

The markets were speaking: Five-year CDSs, the cost of default protection, were moving much faster and getting more expensive at a number of regional banks.

"In recent years," Hack said, "under normal conditions, the credit risk at regional banks is much lower than the big banks. But I think the regional banks have four times more exposure to commercial real estate relative to the big banks. CRE loans make up close to 30 percent of assets at the regionals, compared with only 6 percent at big banks. Regional bank New York Community Bancorp has close to 60 percent of total assets in CRE and Webster Financial and PacWest are near 40 percent."

He was looking at CRE loans relative to a bank's total loan book. Total CRE loans outstanding are up 100 percent over the last decade across the banking system. Loans worth hundreds of billions of dollars were made to borrowers at 1.5 percent to 3 percent rates of interest. Now think of our Apple bond, mentioned above, and Luca Maestri grinning from ear to ear. All these bonds were a lot lower now.

Hack concluded, "If the Fed keeps the funds rate near 5 percent for another five to six months, the losses will be staggering. Another federal bailout may be needed."

God bless him, Hack went on to have a record month in March 2023 and now has his eyes on the insurance companies. Default protection costs on Lincoln Financial and MetLife are trading at historical highs. There is more pain to come. Interest-rate risk in 2023 was expected to turn to credit risk in 2024. Another period of banking turmoil would force the Fed to bring out its playbook of unconventional market accommodation. The market will see this coming from a mile away and sell the dollar long before the Fed starts pressing the panic button. If a crisis is global, the dollar is a safe haven, but this is primarily a U.S. problem, to the detriment of the dollar.

Before all this happened, we did see a canary in the coal mine: We have a model that measures the rate of change and performance divergence between the SPDR S&P Regional Banking ETF (KRE) and the SPDR S&P 500 ETF (SPY). By March 2, 2023, the KRE was underperforming the market year to date by 2.5 percentage points and this accelerated to 11 percentage points underperformance by March 9.

Sheikh Rashid bin Saeed al Maktoum of Dubai once said to his son Sheikh Mohammed bin Rashid al Maktoum, "My grandfather rode a camel, my father rode a camel, I ride a Mercedes, my son rides a Land Rover, and my grandson is going to ride a Land Rover, but my great-grandson is going to have to ride a camel again." The coming fate of the U.S. dollar will come with a generational impact.

At some point, the coming commodity boom will see a counter-reaction—reigniting inflation in what could be described as the "afterburner stage." When most investors finally migrate out of financial assets into hard assets and adjust to a world of sustained higher prices, the Fed will step in. The central bankers will mandate an increase in bank reserves and force our largest financial institutions to hold more U.S. Treasuries. In this world, the Fed ought to raise interest rates, perhaps even *above* long-term inflation expectations, to seek their natural level, but their hands will be tied. Interest on the U.S. national debt will crowd out nearly all discretionary spending in that world. As Tytler warned us more than 150 years ago, there is no political will for that outcome.

The only release valve will be the U.S. dollar. Bond yields could spiral out of control. The Fed will be forced into yield-curve control, which will crash the strong dollar. In turn, this will cause a capital flight from the United States, like a great flock migrating south for the winter.

9

Cold, Hard Assets—the Portfolio for the Next Decade

The Democratic Republic of the Congo (DRC), the largest country in sub-Saharan Africa, equivalent in size to Western Europe, is home to more mineral resources than almost anywhere else on earth. The country is like the Saudi Arabia of the green and high-tech industry, because 70 percent of the world's cobalt supply sits just beneath the surface along the eastern border.

Not too long ago, engineers discovered the game-changing properties of cobalt in rechargeable lithium-ion batteries, smartphones, and electric cars. Cobalt has the ideal configuration that facilitates the stability of the battery at high-energy densities. A higher energy density means that the battery can hold more energy. More energy in the battery is crucial because it makes EVs competitive with gasoline cars and keeps iPhones running for twenty hours per charge.

The entire eastern border of the DRC is buzzing with mining activity. Gécamines, the state-owned mining company; Glencore, the company founded decades ago by fugitive commodity trader Marc Rich; and various Chinese miners are all feverishly digging for the cherished commodity. But a horrifying humanitarian crisis is taking place in the areas just outside the perimeter of these industrial open pit mines. There, a web of independent, so-called artisanal shafts is run by locals that complement the production of the major cobalt mining companies. Thousands of local workers, including more than forty thousand children, in addition to women and the elderly, work in these makeshift mines, often for more than twelve hours per day, according to Siddharth Kara, a fellow at Harvard Kennedy School and author of the *New York Times* bestseller *Cobalt Red.* He has spent four years in the Congo and documented the atrocious working conditions in the artisanal cobalt mining industry.

Deep in the holes, more than one hundred feet down, men are spread out in precariously unsupported tunnels, working with flashlights, clawing away at pockets of cobalt with crowbars. At any minute, the tunnels could collapse and nobody would ever save them. Once the cobalt is captured in rocks called heterogenite, the workers must carry the ninety-pound bags for many miles to local buyers, called *comptoirs,* who pay them just $1 per bag.

Although the global mining companies are making a killing, very few in the DRC are getting rich off the cobalt trade. The money is ripped out of their land and sold on the global market to the technology giants and makers of electric cars. Hardly a dime goes into the local economy. The mining pollutes the water supply, kills young men (who die in mine collapses or from toxic cobalt fumes), and strips small villages of their dignity. Despite its billions of dollars in mineral resources, the DRC remains one of the poorest countries in the world. It is also the most exploited, because there's a great force behind the cobalt industry, perhaps the most powerful force in global trade. It is without emotion, is blind to suffering, and has no face. Its name is *unstoppable demand.*

Shaking Hands with Charlie Munger

In the overarching cycles of markets, cycles that last a decade or more, there is a pendulum that swings between growth and value. Timing that pendulum is the key to long-term wealth, and on January 1, 2022, it completed its fourteen-year journey and was at the pinnacle of its arc, in the furthest reaches of the growth phase. For a brief pause, it was at rest. Then the pendulum set off on its long, arcing swing to the other side, toward a forgotten meadow, to a place investors had left many years ago. For the first time since the dot-com bust, the gate to that meadow opened as the first movers arrived—men like David Einhorn and David Tepper, investors who saw trouble in the meme stocks and crypto assets, money managers who no longer believed central bank accommodation could continue.

Among the small gathering of financiers walking through that gate was a man nearly one hundred years old, a University of Michigan Wolverine and a graduate of Harvard Law, class of 1948. In fact, the man wasn't walking through the gate at all; he was holding it open for the other guests, like someone who had been alone for a long time. In his left hand, he held a vintage oxblood leather briefcase, and the dark gray jacket of his suit was slung over his shoulder. On his cheerful face he wore a pair of stylish oval tortoiseshell specs. The man's name was Charles Thomas Munger, but most people simply called him Charlie.

I first met him in 2013 in Omaha, Nebraska. This was his hometown and the place where he met his business partner, Warren Buffett. Together they built the most successful investment company in the world, Berkshire Hathaway, and it was at their legendary annual shareholder meeting that Charlie arranged a one-on-one meeting with me. He had just read my book, *A Colossal Failure of Common Sense.* I suspected he wanted to meet me not because I'd blown the lid off Lehman Brothers but because he disliked the management of the company so much. They determinedly went against all of Charlie's investing beliefs, and that's not to mention their questionable ethics. Maybe he liked the book because a few of the men who tried to save the firm right before the Grim Reaper arrived were Wolverines like Mr. Munger. Whatever his real reasons, I couldn't believe a Hall of Fame value investor like him wanted to meet with a chap from Falmouth, Massachusetts, who had started life as a pork chop salesman along the Cape Cod Canal. That's me, by the way.

It was a Saturday morning in May when I walked into the CenturyLink Center Omaha, a stadium made of mirrored glass and white cement, like something from the Bauhaus movement. Over the years it has hosted the Olympic swimming trials, professional bull-riding events, and NCAA Division I men's basketball tournaments. The size of the place stunned me—a million square feet, nineteen thousand seats, plus another 250,000 square feet of exhibition halls and meeting space. Walking down the wide hallways and entering the auditorium felt like arriving at a World Series game at Fenway, with "Big Papi" at the plate facing ninety-five-mile-an-hour heat. For me, this was no different.

The day lasted close to six hours, with Buffett and Munger on the stage telling jokes and stories, followed by the longest question-and-answer session I had ever known. All around the stadium, shareholders asked their questions of the men on the stage. It was also the most transparency I had witnessed in all my years on Wall Street, especially after Lehman Brothers, which had collapsed under a pile of off-balance-sheet obfuscation. This was different, and as I looked around at the rapt audience, it became clear why Warren Buffett and Charlie Munger, above anyone else, had captured the hearts of investors all over America.

The next day was cold and brisk. I marched across the icy parking lot and into the nearby Marriott Hotel. I walked quickly through the busy foyer crowded with people in business attire. I glanced left, through a glass door, and saw Buffett locked in a meeting with representatives of sovereign wealth funds, guys who looked after their countries' investments. Across the hall was his friend and bridge partner Bill Gates, who was holding court in a room packed with pension fund managers. I kept moving down the hallway, shaking off the nerves. Then I walked into a room and waited, all alone. It was right here that I was scheduled to meet one of the greatest value investors in the world. I glanced at the austere walls. There was nothing to take my mind off the next half hour. And then, like a miracle, Charlie Munger walked right into the room with his personal assistant, Doerthe Obert, who had called me all those months ago to arrange this meeting.

He was affable and about as down-to-earth as any other Nebraska native. His handshake was powerful, the kind you would expect from a World War II veteran. And he is a market contrarian, a man who never veers from his core investing principle: value. Never tempted by the fashionable, the flashy, or lofty valuations, Charlie sticks rigidly to old-fashioned common sense and puts a lot of emphasis on good management. People such as Buffett and Munger almost seem out of touch when investments like crypto take over the world, when managers like Cathie Wood charge into highly speculative growth companies and grab headlines.

We covered myriad topics in the meeting, from Lehman Brothers to how Charlie loved my book, and then value stocks and healthy balance sheets. We wrapped things up with one of his most profitable mantras. And it was something that had taken me twenty years to figure out.

"Human nature," said Charlie, "is your greatest enemy at market lows.

At your absolute climax of fear, you must do the exact opposite of what you want to do. And once you've done that, leave it alone. Because the real money is in the waiting. Larry, the hardest thing to do is stare at a screen all day and do nothing."

The ultimate lessons? First, trade and invest less. Sit back and wait for those top two or three opportunities that come along each year. Second, measure your level of conviction and allocate your capital accordingly. Above all, never trade or invest out of boredom or a desire to find something to do.

As we walked out the door that day, Charlie said, "Larry, keep up your high level of passion for markets. Growing wiser is a combination of humility and diligent curiosity. Without the first, the second is useless." What a man, and what a meeting in Omaha!

All market valuations are ultimately governed by either inflation or disinflation. The latter causes growth stocks to reach dizzying valuations, where the entire market is filled with people buying stocks at twenty times sales, hoping they will go to forty times sales. Eventually, those people sell their holdings to even greater fools. And those fools in turn hope the stock will go to sixty times sales and they can sell their position to still greater fools for eighty times sales. And so on and so forth, until the market becomes another tulip bubble, on the back of this "greater fool theory." But during times of inflation, the place where we are today, growth gets wiped out, and it wipes out the greater fools, too, while the rest start to flock to companies based on value metrics.

If you look at all the cash cows of 2022, they far outperformed Cathie Wood's darlings. Buffett's and Munger's Berkshire shares finished the inflation-rattled year up 4 percent, compared to a -67 percent plunge for ARK Innovation shares. And once again, this goes back to the Federal Reserve and to central bank accommodation. Growth regimes flourish primarily when the Fed supports markets, without the worry of inflation. But once that tyrant wakes from its long winter of hibernation, it drives money into value stocks and forces the Fed away from its dovish policies. That's when the battle begins. And that's what Jerome Powell has been fighting in 2022 and will continue to fight for many years.

Inflation weakens the value of cash, and it also compresses market multiples. In a deflationary period, a hot tech stock might trade at a price-to-earnings ratio of 35:1, whereas that of a tried-and-true oil stock might be just 7:1. So when market multiples compress, technology and growth stocks have a lot further to fall.

On the other hand, inflation drives up the value of commodities. They preserve their value when fiat currencies are being eaten away by inflation. That's when people want a hedge against inflation, and hard assets become the most popular of all. That's when investors buy stocks like Newmont, Cameco, Alcoa, Arch Resources, Energy Transfer, Teck Resources, U.S. Steel, Chevron, and Southwest Energy—stocks with exposure to precious metals and hard assets, or the established giants of the industrial sector. But it's a slow transition. First, months of discontent must pummel growth-stock investors, until they finally learn their lesson. Right now we might only be at the top of the second inning. This story has a long way to go. Some people believe it could last for twenty years. That's why Charlie Munger was right there holding that gate open, welcoming the first movers to that forgotten investment landscape, one that will last for a decade or more. The great market pendulum is swinging once more into the value sector and into cold, hard assets.

Bloomberg Commodity Index vs. S&P

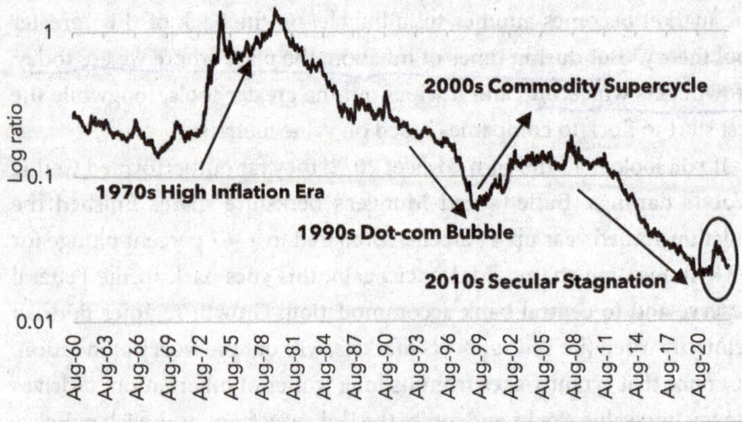

For investors who wanted to expose themselves to less financial risk during the 2010–2020 period, the "risk parity" portfolio of 60 percent stocks and 40 percent bonds was highly popular. This portfolio is dead, in our view. In the 2020–2030 regime, 10 percent cash, 40 percent stocks,

30 percent bonds, and 20 percent commodities makes a lot more sense to us. Yes, if a recession hits, that's deflationary. However, tax receipts will plunge at the same time, and the government's money printing will have to surge again from a much higher trajectory going forward. That creates the foundation for a sustained inflationary regime, and an entirely new thought process is needed around portfolio construction.

In chapter 5, I described the pending global energy crisis and the constant battle between green energy and fossil fuels, which is really morphing into a tussle between East and West. Asia will be a huge driver of fossil fuel demand—oil, natural gas, and coal. And so will the West, but politicians can't admit that yet. When we mention coal, it's important to remember that there are two types: thermal coal, which provides heat and electricity by driving those big steam turbines at the power stations, and metallurgical coal. The latter makes steel, by first melting the coal in a furnace at 1,100 degrees Celsius until it becomes pure carbon, then adding it to a blast furnace with iron ore.

We realize nobody would pass an exam with this quasi-scientific explanation, but that's not important for us. As value investors, we need to know that half the planet is on an upward trajectory, and the demand for steel will be insatiable in Asian and African construction markets. The best stock to own in this space is BHP Billiton, a company with a $175 billion market cap providing the building blocks for the modern world—nickel for the EV revolution, copper for electrical grids, and iron ore and metallurgical coal for steel. In 2022, BHP produced 29.1 million tons of metallurgical coal. We see nothing on the horizon to slow this down. It also pays an 8 percent dividend, so it's a marvelous place to deploy cash. That alone will dodge the persistent inflation coming right at us.

Let's talk about solar. Years ago, the panels used to be one-sided pieces of plastic with some base metals on the interior to conduct electricity, along with 20 grams of silver. But nowadays, the latest panels coming out of China are two-sided. This gives a huge industrial use case for silver, not just as a metal to hedge against inflationary pressures on the currency but also as a serious contender in clean energy. Looking into the next decade, the Silver Institute projects that between 2024 and 2030, solar demand for silver will vary between 70 and 80 million troy ounces per year, or 8 percent of the annual silver production in the world. In the silver-mining space, our strongest conviction is about Hecla Mining Company, founded in 1891 and now the biggest silver miner in the United States. Hecla is also the oldest silver-mining company trading on the New York Stock Exchange, and its mines include Greens Creek, Alaska, and Lucky Friday, Idaho—the latter one of the top seven primary silver mines in the world, seventy-five years old and projected to have another thirty years of life. Then it has Casa Berardi in Quebec, an area with solid government regulation and geopolitical safety, and the giant operation at Keno Hill in the Yukon Territory, an area so vast and so mineral-rich that it has the potential to become the largest silver producer in Canada. That allusion to geopolitical risk is critical because mining is a global game, with war chests of money on the line.

We are fortunate to call one of the top investors in the global resource (global metal and mining) space our trusted adviser. Longtime hard asset adviser Adrian Day will tell anyone about the big dangers of the mining business. He has spent his career studying the sector, an interest sparked at the London School of Economics, and he told me the entire business is pockmarked with risks, some unforeseen, but mostly well-understood risks involving governance, local communities, taxation, corruption, transportation, and political uncertainty. If you're not in the mining business, stay away from small enterprises. That is pretty much the highest risk you can take as an investor. You don't need to go to every wedding, but you do need to avoid funerals. Stick with the giants, ones with multiple mines in their portfolio spread out across the globe. Some will be in areas of political uncertainty, others in the African jungle, some in South America with no transportation. But things can really go wrong.

A civil war could shut down operations for months. This will cost a small operation its life, but a giant in the mining game can take the pain. It's like having 5 percent of your portfolio crash by 50 percent. It really doesn't matter. But if your entire portfolio crashes, it's death. Or a government might raise taxes on the mining company, charging twice what it once promised. A perfect example is Chile, until recently a nirvana for the global mining giants and responsible for 25 percent of global copper mining. For decades the country invited the biggest mining companies to explore its abundant copper, gold, molybdenum, and lithium reserves. BHP, Anglo American, Rio Tinto—all the mining giants have big operations there. Then in the spring of 2023 the newly elected government

INVESTORS TAKE NOTE:

Adrian Day's Six Investing Signs to Watch

1. Underinvestment Bias

"In Q3 2023," Adrian Day told our team, "the XAU [Philadelphia Gold and Silver Index] is cash-flow-positive. This is a staggering fact relative to a heavy capital-intensive industry." As in the uranium and natural gas space, over the last decade a lot of CFOs made poor investments. If you are sitting in their seat today, and you just watched your last two bosses get fired, your capital discipline approach to making investments (capital expenditures) is going to be far more conservative. This is classic behavioral psychology across the commodity space, and it fuels large boom-and-bust cycles. CFOs tend to overinvest at the top of the cycle—see 2011 in the gold space; see 2014 in the oil-and-gas space. At the bottom of the cycle, there is a classic underinvestment bias. Bottom line, across much of the commodity space, the balance sheets are much stronger than the last cycle. And most important of all, underinvestment, or less supply, will support the foundation of the next multiyear bull market.

2. Asset Location

Clearly, there are always high-risk spots in the mining space globally, but Adrian sees a shift toward a multipolar world where asset location premiums may start to expand. "Barrick Gold Corporation has done a great job at spreading out their jurisdictional risk," he told me. "They have mines in some hot spots, but their production trends overall are diversified." Across the commodity space, we see a trend where high-quality safe asset locations will start to develop a premium globally. Access is key.

3. Production Capacity

Adrian looks at assets and asks himself, "Okay, how much gas is left in this tank?" For instance, how many years of quality gold and silver production are left in a company's key mines? Sixteen of the world's twenty largest gold miners—including top producers such as Newmont Corp., Barrick Gold Corp., AngloGold Ashanti Ltd., and Kinross Gold Corp.— saw their aggregate remaining years of production fall between the 2010 and 2019 period. At the end of 2019, Kinross had just nine years remaining, down dramatically from twenty-four years at the start of the decade.

4. Price to Free Cash Flow

"As we sit here in the second half of 2023, looking back forty years," Adrian told me, "the price to free cash flow across the gold and silver mining space is around the 90th percentile." In other words, in the top 10 percent if you look at the equity market capitalization of the gold mining companies relative to the free cash flow. Historically, this is an attractive entry point. Remember, there are large cap, small cap, and pure high-risk exportation companies, so measuring the risk is difficult. Most retail investors are far better off in a fund like Adrian's or an ETF.

5. Price to NAV

Adrian's team looks at the equity market capitalization of any company against the ground reserves and total value of the assets. Again, at this point in time, stocks are cheap relative to NAV historically.

6. Maybe Most Important—Management

"We look for low turnover in the C-suite," Adrian told me. "One of the most dangerous phrases in investment might be 'I am going to step down and spend more time with the family.' Larry, it's all about a history of execution. Poor management teams overpromise and underdeliver. And if there are consistent misses,* relative to a prior forecast, there very well could be more there than meets the eye. Dr. Dennis Mark Bristow is a first ballot Hall of Famer at Barrick. Over the years

*How to listen when markets speak? If there are consistent misses on earnings, they probably have big cost overruns and are delivering the bad news one drop at a time, spreading it out over two to three quarters. There are so many tricks in this trade to be on the lookout for. This applies to many different stocks across different sectors.

he's been exceptionally talented on the execution front, and he has a unique ability in managing risk in some of the unfriendly hot spots around the planet. What a fine talent. Sean Boyd at Agnico is another standout. AEM equity has a $24 billion market capitalization and only $2 billion of debt; we think they can do $1 billion to $1.2 billion free cash flow in 2024. He has put them in a nice spot ahead of the next up cycle."

announced that new lithium contracts would be public-private partnerships in which the state has a majority control over mining. The announcement caused a shock wave through the mining world, and the stocks of the two largest lithium miners in the country, Química and Albemarle, plunged by 17 percent and 11 percent, respectively, in one day.

This is not the only example. One of the largest copper mines in the world is Indonesia's Grasberg mine. For decades copper and gold giant Freeport-McMoRan, based in Phoenix, Arizona, mined the property in a joint venture with the government in Jakarta. The deal was forged in the Suharto era in the 1960s, but the new progressive government in Jakarta has been using the expiring contracts to wrest control over mines away from the international mining companies. Freeport-McMoRan used to own more than 90 percent of Grasberg, but in 2018 the Indonesian government won the battle over control, and now it owns just 51 percent of the mine. Late last year, even Panama, which is one of the very few pro-American countries left in Latin America, forced First Quantum to halt operations in the giant Cobre Panamá copper mine for months over a quarrel about royalty payments. Another example is South Africa, which for years has been working toward an accelerated redistribution of land and mines to the Black majority in the country.

For decades, miners have been dealing with the occasional local uprising: roadblocks with machete-wielding and machine-gun-toting rebels who prevent workers from getting to the mine. This has always been a risk, but one that is dwarfed by the risk of expropriation or forced ownership changes. Anglo American's CEO has warned that "if ownership of mining lands is not guaranteed investors will flee." Only real insiders should invest in these small mining companies, and only if the local government is on their side. They say Murphy's Law works overtime in the mining business. Because of this, stick with the mining giants, companies that have been around for decades, with mines as old as time.

Rent Gold Companies, Do Not Marry Them

Markets are speaking to us all the time, especially in sectors like precious metals. As with crypto, people often get caught up in narratives. From

INVESTORS TAKE NOTE:

How to Value Gold Companies

Valuing gold companies is comparable to valuing other natural resource companies. We look at the amount of gold and silver the miners have in the ground. This is listed in their annual report as proven and probable reserves. We also look at the cost of each miner to take the ore out of the ground. Often, by-products of gold mining are other minerals such as copper, zinc, or lead. The miner accounts for these by-products as credits that lower the cost of mining the gold ore. The by-products therefore can improve the miner's efficiency. We therefore also consider the cash costs each miner incurs to bring the precious metal ores to the surface. The more efficient the miner is, the lower the cash costs per troy ounce. As the accompanying chart demonstrates, there is a relationship between the valuation and the cash costs, whereby miners with lower cash costs tend to have a higher valuation.

Besides gold miners, there is a separate group of gold royalty companies. These royalty companies receive a percentage of the gold production or revenue in exchange for an up-front payment. These royalty companies can use these payments to finance other mining companies, but they don't do any mining themselves. Some of the major gold royalty companies are, for example, Franco Nevada, Osisko, Royal Gold, and Sandstorm. These companies receive

April 2021 to August 2023, during the most significant currency debasement period in the history of the United States, Bitcoin lost 56 percent even though "debasement" and "ugly fiscal deficits in D.C." were touted as the main reasons to own Bitcoin by the crypto fans. It's similar in gold and silver.

Bottom line, if Uncle Sam is willing to give you 5 percent on "risk-free" one-year T-bills, this is a serious headwind for gold, especially if short-term inflation expectations start to come down. If the Fed is aggressively pulling back accommodation, hiking interest rates, no matter

Gold Miners Valuation

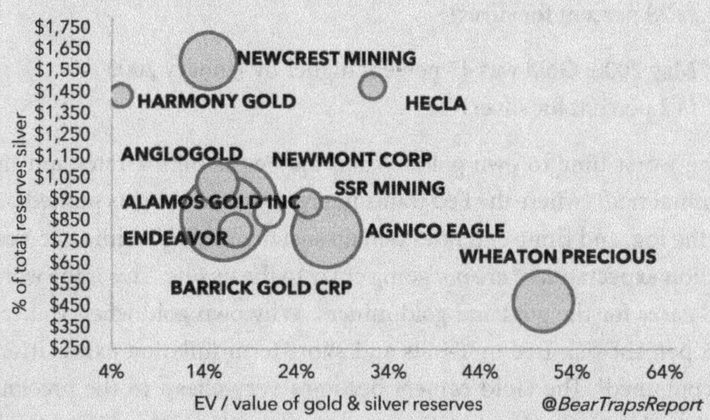

royalties from major gold mines that are operated by other mining companies. Osisko has a stake in the Eleonore mine in Canada, but the mine is operated by Goldcorp. Franco Nevada owns the Cobre Panama mine, but it lets First Quantum mine the property. Franco Nevada also owns the Candelabria mine in Chile, but Lundin Mining operates the property. Some gold royalty companies do outperform the miners by a lot, as their risk profile is lower due to minimal operational risk. Franco Nevada has appreciated by 250 percent over the last five years, whereas the Gold Miners ETF (GDX) has appreciated by only 120 percent over that period.

how sexy the narrative, that is typically a *bad* time to own precious metals, or Bitcoin for that matter. Goldbugs don't get this, or they are too emotionally attached to the narrative to care. Returns have been terrible in the last thirty years during hiking cycles, especially when the Fed enters the warm-up stage, the period when it is just starting to hike rates. Conversely, when the Fed starts to tip its hand that the rate hiking cycle is coming to an end, that is a period where gold and silver typically shine.

How did gold perform after final Fed rate hikes?

> December 2018: Gold was 47 percent higher by July 2020
> (+42 percent for silver)
>
> June 2006: Gold was 50 percent higher by February 2008
> (+78 percent for silver)
>
> May 2000: Gold was 47 percent higher by January 2003
> (+2 percent for silver)

The worst time to own gold? When the Fed is hiking rates and the "terminal rate" (where the Fed wants interest rates to be) gets pushed out into the fog, and front-end rates remain sustainably high while one-year inflation expectations* are *not* going crazy to the upside. This is the worst of all cases for the gold and gold miners. Why own gold when you can get 5 percent risk-free in T-bills and short-term inflation expectations are contained? The Gold Miners becomes very cheap to the precious metal (gold) in that world. We measure the ratio of the Gold Miners (ETF: GDX) versus Gold (ETF: GLD). For us, the buy zone for the miners is 0.15 or below and the sell zone of Gold Miners versus Gold is 0.20 and above. There are clearly times that you want to own one over the other.

Once the terminal rate comes into view and investors can see the end of the hiking cycle, gold miners start to outperform gold. Likewise, the gold miners will typically outperform gold and stocks in general. In a more extreme case, if front-end inflation expectations really start to

* Inflation expectations: Break-even inflation is the difference between the nominal yield on a fixed-rate investment and the real yield (fixed spread) on an inflation-linked investment of similar maturity and credit quality.

move higher and the Fed can't contain them, like in the 1970s, the stars are aligned for gold and the miners. In that world the gold miners will dramatically outperform gold and the overall equity market.

And this brings us to the first part of any cycle, to the moment when the best companies start to rally. They all begin this way, whether it's a growth or a value cycle. People trust the big companies first, the Goliaths of any sector, long before the smaller enterprises. If they're wrong, or too early, they are happier to hold stocks in companies that will be around for a long time. But in 2022 we saw a definitive migration into hard assets, especially into the metals and oil markets. We see huge tailwinds in precious metals as central governments unwind enormous dollar holdings and buy gold, something we discussed in chapter 8. China is unequivocally proving this to be true. According to the International Monetary Fund, by the end of Q2 2023 its holdings had risen to $136 billion, an increase of 46 percent year over year. As the world seeks an alternative to holding too many dollars, as inflation continues to eat away at global GDP, and as the net present value of all future cash flows diminishes across the corporate world, gold will continue its steady climb.

We love Barrick Gold Corporation out of Toronto, one of the world's largest gold miners, operating sixteen mines—copper and gold—in thirteen different countries. It's about as well managed as any operation in the world, and it matches our risk profile of strong diversification and limited geopolitical risk. And of the top ten gold mines in the world, Barrick owns and operates three of them, including the number one gold mine on earth—Nevada Gold Mines, which produces a steady 3.3 million ounces of gold a year. Its direct competitor is Newmont Corporation, now the largest gold miner in the world, after buying Australia's Newcrest Mining for AUD$28 billion. We recommend them both. Grab some gold-mining stocks, either company-specific or the GDX, an ETF.

This brings us neatly to the topic of electricity, one of the thorniest issues in the world, and one that a portfolio designed for the next decade cannot ignore. Right in the middle of the discussion is an unavoidable metal, which for that reason might be the most important one on earth. At temperatures of minus 400 degrees Fahrenheit, its strength increases. It's also an excellent conductor of heat and electricity. It happily resists corrosion and biofouling. I'm talking about copper. A reddish-brown metal, it is essential and highly sought after in every economy, and it's used in every power line and just about every circuit board in the industrialized world. And the big miners of copper belong in your portfolio.

The West has created a demand crisis through its dream of unloading the internal combustion engine by the year 2035 and replacing it with the electric engine. But that's way too soon, according to our estimates. We are not ready for it in terms of charging stations. The amount of copper required to pull this off would be nothing but a fantasy, so all those dreams on Capitol Hill might remain just that: dreams. Because there is currently a $2 trillion, 600,000-mile-long problem standing in the way.

I refer to the aging electric grid of the United States—and unless somebody fixes it, we'll be driving four-stroke engines until the year 3000. Therefore, I believe copper is in a long-term bull market, currently with demand increases of five hundred thousand tons a year, all without renewing one strand of the aging power lines and transformers. There is simply not enough copper and too much demand. Tesla's manufacturing projections alone will require 80 percent of the world's copper. Building charging stations and new electricity power lines and updating an American grid that is beyond its fiftieth year and will need massive renovations to accept the demands of an EV revolution cannot happen with the amount of available global copper. There simply isn't enough. And any dialogue around axing the combustion engine by 2030 is just plain silly. An electric vehicle uses four or five times the amount of copper anyway, so the entire thesis is like something Mickey Mouse invented.

If we put green energy aside, the outlook for copper is still very bullish based just on regular industrial demand. China is once again embarking on more infrastructure spending, and it still has only 350 million cars for its 1.4 billion citizens. This is not to mention the billions of people across the world's tropical regions who will demand access to air-conditioning over the next decade. Think of the power lines that will be needed, each one consisting of miles and miles of copper cabling. In the media, there is endless chatter about commodity shortages, but they don't really exist. There are shortages only at certain price points, meaning there will be new supply if the price gets high enough. Not so with copper. Its shortages are permanent. It's impossible to produce more in a short time frame. Copper mines are huge, and developing one takes years and costs more than $1 billion. The top ten mines today are all over 50 years old, some older than 100, such as Bingham Canyon southwest of Salt Lake City, with an open pit that's two and a half miles across and nearly a mile deep; it's been around for about 125 years. Then there's the high-altitude Chuquicamata mine in northern Chile, 9,300 feet above sea level. This mine is owned by Chile's Codelco and is the world's largest open-pit copper mine, spanning almost three miles from end to end and two miles wide. Operations at this South American behemoth started in 1882, making it about twenty years older than Bingham, but it's not as deep. Almost, but not quite. Big mines like these are very, very rare, and creating a new one is a long, expensive, arduous process. What's more, one of the chiefs at Freeport-McMoRan said recently, "Any new copper mine will take five to ten years before it starts producing." Therefore, when demand outstrips supply, the price must go up. This is why we're bulls, and we highly recommend getting exposure to copper through the Global X Copper Miners ETF (COPX). Most of the big hitters are inside this. Its top holding, for example, is Antofagasta PLC—the operator of the Chuquicamata mine.

An alternative play on copper could be via aluminum. For certain applications, copper can be substituted with aluminum for the transmission of electricity. If the copper shortages become too extreme, the industry will have no choice but to resort to more substitution. By 2035, the copper supply shortfall could be as much as 9.9 million metric tons, representing 20 percent of what is needed to meet global 2050 net-zero goals. This could be a real demand driver for aluminum, and some estimate that it could raise aluminum demand by 5.8 million tons by 2040. A cheap way to play aluminum is Alcoa, a vertically integrated aluminum producer that has managed to reduce its leverage significantly in recent years. As of 2023, Alcoa has 3.6 times more equity than debt and a potential free cash flow generation of around $400 million for 2024. This is great for a capital-intensive business, and the company has no debt maturities until 2027, which gives it a lot of financial flexibility.

We've had Teck in our high-conviction portfolio since 2020. Every time it has touched the 100-week moving average, it's been a moneymaker; the setup now is no different. With a market cap just shy of $20 billion, Teck is set to throw off $5 billion in EBITDA next year—and up to $8 billion by 2026. That's cheap—very cheap. Their Highland Valley

Copper mine in British Columbia is monstrous, as it is one of the largest open-pit copper mines in Canada. It produces 140,000 metric tons a day, has been operating since the 1960s, and is still expected to churn out between 128,000 and 133,000 metric tons of copper this year.

Teck's stock has taken a hit as a result of U.S.-Canadian trade tensions. That's noise, and it's given us a buying opportunity. But that's just one piece. Teck also owns a slice of the Antamina mine in Peru, one of the biggest copper-zinc mines on the planet. And the crown jewel? Quebrada Blanca in Chile, a 300,000-metric-ton-per-year copper engine. When it ramps fully, it will rank among the largest copper producers in the world.

This is a real copper story. A geopolitical discount. And a gift, if you're paying attention.

The copper setup over the next five years will be explosive. Wildfires in Los Angeles alone destroyed nearly 16,000 structures. With each home using about 450 pounds of copper, that's 3,600 tons just to rebuild the houses. Now add in the rebuild of data centers. The rebuild of Ukraine. The rebuild of Gaza. The rebuild of the U.S. grid.

But not all electricity travels directly to consumers from power plants through copper wiring. Particularly as the ranks of the global electric vehicle fleet swell, more and more of it will also be transitionally stored in batteries. Seventy-five percent of the world's lithium-ion battery production occurs in China, not only because of the country's manufacturing capacity but also because of its raw materials processing capacity. These raw materials include graphite (a form of carbon); metals like copper, nickel, cobalt, manganese, and lithium; and so-called rare-earth elements like cerium, lanthanum, and neodymium. Conventional cars use barely any of these. The average combustion-engine vehicle requires only about 20 kilograms of copper and 10 kilograms of manganese. On the other hand, electric cars and their batteries are chock-full of these difficult-to-mine, largely Chinese-controlled metals. China not only controls the mines but also the energy-intensive and sometimes highly pollutive capacity to process these minerals. The average electric vehicle uses 50 kilograms of copper, 40 kilograms of nickel, 25 kilograms of manganese, 15 kilograms of cobalt, 10 kilograms of lithium, and 600 grams of rare-earth elements. Every week, Giga-One ships nearly nine thousand batteries to the Tesla Freemont Factory, and another thousand to Tesla Austin, but these numbers are constantly shifting. The latest estimates for total cobalt consumption by Tesla in North America alone was around 7 million pounds a year.

Robotics? Twenty million need 300,000 metric tons of copper—about fourteen days of global supply—just for the machines.

Data centers are worse. According to the International Copper Association, U.S. data centers will need 300,000 to 400,000 metric tons of copper per year. For perspective, total U.S. copper production is only 1.2 million metric tons. And we already import nearly half of what we use.

Microsoft is dropping $80 billion on data centers in 2025—over half of it in the U.S.—driven by its OpenAI partnership. Meta's in for up to $65 billion this year. There's even chatter about a $200 billion AI data center build. Amazon is outspending its e-commerce warehouses, with over $75 billion expected.

Now, Google is boosting capex guidance from $58 billion to $75 billion. What we're witnessing is a full-blown AI arms race. The tech cash cows are morphing into capital-guzzling machines, desperate to outbuild each other.

We've seen this before: the fiber-optic boom and bust of 1998–2001; the shale boom and bust of 2010–2014. AI is starting to rhyme. If these massive capex plans get too far ahead of practical revenue, we'll be seeing the same movie again.

The IEA predicts that if current trends hold, meeting the global demand of the electric vehicles market could require six to thirty times the current supply of all these critical minerals, especially cobalt and lithium. The European Union alone estimates that to meet its climate-neutrality goal, it will need up to five times more cobalt and eighteen times more lithium by 2030. The forecasts rise to sixty times more lithium and fifteen times more cobalt by 2050.

Let's talk about cobalt once more. The year 2016 saw a full-blown commodity bear market, after the boom years of the previous decade incentivized excess exploration and triggered a massive supply glut. When the Fed tried to hike rates, the U.S. dollar ripped higher and crashed commodities. That's what pushed Aubrey McClendon over the edge on that March morning (see chapter 5). It also placed one of America's darlings of the mining business in deep trouble, when it suddenly found itself faced with a $20 billion debt it couldn't pay. Business conditions were dismal, and the price of copper crashed to $1.95 a pound. That was a real low point for so many in the copper-mining world. And that's when Freeport-McMoRan had to unload assets.

The U.S. government rarely keeps a close eye on grand strategy and global businesses. America should take a leaf out of China's playbook, which never wavers from the long game. That's why China now owns the global battery market, and in 2016 it made a fiendishly intelligent move. With the explicit blessing of the White House, Freeport-McMoRan sold its 56 percent of Tenke Fungurume, one of the largest copper-cobalt mines in the DRC, for $2.65 billion to the Chinese mining giant China Molybdenum, known today as the CMOC Group Limited. Two years later, Freeport-McMoRan also unloaded 95 percent of the Kisanfu copper-cobalt-ore project in the DRC, also to China Molybdenum, for $550 million. Again, Washington approved the deal without any conditions or objections. These transactions made China the world's most powerful controlling arm in the cobalt market. Today, some sources still maintain that Apple buys its cobalt from Zhejiang Huayou Cobalt Company, headquartered in the eastern coastal province of Zhejiang, in mainland China. That's the largest artisanal middleman in the DRC, buying sacks of cobalt that may have been mined and carried by children. Fast-forward to 2023, and China's state reserves administration has drawn up plans to buy two thousand tons of cobalt. This plan could be put into action by the end of the year. The People's Republic is just getting started.

The new geopolitical chessboard is layered over the mining sector, and Europe and the United States are finally waking up to the fact that they need to control the supply of minerals for the green transition in their own countries.

China dominates the global graphite market, but Tesla has a long-term contract to buy its supply from Australia's Syrah Resources, the largest graphite miner in the world. This isn't for any humanitarian reasons, however. There is a healthy tax break for American companies to use non-Chinese minerals, and CEO Elon Musk loves receiving this benefit. I'm sure he'll also be thrilled by the new lithium mine right on his doorstep. By 2030, when EVs will have a battery range of 1,000 to 1,200 miles, the bulls say the internal-combustion engine will be nearly obsolete. But if this is the case, lithium miners should be a lot higher, given the demand picture.

Since Western politicians are all worshipping at the altar of Saint Greta, the electric car will have an illustrious career. Beyond that, as I previously mentioned, most of the Chinese population is currently without a car. As they grow wealthier, hundreds of millions of them will head to their closest dealership to get themselves some wheels. Many of the new cars they purchase will be electric; in fact, China has been the world's top market for plug-in electric vehicles for eight years running, and that is poised to only intensify because Beijing has mandated to end sales of gasoline-powered cars by 2025. Chinese consumers bought 205,000 of them in 2015, 1.2 million in 2019, and a whopping 5.9 million in 2022. EVs now represent 29 percent of all new cars sold in China. In 2022, electric vehicle sales grew a massive 87 percent in China and 55 percent globally. Similar trends are ramping up across other emerging markets, like India, Indonesia, and Brazil. All told, the global market for electric vehicles was worth $130 billion in 2022 and is projected to grow fivefold in value by 2026. With tailwinds coming from multiple directions, we love the VanEck Rare Earth / Strategic Metals ETF (REMX) and see a healthy rally for it that could easily last a decade. The other classic ETF for every investor in hard assets is the SPDR S&P Metals and Mining ETF (XME), which tracks an equally weighted index of American metals and mining companies. This includes the big guns like Cleveland-Cliffs, Alcoa, Freeport-McMoRan, Newmont Corporation, and U.S. Steel.

But if Washington's leadership wants wind turbines and solar panels, they're going to need tons of steel. Because a megawatt of solar power requires between 35 and 45 tons of steel, and each new megawatt of wind power requires 120 to 180 tons of steel. German chancellor Olaf Scholz recently stated, "The goal needs to be three or four new, large wind turbines in Germany every day." Not to be outdone, the Inflation Reduction Act that Biden signed in 2022 contains provisions to add 30 gigawatts of offshore wind power by 2030. For reference, 1 gigawatt is 1,000 megawatts, and right now the United States has only 42 megawatts of offshore wind capacity. That kind of additional capacity will require at least 2,100 new wind turbines. And just one offshore wind turbine requires 200 to 800 tons of steel, 1,500 to 2,500 tons of concrete, and 45 to 50 tons of nonrecyclable plastic.

These turbines also contain big magnets so that they spin in a frictionless way, which avoids the use of cogs that eventually rust and wear out. Big industrial wind turbines use four-ton neodymium magnets, another rare-earth mineral under a Chinese monopoly.

Who pays for all these trillions of dollars of green investments by governments in the United States and various European countries? Biden's Inflation Reduction Act devotes nearly $400 billion to the adoption of green technologies. A year prior he signed the $1.2 trillion bipartisan Infrastructure Investment and Jobs Act, with more than $200 billion for the environment. The European Union is selling $800 billion of mutualized debt, in part to fund this green revolution. Interestingly, lending billions to environmental green-energy financing and firing that money directly into the global economy both create a dangerous multiplier effect. Government-backed environmental financing is similar to printing money, and it creates inflation. It's fair to say that Chancellor Scholz hasn't just been drinking the Kool-Aid, he's bathing in it. He wants renewable electrical generation to increase by 33 percent by 2030 and another 33 percent by 2045.

As stated before in this book, we are huge advocates for a clean planet—less pollution, clean water, healthy fish stocks. But every time our team dives into the mathematics of the green-energy space, we are left with a sinking feeling that none of it can be achieved in the time frame recommended by the World Economic Forum or COP27. Carbon-neutral 2030 is absurd. Carbon-neutral 2050 is still way too aggressive. It's more like 2100. Despite what Olaf Scholz believes is possible, his dream of carpeting Germany with wind turbines and solar panels will not come true. The previous fifteen years of building wind turbines and solar panels, costing more than half a trillion dollars, was a catastrophic failure. It still forced Germany to power 40 percent of its electrical grid with natural gas from Russia. But that supply is now permanently inaccessible. The Germans have been forced into restarting their self-proclaimed "filthy" thermal coal plants. And if even the smartest engineers in Germany can make this massive miscalculation, what's in store for the emerging markets?

Fossil fuels will bridge the gap, but the only permanent solution, the only way to wean the world off carbon emissions, is something else entirely. We're not talking about wood, of which 1 kilogram will keep a light bulb shining for a day and a half. Neither are we writing about coal or oil; they could keep that bulb alight for only four days. I'm discussing the only sensible solution there is, and it's something most Western governments detest. But 1 kilogram of this source of energy could keep that same bulb brightly lit, day and night, for 25,000 years. And it's called uranium.

The Uranium Market

In the third quarter of 2023, I sat down in New York with one of the brightest minds in the uranium space, my longtime friend Mike Alkin, founder of Sachem Cove Partners. He believes uranium equities offer outstanding risk-reward over the next decade. There had been a fourteen-year bear market. In 1982, the United States produced 44 million of its 50 million pounds of annual uranium consumption. In 2023, it produced a million.

"Walk us through the long-term bull case," I began. "Why uranium?"

"The setup's a real eye-opener. It's like a hundred-year storm—in a good way. Seventy percent of global demand comes from the West, but 70 percent of supply comes from the East. Kazakhstan, Russia, and Niger. Not the kind of neighbors who show up with an apple pie."

"That's just a cultural difference," I added with a smirk. "How tight is the market?"

"Tight. About 45 percent of global enrichment comes from Russia," he replied. "And that could drop to 36 percent by 2030. Over the last decade, Putin has gone all-in on hard assets. And the U.S. still gets 25 percent of its enriched uranium from Russia. During a war. During brutal U.S. sanctions. It's mind-blowing. There is legislation on Capitol Hill to ban the imports of low-enriched uranium from Russia, but it's on ice. Under review."

Mike went on to explain the 175 million pounds of uranium per year of global demand. And the 440 operating plants. The additional 58 under construction. The 150 to 200 in the planning and approval process. This was boom country.

From 2018–2019 there was an excess capacity globally. The Sprott Physical Uranium Trust was near $7.60. Now there was a capacity deficit, and Sprott was near $18.05C. That's a tight market, and potentially dangerous.

Then Mike gave me the stats, as if he'd been rehearsing. But it didn't surprise me; he knew more about this sector than most people on the Street.

"Global capacity versus the enrichment imbalance could trigger a price shock," he said. "State producers are supplying about 115 million pounds of uranium. Cameco is at table max . . . 30 million. Financial speculators are at 10 million, recontracting 15 million. The rest . . . call it 30 million. Net-net, the market is 15 to 30 million pounds short."

"Annually?"

"That's correct. And this data is highly dependent on enrichment capacity. Again, that sits with Putin. His ban on petroleum exports in the fall of 2023 demonstrates his ability to shut off Russia's enrichment capacity for U.S. and European utilities. This could lead to acute shortages of refined uranium to keep the lights on."

After a fourteen-year bear market, the brain drain across the industry is significant. It will take years to bring the vital and necessary engineers back to the uranium industry. We keep hearing that corporate green incentives across the energy sector could drive an acquisition run across the uranium sector at some point, and the sector is still very small, relatively speaking—only 230 million pounds of demand per year, with a $57 uranium price. That's about a $13 billion annual demand. Compared to oil's 100 million barrels a day? That's small.

We believe the global uranium market is dramatically undersupplied relative to surging demand trends. To move ahead of these trends, in 2020 and 2021, we recommended clients invest in Cameco (CCJ) and Sprott Uranium Miners ETF (URNM). These were clearly investments for high-risk tolerance.

These days, everyone is still chasing Nvidia. But we prefer the Range Nuclear Renaissance Index ETF (NUKZ). Its top three holdings are worth just $250 billion. Nvidia alone is $3.3 trillion. That's the problem with passive investing—everyone's money ends up in the wrong trade. As a quick comparison, NUKZ's market cap is just $241 million. SOXX's, the semiconductor ETF, is $2.1 billion. For three years, Wall Street's been pumping semiconductors to retail investors as the way to play AI. Meanwhile, the real AI trade—power infrastructure and uranium—has been quietly crushing it.

Year-to-date, uranium names are up 22 percent. Semis are down 6 percent. Over the past year: uranium up 51 percent, semis down 13 percent.

This is turning into a World War II–style mobilization. National security is now front and center. The U.S. is miles behind China—and scrambling to catch up; expect executive orders to be the weapon of choice. The White House wants to quadruple domestic nuclear output in twenty-five years. Elon Musk has been making this point for thirty-six months.

In the last decade, China added over 34 gigawatts of nuclear power. They now operate fifty-five reactors (with a total net capacity of 53.2GW as of April 2024) with twenty-three more under construction. The U.S.? We have zero reactors under construction as of 2024.

That's changing, though. Fast. A new executive order just gave the U.S. energy secretary authority to greenlight advanced reactor projects, bypassing the bureaucratic logjam that's stalled the industry for fifty years.

This is where the puck is going, and hardly anyone's skating there yet.

Demand is mounting. Japan, Korea, and Sweden are leading the charge among a growing list of countries raising their nuclear power targets. Eventually, nuclear will become a large portion of the grid in India and China, too. India has twenty-two operational plants and is building eleven more as we speak. China has fifty-three nuclear reactors powering cities across the country and more than twenty underway. Numbers in both countries are set to double over the next ten to twenty years. Now add in the nearly recession-proof nature of uranium and nuclear energy—that's because power plants consume uranium at the same rate, irrespective of energy demand. That's a master recipe for strong performance in the coming years. We suspect that spot prices for uranium will jump from $41 to $100 or $150 in the next three to four years.

At Lehman Brothers, I worked under Mike Gelband, head of fixed income. In 2017, he co-founded one of the fastest-growing hedge funds out there; ExodusPoint began managing investor capital in 2018. By 2023, ExodusPoint's assets under management had reached $13.2 billion. Long before 2008, while extolling the virtues of the housing market, Mike Gelband was known at Lehman for asking, "Are you long because you like it, or do you like it because you're long?"

INVESTORS TAKE NOTE:

Leaders in the Value and Hard Asset Space

Our team did a deep dive across all the ETFs and asset management strategies in the value and hard asset space. Greenlight Capital has for years been one of our top choices. Here are some other attractive options in the public markets space (all of which are incorporated in the United States):

The Kopernik Global All-Cap Fund (KGGIX) is an open-end fund that provides long-term capital appreciation. It invests at least 80 percent of its net assets in equity securities of U.S. and non-U.S. companies of any size.

The Alpha Architect U.S. Quantitative Value (QVAL) also offers long-term capital appreciation, employing a multistep, quantitative, rules-based methodology to identify a portfolio of approximately fifty to one hundred undervalued U.S. equity securities. Meanwhile, the Alpha Architect International Quantitative Value ETF (IVAL) identifies a portfolio of approximately fifty to one hundred undervalued international equity securities.

The Pacer U.S. Cash Cows 100 ETF (COWZ) uses a proprietary methodology to provide exposure to large and midcap U.S. companies with high free cash flow yields. The Pacer U.S. Small Cap Cash Cows 100 (CALF) targets small-cap U.S. companies with the highest free cash flow to enterprise value ratios in the S&P Small Cap 600. And the Pacer Developed Markets International Cash Cows 100 ETF (ICOW) provides exposure to international companies with high free cash flow yields.

The Goehring & Rozencwajg Resources Fund (GRHIX) is an open-end fund that seeks total return, which consists of income on its investments and capital appreciation. It invests in securities of natural resources companies and other instruments that offer exposure to this sector.

High beta stocks, like uranium miners, move far more violently than the market in both directions. The higher the beta of a stock, the more it can rise when markets rally—and the faster it can go down in corrections. I often think about Mike's words when investing in the uranium space. The five-to-ten-year investment thesis is very bullish, but the volatility is not for the faint of heart. If the S&P 500 is down 10 percent, high beta equities can be down 20 to 30 percent. The names just aren't as liquid, so if a few large sellers come in simultaneously, elevator-shaft drops are common, and more often than not bargains can be found. Keep in mind, with the miners, every few years the tourists are *always* coming on and off the bus. It's very hard to quantify, but through the bull and bear market trends a lot of the trading volume comes down to hot-money inflows and outflows. This is high beta fuel. Testosterone is everywhere. The swings are violent, and the momentum shifts are fierce. Investing in the S&P 500 is like riding a white pony in the midday sun relative to a bucking bronco at midnight under a waning crescent moon in the uranium mines. That said, we want to strategically use the volatility to our advantage. With high beta sectors, our mission is clear.

Using Capitulation to Trade Miners

We must meticulously measure the breadth and power of capitulation selling. In 2010, Larry McCarthy, one of the best junk-bond traders of all time in the junk bond space, gave us the framework for our seven-factor capitulation model. It's all about listening when markets speak and measuring the pain. We look for an exponential acceleration in capitulation volume. This comes down to measuring the speed at which those proverbial tourists are getting off the bus. Indeed, high beta sectors come with a lot of tourists. Larry used to say, "As in poker, the weak hands are your friend. We must use them to our advantage." In March 2006, Jack Dorsey, Noah Glass, Biz Stone, and Evan Williams created Twitter. They didn't know it at the time, but they really did change technical analysis forever. Per the CFA Institute, *technical analysis* is a form of security analysis that uses price data and volume data, typically displayed graphically in charts. On Twitter, there are some good chartered market technicians (CMTs) who have studied their craft for years. But there are thousands of pretenders, literally making it up as they go along. Back in late 2009, at an ideas dinner in New York City, one of the best technicians I have ever met, Herb Lust, said, "Larry, if this Twitter thing continues to take off, the rate of change inside and the speed of information flow behind technical analysis will likely change forever. There will be thousands of pretenders all using approximately the same stops." (A stop loss is a trigger point that forces an exit or a sale out of a position.) "You are far better off trading against them than with them. The hot-money flush will be spectacular when they all walk out the door at the same time."

This really hit me like a sharp slap upside the head. Herb was describing capitulation in the twenty-first century. In the previous century, it could take weeks for the capitulation process to develop; now it can take hours, if not minutes.

We look to measure the capitulation selling process; our model attempts to calculate the highest probability of what we call a climax. We want to add to the pain, lighten into strength, and be there for "the turn," the moment a new bull market is born. In high beta sectors, we always build new positions in thirds. Everyone knows, only monkeys pick bottoms. We are *not* trying to pick an exact bottom, but we will attempt to develop an attractive cost basis near a bottom. Our model also looks at the distance below the lower Bollinger band, the daily and weekly relative strength index (RSI) readings, and other important factors. Investing in high beta sectors, your entry point is like dancing with a serpent. Don't let the mad mob suck you in; use capitulation selling to your advantage.

We will scale in one third at a time, averaging into the Sprott Uranium Miners ETF (URNM). At one point in 2021, during the growth-stock overdose, shares of exercise bike maker Peloton (PTON) were worth an astounding $37 billion on just $4 billion of revenues, while the entire uranium sector was valued near $29 billion. The uranium sector's largest player, Cameco (CCJ), started that year valued under $7 billion on close to $2 billion of revenues. Central bankers created colossal dislocations, and the hard-asset sector was left for dead in a world with perceived low inflation. All the capital was rushing into growth stocks and financial assets. Elon Musk's net worth touched $160 billion, five times the value of all the uranium miners combined. Back then we argued, looking out twenty years, that the only mathematically sustainable way Tesla would grow into its colossal valuation was through a 2x-to-3x build-out of the planet's green nuclear-power fleet. EVs desperately need nuclear power; most of the current fleet is powered by coal plants.

Finally, there's another reason why we are bullish on demand for oil, gas, and coal. "Green" energy may be clean in terms of carbon emissions, but it often fails on the level of morals and environmental impact. As I noted, an estimated forty thousand Congolese children dig for the cobalt needed for electric cars, wind turbines, and solar panels in terrible conditions. Similar issues crop up with lithium and copper. Chile's Atacama Desert produces 28 percent of the world's copper and 21 percent of its lithium. Unfortunately, almost all the mines interfere with the indigenous communities there and destroy their land. Mining for rare-earth elements in China and elsewhere has had terrible consequences for several regions, where toxic metallic waste has poisoned the rivers and the groundwater. The overzealous efforts of the West to replace fossil fuels with any alternative has destroyed a big part of the oldest and the most biodiverse rainforest in the world. The majority of biodiesel, which has become popular since the start of this century, is made from palm oil. Researchers at the University of Wageningen, in the Netherlands, estimate that palm plantations were responsible for one third of Indonesia's loss of rainforest since the year 2000, or 10 million hectares burned to the ground. The palm oil industry destroyed an area of the rainforest the size of Pennsylvania, and countless animals, including the orangutan, the tiger, and the white rhino, have become critically endangered as a result.

It's not necessarily these moral or environmental abuses themselves that will impede the transition to a green economy. Rather, it could be the reaction of people in the developed world. If they knew about it, most people would rightly see the children mining cobalt, the displacement of indigenous peoples, or the mining pollution as abominations. Perhaps they would start having second thoughts about this entire system that has been incentivized by political agendas and ESG investing. It's unlikely that the push for carbon-neutral energy will be abandoned, but there's a high probability that we will see a backlash against green-related mining from social and environmental activists in the next twenty years. They could push for Western governments and companies to start putting higher standards on the resources they need for green energy. These could come in the form of tighter labor and environmental standards and reshoring whatever can be done at home. This will make the resources needed more expensive. And since the price of energy affects just about everything, this will raise the global level of inflation. It will also slow down the transition, which inevitably increases the demand for fossil fuels and extends their use further into the future.

The Shifting Desert Sands

Since the end of the Cold War, the market has experienced an almost perpetual state of disinflation. The deflation trade was so entrenched in the narrative that $80 trillion of the world's wealth became concentrated in growth stocks and bonds, and much of it still is. Nobody had a second thought about inflation. At one point, the Nasdaq 100 had $20 trillion in it—mostly piled into fifteen megacap stocks. That amount of money in $1 bills, laid end to end, could go back and forth to the sun ten times. Almost the opposite was true in the inflationary years between 1968 and 1981, when deflation seemed like a market phenomenon that could never appear. The danger of these long cycles from an investing standpoint is that the belief lives on for much longer than markets allow. How many millennials are thinking the next crypto rally is just around the corner? Who still thinks the biggest tech stocks will outperform the market over the next decade? There are investors all over America who are so badly positioned for the next market cycle.

Financial markets, much like the fashion industry, have hot sectors and boring sectors, and these are constantly shifting like desert sands. Places where billions are made will not always be that way. And sectors that once delivered tiny returns, if any at all, could one day be highly profitable. Precious metals, coal miners, uranium, copper, rare earths, oil and gas—once the great laggards of the stock market—will be among the most heavily populated sector in the coming years, and big tech will fall into the shadows. The world is about to witness the most epic migration of capital in the history of financial markets. Will your family's wealth play a role in this and walk into that neglected meadow of value stocks, commodities, and hard assets, or will it fade away with the last decade's portfolio? The choice is yours.

ACKNOWLEDGMENTS

Mosaic research is taking a piece of information and then surrounding it with other pieces of information and wisdom. The goal is to determine its value and validity. The deeper and broader your bench and resources, the closer you are to finding truth. It takes a ton of hard work, but above all, a lot of asking. A man with many of the answers is Robbert van Batenburg. A trusted friend and colleague for more than a decade, he led this project with passion, drive, and determination. There is no investment strategist in the business with a deeper understanding of the intersection of public policy trends and capital markets. On the corner of Washington and Wall Street, there is where you will find Robbert.

Going back to my days as a trader at Lehman, Herbert C. Lust III has been an invaluable friend and mentor. Besides being known as the J. P. Morgan analyst who outed Enron over a year before the company plunged into bankruptcy, Herb trained the best distressed research team on Wall Street at Lehman.

As my longtime friend and coauthor, I thank James Robinson for his constant support, meticulous research, and unique ability to connect Wall Street and the literary world. James has a gift for lifting the world of boring finance out of the cobwebs and delivering gems to a wide audience with flair and entertainment.

On the publishing and editing team, thanks to Leah Trouwborst of Crown—whose passion for perfection is only surpassed by her extraordinary talent—and to the finest literary agent in the business, Jim Levine of the Levine Greenberg Rostan Literary Agency. Without Jim's experience and raw talent, this project never would have been possible.

To the finest products out of the legendary asset management firm Moore Capital: Brian Yelvington, Marc Cheval, Ben Giesmann, and Jonathan Turek have always been there looking over rates, Eurodollars (SOFR), and foreign exchange futures.

To the best economist on Wall Street, thank you, Joe Lavorgna.

My longtime friends in Washington are priceless. Thanks to ACG Analytics' managing partner, David Metzner, and his fine team led by John

East and Chris Czerwinski. We have traveled the world together leaving no stone unturned. I am so grateful to have had you by my side.

A restructuring legend and former adviser to President Obama, Jim Millstein has always been there to make me think and dig deeper.

Thank you, Nigel Farage, for your thoughtful analysis of political risks in our multipolar world.

I am fortunate to work with one of the brightest minds out of Brookings and the U.S. Treasury Department. Thank you, Aaron Klein.

When it comes to economic trends, there is no better team to run new ideas past than the one that includes the following: Robbert Ax, Josh Ayers, Kevin Bambrough, Rohit Bansal, Jenna Barnard, Manas Baveja, Drew Casino, Porter Collins, Vincent Daniel, Bob Davenport, James Davis, Adrian Day, Bobby "D" Dziedziech, David Einhorn, Mohamed El-Erian, John Fath, Niall Ferguson, Tony Frascella, Mike Gelband, Jon Glaser, Alan Guarino, Mike Guarnieri, David Hall, Alan Higgins, Munib Islam, Doug Kass, Ravi Kaza, Lord Mervyn King, Alex Kirk, David LaPlaca, Jerry Levy, Andrew McCaffery, Bart McDade, Joe Mauro, Ben Melkman, Edward Misrahi, Jeff Moskowitz, Jon Najarian, John Renato Negrin, Jens Nordvig, Ed Oppedisano, Tim Pagliara, John Pattullo, Ralph Reynolds, Joe Scafidi, Peter Schellbach, Eric Schiffer, Geoff Sherry, Marc-Andre Soubliere, Rafi Tahmazian, James Ter Haar, Ram Venkatraman, Caesar Yuan, and Shahar Zer.

To Mark Cuban, I am so grateful to you, my friend. Thank you for always making me think. Your "around the corner" vision now spans multiple decades.

Thanks to my longtime friend and confidant John Coen. And to Dan Hoverman and Terence Tucker in regional bank finance. Special thanks are in order to my mentor, Bernie Groveman. Also to Brendan Ahern, Mike Alkin, Adam Barratta, Arthur Bass, Larry Berman, Ben Brey, John Ciampaglia, Alejandro Cifuentes, Jack Corbett, Robinson Dorion, Keith Dubauskas, Dani Egger, Paul Hackett, Bob Hamil, John Helmers, Stan Jonas, Brian Joseph, Brian Kelly, Adam Kramer, Tom Kurtz, Rogerio Lempert, Ben Levine, Brandt McDonald, Jim McGovern, Peter Obermeyer, John O'Connor, Raoul Pal, Luke Palmer, John Parker, John Paul Parker, David Patterson, Jason Polansky, Steve Purdom, Loren Remetta, Hugh Sconyers, Seth Setrakian, Scott Skyrm, John Smyth, George Whitehead (the Godfather of Gilts), Greg Williams, and Tian Zeng.

My friend Paul C. Jenkins spent more than thirty years as an economist and in supervisory positions at the Canada Department of Finance, the Bank of Canada, and the International Monetary Fund. I have been more than fortunate to have his lens on this book through the development process over the last year. His contributions helped shape the book's direction and enhanced the quality of our findings.

To Roberto Brenes, Sergi Lucas, and Andre Estevez, thank you. Your understanding of Latin American political risk and opportunities is second to none!

The production team was led by Valentina Sanchez-Cuenca and Jose Tutiven. I am so grateful to you both. Your energy and focus helped me reach the finish line.

NOTES

Introduction

xxii ***history moves through predictable phases:*** William Strauss and Neil Howe, *The Fourth Turning: An American Prophecy* (New York: Broadway Books, 1997).

Chapter 2

23 ***But for every winner:*** Stephen D. Cohen, "The Route to Japan's Voluntary Export Restraints on Automobiles" (Working Paper No. 20, National Security Archive, 1997).

24 ***In response to this, Tokyo:*** "Global Prospects and Policies," International Monetary Fund, April 2011.

26 ***At its peak, Tokyo's real estate:*** Douglas Parkes, "Japan in the 1980s," *South China Morning Post,* July 1, 2020.

27 ***Ben Bernanke, who became chairman:*** Ben S. Bernanke, "Deflation—Making Sure 'It' Doesn't Happen Here," speech, National Economists Club, Washington, D.C., November 21, 2002, bis.org/review/r021126d.pdf.

28 ***He had a face still plump with youth:*** Roger Lowenstein, "Long-Term Gamble That Failed to Deliver the Expected Result," *The Times* (UK), September 1, 2000.

32 ***In other words, Asian central banks:*** Giancarlo Corsetti, Paolo Pesenti, and Nouriel Roubini, "What Caused the Asian Currency and Financial Crisis?" (Working Paper 6833, National Bureau of Economic Research, December 1998).

34 ***"coming apart at the seams":*** Floyd Norris, "Editorial Observer; Is the Global Capitalist System Collapsing?," *New York Times,* September 21, 1998.

35 ***"Markets would . . . possibly cease to function":*** "After Losing Billions, Life Goes on for Long-Term Capital's Partners," *Journal Record,* September 26, 2000.

Chapter 3

44 ***How Much Did the Government Spend:*** James Felkerson, "$29,000,000,000,000: A Detailed Look at the Fed's Bailout of the Financial System" (One-Pager No. 23, Levy Economics Institute, December 2011).

46 ***The Demise of the U.S. Auto Industry:*** "Domestic Auto Production," FRED, July 28, 2023, https://fred.stlouisfed.org/series/DAUPSA.

49 ***The spending plans:*** Board of Governors of the Federal Reserve System, "Distribution of Household Wealth in the U.S. Since 1989," https://www.federalreserve.gov/releases/z1/dataviz/dfa/distribute/chart.

54 ***Princeton professors Anne Case and Angus Deaton:*** Atul Gawande, "Why Americans Are Dying from Despair," *New Yorker,* March 16, 2020.

54 ***manufacturing job losses predict:*** Nathan Seltzer, "The Economic Underpinnings of the Drug Epidemic," *SSM Population Health* 12 (December 2020), doi: 10.1016/j.ssmph.2020.100679.

54 ***If we look at the map:*** Alicia Sasser Modestino, "How Opioid Overdoses Reached Crisis Levels," *Econofact,* November 19, 2021.

Chapter 4

79 ***"to reimagine and rebuild":*** "Fact Sheet: The American Jobs Plan," The White House, March 31, 2021, https://www.whitehouse.gov/briefing-room/statements-releases/2021/03/31/fact-sheet-the-american-jobs-plan/.

Chapter 5

84 ***Aubrey McClendon's gray hair:*** Bryan Gruley, Joe Carroll, and Asjylyn Loder, "The Incredible Rise and Final Hours of Fracking King Aubrey McClendon," *Bloomberg Businessweek,* March 10, 2016.

86 ***Ben Bernanke admits:*** Edison Yu, "Did Quantitative Easing Work?," *Economic Insights* (a publication of the Research Department of the Federal Reserve Bank of Philadelphia), First Quarter 2016.

92 ***Leigh Goehring and Adam Rozencwajg's research:*** "The Truth About Renewables—Featuring Leigh Goehring and Adam Rozencwajg," Goehring & Rozencwajg: Natural Resource Investors, September 9, 2021, https://blog.gorozen.com/blog/the-truth-about-renewables-featuring-leigh-goehring-and-adam-rozencwajg.

95 ***"Modern nuclear energy":*** Bill Gates, quoted in azhuk, "The Advantages of Nuclear Energy," blog post, Frontier Technology Corporation, April 20, 2023.

96 ***"Germany should not only not shut down":*** Elon Musk, quoted in Luc Olinga, "Elon Musk Says Germany Is Making a Dangerous Mistake," April 16, 2023.

97 ***"The global volume of solar-panel waste":*** Dieter Holger, "The Solar Boom Will Create Millions of Tons of Junk Panels," *Wall Street Journal,* May 5, 2022.

100 ***California has seen multiple devastating fires:*** Judge Glock, "Why Is PG&E Failing California? All the Wrong Incentives," Cicero Institute, September 9, 2020.

103 ***"Every sector will be transformed":*** Larry Fink, "Larry Fink's 2022 Letter to CEOs: The Power of Capitalism," BlackRock, January 18, 2022.

104 ***For copper, 40 percent of the future demand growth:*** Andrew Mitchell and Nick Pickens, "Nickel and Copper: Building Blocks for a Greener Future," Wood Mackenzie, April 4, 2022.

106 ***according to the Oregon Group:*** Anthony Milewski, "A Lot More Copper Needed to Expand Global Electricity," The Oregon Group, July 26, 2023.

106 ***it will cost as much as $7 trillion:*** Leonard Hyman and William Tilles, "The $7 Trillion Cost of Upgrading the U.S. Power Grid," OilPrice.com, February 25, 2021.

Chapter 6

123 ***an immense amount of liquidity to the markets:*** "Assessing Liquidity—Revisiting Whether Book Depth Is a Sufficiently Representative Measure of Market Liquidity," CME Group, June 17, 2020, https://www.cmegroup.com/education/articles-and-reports/assessing-liquidity.html.

128 ***deterioration in Treasury liquidity:*** Jordan Barone, "The Global Dash for Cash in March 2020," *Liberty Street Economics,* July 12, 2020.

Chapter 7

149 ***With the Sequoia brand in its sales pitch:*** Vicki Auslender, "How Did Some of the World's Largest VCs Miss All the Warning Signs and Invest in FTX?," CTech, November 22, 2022.

150 ***"Who the fuck is this goofball?":*** Marc Cohodes and Larry McDonald, interview minute 19–20:15. Zoom, December 14, 2022. Quote: "FTX put up billboards of SBF himself. . . . and who is he, he's a total f****** nobody. So the whole focus on the shiny object, which was him, this goofball, and ignore everything else, lulled everybody. It lulled the regulators."

154 ***"10 largest female-run funds by total net assets":*** "Cathie Wood's 'Phenomenal Rise' Brings ETF Assets to $60 Billion," Bloomberg.com, February 17, 2021.

154 ***bragging about her:*** Evie Liu, "Red-Hot Ark ETFs Add $12.5 Billion in New Cash in 2021," *Barron's,* February 10, 2021.

Chapter 8

178 ***This is the country that was eavesdropping:*** Tim Starks and Karen DeYoung, "U.S. Eavesdropped on U.N. Secretary General, Leaks Reveal," *Washington Post,* April 17, 2023.

180 ***On the other side of the Persian Gulf:*** Zahra Tayeb, "Russia and Iran Are Working on a Gold-Backed Cryptocurrency to Take On the Dominant Dollar," *Business Insider India,* January 17, 2023.

181 ***60 percent of the world's reserves in natural gas:*** Daniel Onyango, "Russia and Iran Move to Create One of the Largest Global Natural Gas Cartel," *Pipeline Technology Journal,* August 26, 2022.

181 ***These are early indications:*** "Asian Nations Sign Pact to Shift Away from Dollar," Mehr News Agency, May 3, 2023.

182 ***In April 2023, the BRICS:*** Tanupriya Singh, "Towards De-dollarization," *Peoples Dispatch,* April 7, 2023.

182 ***In May 2023, Brazil:*** "Argentina and Brazil to Discuss Trade Agreement to Skip Dollar," *Buenos Aires Herald,* May 2, 2023.

185 ***The report blamed "significant financing issues":*** Peter G. Peterson Foundation, "Without Reform, Social Security Could Become Depleted Within the Next Decade," June 29, 2023.

188 ***valuing gold in terms of outstanding dollars:*** Laura Brothers, "Gold vs. Money Supply," Vaulted.com, August 20, 2021.

195 ***"My grandfather rode a camel":*** "Dubai Sheikh's Words Lost in Translation with Viral Quote," Australian Associated Press, April 26, 2021.

Chapter 9

197 ***forty thousand children:*** Annie Kelly, "Children as Young as Seven Mining Cobalt Used in Smartphones, Says Amnesty," *The Guardian,* January 19, 2016.

207 ***an accelerated redistribution:*** Eric Oteng, "South Africa's Dilemma of Land Reform and Mining Investment," *Africanews,* February 10, 2019.

207 ***"if ownership of mining lands is not guaranteed investors will flee":*** Oteng, "South Africa's Dilemma of Land Reform and Mining Investment."

212 ***Building charging stations:*** Alex Woodrow, "2022–2040 Powertrain Outlook," *KGP Automotive Intelligence,* October 2022.

213 ***"Any new copper mine will take five to ten years":*** "Copper Production Takes 5–10 Years, and That Causes Supply Delays, Says Freeport-McMoRan CEO," YouTube, 2022, https://www.youtube.com/watch?v=7PtXQP0kmuo.

214 ***These raw materials include graphite:*** Joseph Quinlan and Lauren Sanfilippo, "China Is Leading the World on Manufacturing, but the Race Isn't Over," *Barron's,* August 31, 2020.

215 ***cobalt consumption by Tesla:*** Frik Els, "All the Mines Tesla Needs to Build 20 Million Cars a Year," Mining.com, January 27, 2021.

217 ***"The goal needs to be":*** Olaf Scholz, quoted in Chris Reiter, "Germany Targets Three New Windmills a Day for Energy Reboot," Bloomberg.com, January 14, 2023.

INDEX

ABOUT THE AUTHORS

© Jesus Obando

Lawrence G. McDonald is a *New York Times* bestselling author and the founder of the advisory platform *The Bear Traps Report,* which has clients across twenty-three countries. One of Wall Street's most respected financial experts, McDonald has made more than 1,400 media appearances and was featured prominently in the Academy Award–winning documentary *Inside Job,* narrated by Matt Damon. Previously, he was a vice president of distressed debt and convertible securities trading at Lehman Brothers.

James Patrick Robinson is the CEO of Robinson Speakers Bureau. With a background in English literature and creative writing, he's written six feature-length screenplays.